# Desktop Guide to Basic Contracting Terms

*Sixth Edition, Revised and Expanded*

Originally Compiled by Regina Mickells Bova
Revised by Margaret G. Rumbaugh, CPCM

National Contract Management Association

Printed in the United States of America
ISBN 0-9700897-3-2

# Dedication

I dedicate the sixth edition of NCMA's *Desktop Guide to Basic Contracting Terms* to W. Gregor Macfarlan. I first worked with Greg when I was a technical writer on the NCMA staff and he was the national vice president for education and certification (NVP–EC) (1990–91). Under his leadership, NCMA's educational products department developed National Education Seminars, books, and workshops, as well as a subscription series, *Topical Issues in Procurement*. He always took the time to read each product, making constructive comments to ensure it was the best it could be. He handwrote encouraging notes to me for virtually every product; I still have and treasure those notes. While working for him as a member of the NCMA staff, I set a personal goal to become the NVP–EC. In 1997–98, I met that goal. It was quite an honor to walk in his path that year. Even after being the national president, he remained a leader in NCMA by participating on the Education and Certification Policy Review Board.

Later in my career, I became an independent consultant and again had the privilege of working with Greg at the Logistics Management Institute. Always a mentor, he encouraged me to continue consulting and training, which I still do almost 15 years later. In more than 20 years as an acquisition professional, I have never encountered anyone as wise, caring, and committed to professionalism as Greg Macfarlan. His high standards for quality, professionalism, and simply doing the right thing will remain with me throughout my career.

—Marge Rumbaugh, CPCM

*The secret of joy in work is contained in one word—excellence.*
*To know how to do something well is to enjoy it.*
—Pearl Buck, *The Joy of Children*, 1964

# Introduction

Although the 2006 edition of NCMA's *Desktop Guide to Basic Contracting Terms* provides useful information on the fundamental meaning and everyday use of more than 1,300 contracting terms, the *Guide* is not meant to provide complete technical definitions, especially as they apply to various specialized contracting situations. Readers are encouraged to refer to the *Federal Acquisition Regulation (FAR)* and other official sources for more detailed definitions.

NCMA's *Desktop Guide to Basic Contracting Terms* can serve as an on-the-job reference for new entrants into the field, a review for more seasoned practitioners, and a study tool for the certified federal contracts manager (CFCM) section of the certified professional contracts manager (CPCM) exams. Other study manuals for professional certification exams are available from NCMA.

The contract management profession relies largely on precision and proper interpretation of language. Therefore, this edition of *Desktop Guide to Basic Contracting Terms* has been expanded to cover definitions that acquisition personnel may expect to encounter; all obsolete terms have been removed.

We invite readers to submit additional terms for inclusion in future editions of this publication. If you are able to provide an existing written definition along with the term itself, please supply a reference for the definition. Please send your definitions to NCMA at **learning-center@ncmahq.org**.

# Index to Source Codes

**ACC**
Acquisition Community Connection Web site. Defense Acquisition University. **https://acc.dau.mil/simplify/ev_en.php** (posted October 2002, accessed April 2006).

**AFIT**
Air Force Institute of Technology. *Compendium of Authenticated Systems and Logistics Terms, Definitions and Acronyms.* Wright-Patterson Air Force Base, OH: Air Force Institute of Technology, 1981.

**AH**
*American Heritage Dictionary.* 2nd college ed. Boston: Houghton Mifflin Company, 1982.

**AI**
Chierichella, John W., and Douglas E. Perry. "Negotiating Teaming Agreements." *Acquisition Issues.* Vienna, VA: Holbrook & Kellogg, Inc., 1991.

**ASPM**
Department of Defense. *Armed Services Pricing Manual.* "Vol. 1, Contract Pricing." Washington, DC: Department of Defense, 1986.

**BLD**
Black, Henry C. *Black's Law Dictionary.* 5th ed. St. Paul, MN: West Publishing Co., 1979.

**BLD2**
Black, Henry C. *Black's Law Dictionary.* 6th ed. St. Paul, MN: West Publishing Co., 1990.

**DCG**
*Business Conduct Guidelines.* Seattle, WA: The Boeing Company, 1987.

**BP(89-13)**
Vacketta, Carl L., Richard H. Mays, and Gail D. Frulla. "The Government Contractor Defense in Environmental Actions." *Briefing Papers* (no. 89–13). Washington, DC: Federal Publications, Inc., December 1989.

**BP(90-11)**
Albertson, Terry L., Edward Jackson, and Linda S. Bruggeman. "Compensation Costs." *Briefing Papers* (no. 90-11). Washington, DC: Federal Publications, Inc., October 1990.

**BP(91-8)**
Allen, Rand L., and Jeffrey M. Villet. "Implied Warranty of Specifications." *Briefing Papers* (no. 91–8). Washington, DC: Federal Publications, Inc., July 1991.

## CE
Stewart, Rodney D. *Cost Estimating*. 2nd ed. New York: John Wiley & Sons, Inc., 1991.

## CM-1/99
Myers, James A. "Federal Financial Management Reform: An Emphasis on Accountability and Agency Performance." *Contract Management* 39, no. 1 (January 1999): 32.

## CM-4/98
Johnson, Kevin W. "The Blair House Papers: A Prescription for Change to Reshape Government Procurement." *Contract Management* 38, no. 4 (April 1998): 12.

## Cohen
Cohen, Cary. *The Handbook of Effective Contract Administration*. Richmond, VA: Caldwell Consulting Associates, 1985.

## Culver
Culver, C. M. *Federal Government Procurement—An Unchartered Course Through Turbulent Waters*. McLean, VA: National Contract Management Association, 1985.

## DAAT
*Defense Acquisition Acronyms and Terms*. 12th ed. Fort Belvoir, VA: Defense Acquisition University, July 2005.

## DBL
Dobler, Donald W., David N. Burt, and Lamar Lee Jr. *Purchasing and Materials Management*. 5th ed. New York: McGraw-Hill Publications, 1990.

## DGCQI
*Desktop Guide for Continuous Quality Improvement*. Seattle, WA: Boeing Defense and Space Group, 1990.

## DLA
Defense Logistics Agency. "Understanding the DOD Budget." *Dimensions*. Alexandria, VA: Defense Logistics Agency (April 1991): 2–3.

## DOD
Office of the Inspector General. *Acquisition Alerts for Program Managers*. Washington, DC: Department of Defense, 1987.

## DOD-MMH
Defense Systems Management College. *Department of Defense Manufacturing Management Handbook for Program Managers*. 2nd ed. Fort Belvoir, VA: Defense Systems Management College, 1984.

## DSMC
Defense Systems Management College. *Subcontracting Management Handbook*. Fort Belvoir, VA: Department of Defense, 1988.

**ECON**
Waud, Roger N. *Microeconomics.* 3rd ed. New York: Harper & Row, Publishers, 1986.

**EDI**
Emmelhainz, Margaret A. *Electronic Data Interchange: A Total Management Guide.* New York: Van Nostrand Reinhold, 1990.

**EDIW**
*EDI World.* Hollywood, FL: EDI World, Inc.

(1-11)— Ugljcзa, Juaii M. "A&D Contract Management Discovers EDI." Vol. 1, no. 11 (November 1991): 25.

(2-1)—Millhorn, Tom, and Javier Romeu. "EDI Capabilities Grow to Include Complex Data Transfer." Vol. 2, no. 1 (January 1992): 31.

**EVM**
**www.earnedvaluemanagement.com**
(accessed April 2006).

**EVMIG**
*Earned Value Management Implementation Guide.* Washington, DC: Department of Defense. April 7, 2005.

**FAI**
Federal Acquisition Institute. *Basic Procurement Course Materials.* Washington, DC: Federal Acquisition Institute, 1991.

**FAI-web**
**www.fai.gov/index.htm**
(accessed April 2006).

**FAR**
*Federal Acquisition Regulation.* Government Printing Office, Washington, DC.

**FBL**
Scaletta, Phillip J. Jr., and George D. Cameron III. *Foundations of Business Law.* 2nd ed. Homewood, IL: Richard D. Irwin, Inc., 1990

**FCR**
*Federal Contracts Report.* Vol. 61, no. 5. Washington, DC: Bureau of National Affairs, February 7, 1994, 173.

**F&F**
*The Government Contractor's Glossary.* Rockville, MD: Friedman & Fuller, PC, 1992.

**Foglia**
Foglia, Joseph T. *How to Market to the Government.* Richmond, VA: Baruch Defense Marketing, Inc., 1989.

**GAO**
U.S. General Accounting Office. *Quality Assurance Concerns About Four Navy Missile Systems.* Washington, DC: U.S. General Accounting Office, 1987.

## Garrett
Garrett, Gregory A. *Contract Negotiations: Skills, Tools, and Best Practices*. Chicago: CCH, Inc., 2005.

## GSA
U.S. General Services Administration. *Small Purchases/Schedule Contracts Student Manual* (#220A). Washington, DC: U.S. General Services Administration, January 1989.

## GSA SSEB
U.S. General Services Administration. *Guide for Source Selection Evaluation Board Members*. Washington, DC: U.S. General Services Administration, Office of Acquisition Policy, May 1992.

## GUIDE
Arnavas, Donald P., and William J. Ruberry. *Government Contract Guidebook*. Washington, DC: Federal Publications, Inc., 1986.

## GW
GovWorks, a Federal Acquisition Center under the Department of the Interior. **www.govworks.gov** (accessed April 2006).

## IAE
Integrated Acquisition Environment Web site. **http://acquisition.gov** (accessed April 2006).

## Linster
Linster, Bruce G., PhD, and David R. Mullin, PhD. *Auctions in Defense Acquisition: Theory and Experimental Evidence*. Defense Acquisition University. *Acquisition Review Quarterly* (Summer 2002).

## L&P
Lamm, David V., and William C. Pursch (with assistance from John E. Cannaday, Daniel L. Downs, Richard A. Florek, William J. Hauf, Randal Indvik, Dean R. Matro, Laureli M. Moyle, Michael W. Robinson, Daniel F. Ryan, and Robert Eric Wilson). "A Dictionary of Contracting Terms." *Contract Management* (May 1991): 41.

## MCS
Anthony, Robert N., John Dearden, and Richard F. Vancil. *Management Control Systems*. Homewood, IL: Richard D. Irwin, Inc., 1972.

## McVay
McVay, Barry L. *Getting Started in Federal Contracting*. Westbury, NY: Asher-Gallant Press, 1986.

## MGMT
Horngren, Charles T., and Gary L. Sundem. *Introduction to Management Accounting*. 7th ed. Englewood Cliffs, NJ: Prentice-Hall, 1987.

## MSA
*The Management of Security Assistance*. Defense Institute of Security Assistance Management. **www.disam.dsca.mil/pubs/DR/greenbook.htm** (posted January 2005, accessed April 2006).

**Navy**
Richardson, Judith V. *Handbook for Contract Specialists.* Washington, DC: Naval Air Systems Command, 1989.

**NC-A**
Cibinic, John Jr., and Ralph C. Nash Jr. *Administration of Government Contracts.* Washington, DC: George Washington University, 1985.

**NC-F**
Cibinic, John Jr., and Ralph C. Nash Jr. *Formation of Government Contracts.* Washington, DC: George Washington University, 1982.

**NCMA-CA**
*Cost Accounting Basics.* Rev. ed. Vienna, VA: National Contract Management Association, 1990.

**NCMA-CP2**
*CPCM Candidate's Workbook Supplement 2.* Vienna, VA: National Contract Management Association, 1989.

**NCMA-SB**
*Solicitations, Bids, and Awards.* McLean, VA: National Contract Management Association, 1984.

**NCMA-SP**
*Specifications and Standards.* McLean, VA: National Contract Management Association, 1984.

**NCMA-SS**
*Source Selection.* McLean, VA: National Contract Management Association, 1984.

**NDIA**
National Defense Industrial Association (NDIA). *Program Management Systems Committee (PMSC) ANSI/EIA-748-A Standard for Earned Value Management Systems Intent Guide.* Arlington, VA: National Defense Industrial Association, January 2006.

**NES-00**
*The Contracting Professional as a Business Manager.* Vienna, VA: National Contract Management Association, 2000.

**NES-02**
Droms, William G., and Neal J. Couture. *Financial Analysis: Contract Management Applications.* Vienna, VA: National Contract Management Association, 2002.

**NES-87**
Arnavas, Donald P., Gilbert J. Ginsburg, Matthew S. Simchak, and John S. Pachter. *Managing Contract Changes.* Vienna, VA: National Contract Management Association, 1987.

**NES-89**
Marks, H. Philip, and Donald L. Brechtel. *Subcontracts: Government and Industry Issues.* Vienna, VA: National Contract Management Association, 1989.

## NES-90

Jacobs, Daniel M., Janice M. Menker, and Chester P. Shinaman. *Building a Contract: Solicitations/Bids and Proposals.* Vienna, VA: National Contract Management Association, 1990.

## NES-92

Hernandez, Richard J., and Delane F. Moeller. *Negotiating a Quality Contract.* Vienna, VA: National Contract Management Association, 1991.

## NES-93

Baker, Keith L., William A. Erie, and Scott J. Parkinson. *Financial Issues for the Contracts Professional.* Vienna, VA: National Contract Management Association, 1992.

## NES-94

National Contract Management Association. *Commercial, Environmental, and International Contracting: An Evolving Focus.* Vienna, VA: National Contract Management Association, 1994.

## NES-96

Bauman, Lt. Col. Christine M. (Select), CPCM; Greg S. Bingham; William J. Esmann, et.al. *Program and Contract Changes.* Vienna, VA: National Contract Management Association, 1996.

## NES-97

Gaudio, Louis M., Eric L. Gentsch, Phillip H. Harrington, et.al. *Commercial Item Acquisition.* Vienna, VA: National Contract Management Association, 1997.

## NES-98

Moeller, Col. Delane F., U.S. Army (Ret.), CPCM; and Lt. Col. Herbert L. McCulloch, U.S. Army (Ret.). *Electronic Contracting.* Vienna, VA: National Contract Management Association, 1998.

## NES-99

Ablard, John H.; L.A. Barvinchak, CFCM; Paula P. Cushman, CPCM, et.al. *Innovative Contracting: Practical Approaches.* Vienna, VA: National Contract Management Association, 1999.

## NS

Nash, Ralph C. Jr., and Steven L. Schooner. *The Government Contracts Reference Book.* Washington, DC: George Washington University, 1992.

## OMB A-109

Office of Management and Budget. *OMB A-109 Circular No. A-109.* "Major Systems Acquisitions." Washington, DC: Office of Management and Budget, April 5, 1976.

## OMB A-11

Office of Management and Budget. *OMB A-11.* "Planning, Budgeting, Acquisition, and Management of Capital Assets." Executive Office of the President, Office of Management and Budget, July 2003.

## OMB A-130

Office of Management and Budget. *OMB A-130 Circular No. A-130.* "Management of Federal Information Resources." Washington, DC: Office of Management and Budget, February 8, 1996.

## OMB A-131

Office of Management and Budget. *OMB A-131 Circular No. A-131.* "Value Engineering." Washington, DC: Office of Management and Budget, May 21, 1993.

## OMB A-76

Office of Management and Budget. *OMB A-76 Circular No. A-76.* "Performance of Commercial Activities." Washington, DC: Office of Management and Budget, May 29, 2003.

## OPM

U.S. Office of Personnel Management. *Position Classification Standards for the Contract and Procurement Series, GS-1102.* Washington, DC: U.S. Office of Personnel Management, 1981.

## OTB

*Over Target Baseline and Over Target Schedule Handbook.* Acquisition Community Connection. Fort Belvoir, VA: Defense Acquisition University. **https://acc.dau.mil/simplify/ev.php?ID =17993_201&ID2=DO_TOPIC** (posted May 7, 2003, accessed April 2006).

## P&L

Pursch, William C. and David V. Lamm (with assistance from John E. Cannaday, Daniel L. Downs, Richard A. Florek, William J. Hauf, Randal Indvik, Dean R. Matro, Laureli M. Moyle, Michael W. Robinson, Daniel F. Ryan, and Robert Eric Wilson). "A Dictionary of Contracting Terms Part II." *Contract Management* (November 1991): 42.

## PW

Price Waterhouse. *Contracting with the Federal Government.* 2nd ed. New York: John Wiley & Sons, 1988.

## SBA

Small Business Administration Web site. **www.sba.gov** (modified August 31, 2001, accessed April 2006).

## Sherman

Sherman, Stanley N. *Contract Management: Post Award.* Gaithersburg, MD: Wordcrafters Publications, 1987.

**Sherman2**

Sherman, Stanley N. *Government Procurement Management*. 2nd ed. Gaithersburg, MD: Wordcrafters Publications, 1985.

**Sherman3**

Sherman, Stanley N. *Government Procurement Management*. Gaithersburg, MD: Wordcrafters Publications, 1991.

**SPP**

Federal Acquisition Institute. *Small Purchase Procurement: An Introduction*. "Desk Guide and Workbook." Washington, DC: Federal Acquisition Institute, 1986.

**Steinhauer**

Steinhauer, Raleigh Fred. "The Intergovernmental Cooperative Purchasing Arrangement in the Metropolitan Washington Area." *A Dissertation Submitted to the School of Government and Business Administration*. Washington, DC: George Washington University, May 1972.

**TIPS**

*Topical Issues in Procurement Series*. Vienna, VA: National Contract Management Association.

(1-6)—"Controlling Consultants." Vol. 1, no. 6 (March 1990).

(1-9)—"Environmental Issues in Government Contracting." Vol. 1, no. 9 (June 1990).

(1-12)—"Who's Reading Your Mail? A Freedom of Information Act Update." Vol. 1, no. 12 (September 1990).

(1-14)—"Technology Transfer and Cooperative Research and Development Agreements." Vol. 1, no. 14 (November 1990).

(1-15)—"The Trade Agreements Act." Vol. 1, no. 15 (December 1990).

(2-2)—"The Wrath of TINA: Understanding the Penalties for Violating the Truth in Negotiations Act." Vol. 2, no. 2 (February 1991).

(2-5)—"The Data Rights Rollercoaster." Vol. 2, no. 5 (May 1991).

(2-6)—"The Mystery of the M Account." Vol. 2, no. 6 (June 1991).

(2-8)—"Expert Systems Applications in the Procurement Field." Vol. 2, no. 8 (August 1991).

(2-9)—"The Pilot Mentor–Protégé Program." Vol. 2, no. 9 (September 1991).

(2-10)—"Exploring Export Opportunities." Vol. 2, no. 10 (October 1991).

**UNI**
Unisys Defense Systems. *Handbook of Ethical Business Practices*. McLean, VA: Unisys Corporation, 1988.

**USCG**
United States Coast Guard. *Contracting Officer's Technical Representative Desk Guide*. September 1991.

**USC-44-35**
United States Code (USC) Title 44, Chapter 35.

**USC-44-3502**
United States Code (USC) Title 44, Part 3502, Paragraph 12.

**Verzuh**
Verzuh, Eric. *The Portable MBA in Project Management*. Hoboken, NJ: John Wiley & Sons, 2003.

**W-**
Workshop Series. Vienna, VA: National Contract Management Association.

AN—*Advanced Negotiations*, 1990.

ATCC—*Analyzing Total Cost Claims,* 1993.

BPA—*Blanket Purchase Agreements*, 1989.

CC—Contract Challenge, 1994.

CCC—*Conducting Contract Closeout,* 1991.

ESCA—*Explaining the Service Contract Act,* 1992.

GCLB—*Government Contract Law Basics,* 1992.

GPB—*Government Property Basics,* 1991.

GSD—*Guidelines for Specification Development,* 1992.

HAP—*How to Avoid Protests,* 1993.

ICPA—*Introduction to Cost and Price Analysis,* 1989.

MFPP—*Mastering the Fundamentals of Progress Payments,* 1993.

PSP—*Practical Small Purchasing,* 1991.

SBC—*Small Business Contracting,* 1990.

# Common Abbreviations and Acronyms

**A-76**    Office of Management and Budget (OMB) Circular Number A-76, Performance of Commercial Activities

**A-109**    Office of Management and Budget (OMB) Circular Number A-109, Major Systems Acquisition

**A-120**    Office of Management and Budget (OMB) Circular Number A-120, Guidelines for the Use of Advisory and Assistance Services

**ACH**    Automated Clearing House

**AAC**    Advance Acquisition Contract

**ACO**    administrative contracting officer

**ACRN**    Accounting Classification Reference Number

**ACSN**    Advance Change Study Notice

**ACWP**    Actual Cost of Work Performed; also called Actual Cost (AC)

**ADA**    Anti-Deficiency Act

**ADP**    Automatic Data Processing

**ADPE**    Automatic Data Processing Equipment

**ADR**    alternative dispute resolution

**ADRA**    Administrative Dispute Resolution Act of 1990 and 1996

**A-F**    Architect-Engineering

**AEC**    Army Environmental Center or Atomic Energy Commission

**AFARS**    Army FAR Supplement

**AFFARS**    Air Force FAR Supplement

**AGAR**    Department of Agriculture Acquisition Regulation

**AIDAR**    Agency for International Development Acquisition Regulation

**AMC**    Army Materiel Command

**ANSI**    American National Standards Institute

**APB**    Accounting Principles Board

**ARNet**    Acquisition Reform Network

**ASBCA** Armed Services Board of Contract Appeals

**ASPR** Armed Services Procurement Regulation

**ASSIST-Online** Acquisition Streamlining and Standardization Information System

**AUPC** average unit procurement cost

**BA** budget authority

**BAA** Broad Agency Announcement; Buy American Act

**BAC** Budget at Completion

**BCWP** Budgeted Cost for Work Performed; also called Earned Value

**BCWS** Budgeted Cost for Work Scheduled; also called Planned Value (PV) or Performance Measurement Baseline (PMB)

**BLS** Bureau of Labor Statistics

**BOA** Basic Ordering Agreement

**BOE** Basis of Estimate

**BOM** bill of materials

**B&P** Bid and Proposal

**BPA** Blanket Purchase Agreement

**BRAC** Base Realignment and Closure

**BXA** Bureau of Export Administration

**CA** control account

**CAA** Clean Air Act (1955) (Amend. 1990)

**CAAC** Civilian Agency Acquisition Council

**CAD/CAM** Computer-Aided Design/Computer-Aided Manufacturing

**CAGE Code** Commercial and Government Entity Code

**CAIV** Cost as an Independent Variable

**CALS** Computer-Aided Acquisition and Logistics Support or Continuous Acquisition and Life-cycle Support

**CAM** DCAA Contract Audit Manual

**CAO** Contract Administration Office

**CAP** Contractor Acquired Property; Control Account Plan

**CAPS** Center of Advanced Purchasing Studies or Control Account Plans

| | | | |
|---|---|---|---|
| **CAR** | Commerce Acquisition Regulation | **CFSR** | Contract Funds Status Report |
| **CAS** | Cost Accounting Standards | **CFR** | Code of Federal Regulations |
| **CASB** | Cost Accounting Standards Board | **CFTA** | Canadian Free Trade Agreement |
| **CBA** | Collective Bargaining Agreement | **CI** | configuration item |
| | | **CICA** | Competition in Contracting Act |
| **CBB** | Contract Budget Base | **CID** | Commercial Item Description |
| **CBO** | Congressional Budget Office | **CISG** | Convention on Contracts for the International Sale of Goods |
| **CCB** | Configuration Control Board | | |
| **CCF** | Cost Comparison Form | **CL** | car load |
| **CCP** | Contract Change Proposal | **CLIN** | Contract Line Item Number |
| **CDA** | Contract Disputes Act | **CO** | contracting officer |
| **CDR** | Critical Design Review | **COC** | Certificate of Competency |
| **CDRL** | Contract Data Requirements List | **COCO** | Contractor Owned, Contractor Operated |
| **CER** | Cost Estimating Relationships | **COGP** | Commission on Government Procurement |
| **CERCLA** | Comprehensive Environmental Response, Compensation, and Liability Act (Superfund) | **COI** | Conflict of Interest |
| | | **CONOPS** | Concept of Operations |
| **CFC** | Court of Federal Claims | **CONUS** | Continental United States |
| **CFE** | Contractor-Furnished Equipment | **COR** | Contracting Officer's Representative |

**COTR** Contracting Officer's Technical Representative

**COTS** commercial-off-the-shelf

**CPAF** Cost Plus Award Fee

**CPBOSH** Committee for the Purchase from the Blind and Other Severely Handicapped

**CPFF** Cost Plus Fixed Fee

**CPIF** Cost Plus Incentive Fee

**CPI** Cost Performance Index

**CPM** Critical Path Method

**CPPC** Cost Plus Percentage of Cost

**CPSR** Contractor Purchasing System Review

**CR** Clarification Request; continuing resolution

**CRA** Continuing Resolution Authority

**CRAG** Contractor Risk Assessment Guide

**CUPS** Council on the Uniform Procurement System

**CV** cost invoice

**CWA** Clean Water Act

**CWBS** Contact Work Breakdown Structure

**CY** Calendar Year

**DAC** Defense Acquisition Circular

**DAWIA** Defense Acquisition Workforce Improvement Act (1991)

**DAR** Defense Acquisition Regulation

**DARC** Defense Acquisition Regulatory Council

**DBA** Davis-Bacon Act

**DBMS** Database Management System

**DCAA** Defense Contract Audit Agency

**DD FORM** Department of Defense Form

**DEAR** Department of Energy Acquisition Regulation

**DFARS** Department of Defense FAR Supplement

**DID** Data Item Description

**DIG** Designated Industry Group

| | | | |
|---|---|---|---|
| **DLA** | Defense Logistics Agency | **EFAR** | Corps of Engineers Federal Acquisition Regulation |
| **DLAR** | Defense Logistics Acquisition Regulation | **EFT** | Electronic Funds Transfer |
| **DOD** | Department of Defense | **e-COMMERCE** | electronic commerce |
| **DOLAR** | Department of Labor Acquisition Regulations | **EIS** | Environmental Impact Statement |
| **DOSAR** | Department of State Acquisition Regulation | **e-Mail** | electronic mail |
| **DPAS** | Defense Priorities and Allocations System | **e-MALL DOD** | electronic mall |
| | | **EO** | executive order |
| **DR** | Deficiency Report | **EOQ** | Economic Order Quantity |
| **DTC** | Design to Cost | **EPA** | Environmental Protection Agency |
| **EA** | Environmental Assessment; also Evolutionary Acquisition | **EPAAR** | Environmental Protection Agency Acquisition Regulation |
| **EAC** | estimate at completion | **EPCI** | Enhanced Proliferation Control Initiative |
| **EAJA** | Equal Access to Justice Act | | |
| **EAR** | Export Administration Regulations | **EPIC** | Electronic Processes Initiatives Committee |
| **ECP** | Engineering Change Proposal | **EPS** | Electronic Posting System |
| **ECRC** | Electronic Commerce Resource Centers | **ESI** | early supplier involvement |
| **EDI** | Electronic Data Interchange | **EVMS** | Earned Value Management System |
| **EEO** | Equal Employment Opportunity | **FAC** | Federal Acquisition Circular |

**FACNET**  Federal Acquisition Computer Network

**FAD Sheet**  Financial Data Addendum Sheet

**FAI**  Federal Acquisition Institute

**FAR**  Federal Acquisition Regulation

**FARA**  Federal Acquisition Reform Act

**FASA**  Federal Acquisition Streamlining Act (1994)

**FASB**  Financial Accounting Standards Board

**FBO**  FEDBIZOPPS, or Federal Business Opportunities

**FCCM**  Facilities Capital Cost of Money

**FDPC**  Federal Data Processing Center

**FFP**  Firm-Fixed-Price

**FFCA**  Federal Facilities Compliance Act

**FFRDC**  Federally Funded Research and Development Center

**FIFO**  first-in, first-out

**FIP**  Federal Information Processing

**FMS**  Foreign Military Sale

**FOB**  Free on Board

**FOIA**  Freedom of Information Act

**FOUO**  For Official Use Only

**FPAF**  Fixed-Price-Award Fee

**FPDC**  Federal Procurement Data Center

**FPDS**  Federal Procurement Data System

**FPI**  Federal Prison Industries; also Federal Procurement Institute; *also* Fixed-Price-Incentive

**FPMR**  Federal Property Management Regulation

**FPR**  Fixed-Price Redeterminable; also Federal Procurement Regulations; *also* Final Proposal Revision

**FSD**  full-scale development

**FSN**  Federal Stock Number

**FSS**  Federal Supply Schedule

**FTE**  Full-Time Equivalents

**FY**  fiscal year

**G&A** General and Administrative

**GAAP** Generally Accepted Accounting Principles

**GAO** General Accountability Office

**GATT** General Agreements on Tariffs and Trade

**GBL** Government Bill of Lading

**GFE** government-furnished equipment

**GFP** government-furnished property

**GNP** gross national product

**GOCO** Government-Owned, Contractor-Operated

**GPE** government point of entry

**GPLR** Government Purpose License Rights

**GPRA** Government Performance and Results Act (1993)

**GSA** General Services Administration

**GSAR** General Services Administration Acquisition Regulation

**GSBCA** General Services Board of Contract Appeals

**GWAC** Governmentwide Acquisition Contract

**HBCU** Historically Black Colleges and Universities

**HCA** Head of Contracting Activity

**HHSAR** Department of Health and Human Services Acquisition Regulation

**HUBZone** Historically Underutilized Business

**HUDAR** Department of Housing and Urban Development Acquisition Regulation

**IAAR** U.S. Information Agency Acquisition Regulation

**IAE** Integrated Acquisition Environment

**IAIC** Interagency Acquisition Internet Council

**ICC** Interstate Commerce Commission

**ICE** Independent Cost Estimate

**IDAR** Department of Interior Acquisition Regulation

**IDIQ** indefinite delivery/indefinite quantity contract

| | | | | |
|---|---|---|---|---|
| **IDWA** | Interdivision Work Authorization | | **ITAR** | International Traffic in Arms Regulation |
| **IDWO** | Interdivision Work Order | | **ITC** | International Trade Commission |
| **IEC** | International Electrotechnical Commission | | **ITMRA** | Information Technology Management Reform Act (1996) |
| **IFB** | invitation for bids | | **IWO** | Interdivision Work Order |
| **IFSS** | International Federal Supply Schedule | | **J&A** | Justification and Approval |
| **IG** | Inspector General | | **JAR** | Justice Acquisition Regulation |
| **IGCE** | Independent Government Cost Estimate | | **JEPCO** | Joint Electronic Commerce Program Office |
| **ILS** | Integrated Logistics Support | | **JIT** | just in time |
| **IMIP** | Industrial Modernization Incentives Program | | **JTR** | Joint Travel Regulations |
| **INCOTERMS** | International Commercial Terms | | **JWOD** | Javits-Wagner-O'Day Act |
| **IOT** | Interorganizational Transfer | | **LCL** | less than truck load |
| **IPSO** | information processing services organization | | **LIFO** | last-in, first-out |
| **IR&D** | Independent Research and Development | | **LOC** | level of control |
| **IRO** | Independent Review Officer | | **LOE** | level of effort |
| **ISSA** | Interservice Support Agreement | | **LOI** | letter of intent |
| | | | **LTOP** | Lease-to-Ownership Program |
| | | | **LRE** | Latest Revised Estimate |

**LS**  logistics support

**LWOP**  lease-with-option purchase

**MANTECH**  Manufacturing Technology

**MAP**  Military Assistance Program

**MAS**  multiple award schedule

**MEO**  [Government's] Most Efficient Organization

**MILSPEC**  Military Specification

**MILSTRIP**  Military Standard Requisitioning and Issue Procedures

**MIPR**  Military Interdepartmental Purchase Request

**MMAS**  Material Management and Accounting System

**MOA**  Memorandum of Agreement

**MOU**  Memorandum of Understanding

**MPC**  Model Procurement Code

**MR**  management reserve

**MRO**  material release order; also maintenance, repair, and operating

**MRP**  Material Requirements Planning; also Manufacturing Resource Planning

**MTBF**  mean time between failures

**NAFTA**  North American Free Trade Agreement

**NAICS**  North American Industry Classification System

**NAPS**  Navy Acquisition Procedures Supplement

**NASA FAR Supplement (NFS)**  National Aeronautics and Space Administration FAR Supplement

**NDI**  Nondevelopmental Item

**NEPA**  National Environmental Policy Act (1969)

**NESHAPs**  National Emissions Standards for Hazardous Air Pollutants

**NIB**  National Industries for the Blind

**NISH**  National Industries for the Severely Handicapped

**NPR**  National Performance Review

**NRCAR**  Nuclear Regulatory Commission Acquisition Regulation

| | |
|---|---|
| **NSN** | National Stock Number |
| **NSS** | National Security System |
| **NTE** | not to exceed |
| **O&M** | operations & maintenance |
| **OBS** | Organizational Breakdown Structure |
| **OCI** | Organizational Conflict of Interest |
| **ODC** | other direct costs |
| **OFPP** | Office of Federal Procurement Policy |
| **OMB** | Office of Management and Budget |
| **OMI** | Other Minority Institutions |
| **OPIC** | Overseas Private Investment Corporation |
| **OSDBU** | Office of Small and Disadvantaged Business Utilization |
| **OT** | other transactions |
| **OTB** | Over Target Baseline |
| **PALT** | Procurement Administrative Lead Time |

| | |
|---|---|
| **PASS** | Procurement Automated Source System |
| **PB** | President's Budget |
| **PBA** | Performance-Based Acquisition |
| **PBC** | Performance-Based Costing |
| **PBSA** | Performance-Based Services Acquisition |
| **PBWS** | Performance-Based Work Statement |
| **PCA** | Physical Configuration Audit |
| **PCO** | procuring contracting officer |
| **PEA** | Price Evaluation Adjustment |
| **PERT** | Program Evaluation and Review Technique |
| **PHSAR** | Public Health Services Acquisition Regulation |
| **P&L** | profit and loss |
| **P.L.** | Public Law |
| **PM** | Program Manager |
| **PMAT** | Performance Measurement Action Team |
| **PMB** | Performance Measurement Baseline |

| | | | |
|---|---|---|---|
| **PNM** | Price Negotiation Memorandum | **QPL** | Qualified Products List |
| **PO** | Purchase Order or Program Officer | **R&D** | research and development |
| **POR** | planned order release | **RCRA** | Resource Conservation and Recovery Act (1976) |
| **PR** | Purchase Request; Purchase Requisition | **RDT&E** | Research, Development, Test, and Evaluation |
| **PRAG** | Performance Risk Assessment Group | **REA** | Request for Equitable Adjustment |
| **PRR** | Production Readiness Review | **RFI** | request for information |
| **PRS** | Performance Requirements Summary | **RFP** | request for proposal |
| | | **RFQ** | request for quotation |
| **PTAC** | Procurement Technical Assistance Center | **ROI** | Return on Investment |
| **PTACAP** | Procurement Technical Assistance Cooperative Agreement Program | **ROM** | Rough Order of Magnitude |
| | | **SADBUS** | Small and Disadvantaged Business Utilization Specialist |
| **PWS** | performance work statement | **SARA** | Service Acquisition Reform Act; *also* Superfund Amendment and Reauthorization Act |
| **QA** | quality assurance | | |
| **QASP** | Quality Assurance Surveillance Plan | **SAS** | Single Award Schedule |
| **QBL** | Qualified Bidders List | **SAT** | simplified acquisition threshold |
| **QC** | quality control | | |
| **QML** | Qualified Manufacturers List | **SBA** | Small Business Act; *also* Small Business Administration |

**SBAR**  Small Business Administration Acquisition Regulation

**SBCDP**  Small Business Competitiveness Demonstration Program

**SBIR**  Small Business Innovation Research Program

**SCA**  Service Contract Act

**SCCF**  Streamlined Cost Comparison Form

**SCDRL or SDRL**  Subcontractor's Data Requirements List

**SDB**  Small and Disadvantaged Business

**SF**  Standard Form

**SIC Code**  Standard Industrial Classification Code

**SOO**  statement of objectives

**SOT**  Secretary of the Treasury

**SOW**  statement of work

**SPC**  Statistical Process Control

**SPI**  Single Process Initiative

**SSA**  Source Selection Authority

**SSAC**  Source Selection Advisory Council

**SSEB**  Source Selection Evaluation Board

**SSP**  Source Selection Plan

**SV**  Schedule Variance

**TAPR**  Treasury Acquisition Procurement Regulation

**TAR**  Department of Transportation Acquisition Regulation

**TD**  technical data

**TCO**  Termination Contracting Officer

**TDP**  technical data packages

**TIA**  Technology Investment Agreement

**TINA**  Truth in Negotiations Act

**T&E**  Test and Evaluation

**T&M**  Time and Materials

**TL**  truck load

**TQM**  Total Quality Management

**TSCA**  Toxic Substances Control Act (1976)

**TSPR**    Total System Performance Responsibility

**Ts and Cs**  Terms and Conditions

**UCC**    Uniform Commercial Code

**UCF**    Uniform Contract Format

**UNCITRAL**  UN Commission on International Trade Law

**UPS**    Uniform Procurement System

**USC**    United States Code

**USCA**    United States Code Annotated

**VA**    Veterans Affairs

**VAAR**    Veterans Affairs Acquisition Regulation

**VE**    Value Engineering

**VECP**    Value Engineering Change Proposal

**WBS**    Work Breakdown Structure

**WGM**    Weighted Guidelines Method

**WQA**    Water Quality Act

**WP**    work packages

**ZBB**    Zero-Based Budgeting

## ABC ANALYSIS

Application of Pareto's Law, or the 80/20 rule. ABC analysis, as related to inventory, is simply a determination of the relative ratios between the number of items and the dollar value of items purchased repetitively as stock. Typically, five–10 percent of the items (A items) account for 75–80 percent of the investment, 20–25 percent of the items (B items) account for 15–20 percent of the investment, and 70–75 percent of the items (C items) account for five–10 percent of the investment. Inventories should be managed accordingly, with more emphasis placed on the strategic management of the A items.

*Commercial Practices*

## ABSOLUTE STANDARDS

A type of standard used in competitive negotiations to evaluate a pro-posal. Includes both the maximum and minimum acceptable values for all selected evaluation criteria.

*Garrett*

## ABSORPTION OF COSTING

A method of determining the actual cost of a unit of production (either at various stages of completion or when service is provided), which treats fixed indirect costs as product costs. Under absorption costing, a unit's total cost is equal to the sum of the allocated fixed indirect costs and the costs of direct material, direct labor, and applicable overhead.

*P&L*

## ABSTRACT OF BIDS

A list of bidders for a particular sealed bid procurement that shows the significant portions of their bids.

*GUIDE*

## ABSTRACT OF TITLE

A condensed history of the title to property as created from past records.

*Commercial Practices*

## ACCELERATED DELIVERY

The advancing, in whole or in part, of the scheduled delivery of material on order to meet emergency requirements.

*AFIT*

## ACCELERATED PROCEDURE

Procedure under the Contract Disputes Act (CDA) whereby an appellant before an agency's Board of Contract Appeals can elect, for claims of $100,000 or less, to have a decision issued on a claim within six months after making the election. *(Threshold amount revised in sixth edition.)*

### GUIDE
See also "Expedited Procedure."

## ACCEPTANCE
(1) The act of an authorized government (buyer) representative by which the government (buyer) assents to owner-ship of existing and identified supplies, or approves specific services rendered, as partial or complete performance of a contract.

### AFIT

(2) An offeree's manifestation of assent to the terms of an offer made to him or her by an offeror. The acceptance is the act, the oral or written assent, or, in certain instances, the silence that creates contractual liabilities for both the offeror and the offeree.

### FBL

(3) The taking and receiving of anything in good part, and as if it were a tacit agreement to a preceding act, which might have been defeated or avoided if such acceptance had not been made.

(4) Agreement to the terms offered in a contract. An acceptance must be communicated, and (in common law) it must be the mirror image of the offer.

### Garrett

## ACCEPTANCE, IMPLIED
In the case of a bilateral contract, acceptance of an offer need not be expressed, but it may be shown by any words or acts indicating the offeree's assent to the proposed bargain.

### BLD

## ACCEPTANCE SAMPLING
(1) Evaluating a portion of a lot for the purpose of accepting or rejecting the entire lot as either conforming or not conforming to a quality specification.

### DGCQI

(2) A statistical quality control tech-nique used to evaluate the overall condition of a given lot by inspecting only a portion or sample of the lot.

### Commercial Practices

## ACCORD AND SATISFACTION
(1) A method of discharging a claim whereby the parties agree to give and accept something in settlement of the claim and perform the agreement. The accord is the agreement, and the satisfaction is the execution or performance.

### BLD

(2) Two persons agree that one of them has a right of action against the other, but they accept a substitute or different act or value as performance.

### FBL

## ACCOUNTING, COST

Cost accounting seeks to identify and assign relevant costs to distinct business units or projects.

*NES-02*

## ACCOUNTING, MANAGERIAL

Managerial accounting seeks to collect, report, and interpret information needed for managerial decision-making.

*NES-02*

## ACCOUNTING ENTITY

The accounting process recognizes that various enterprises (i.e., companies, government units, etc.) are individual entities, and that economic activity relating to those entities can be identified and measured distinctly from other entities. The accounting entity concept does not apply only to the identification and segregation of economic activity among different enterprises; it may refer to distinctions between departments within a company, individuals within a department, segments within a conglomeration, etc.

*NCMA-CA*

## ACCOUNTING PERIOD

The accounting process recognizes the necessity of providing financial information over specified time periods. This process facilitates a comparison of the entity's performance between time periods and provides relevant financial information on a timely basis to be used in managerial decisions.

*NCMA-CA*

## ACCOUNTING PRINCIPLES BOARD (APB)

See "Financial Accounting Standards Board" (FASB).

## ACCOUNTING SYSTEM

A formal communications network that supplies relevant information for planning, control, decision-making, and evaluation.

*NCMA-CA*

## ACCOUNTS PAYABLE

Amounts owed on open accounts (e.g., materials and services received, wages earned, and fringe benefits unpaid).

*DAAT*

## ACCOUNTS RECEIVABLE

(1) Amounts due from debtors on open accounts. Under appropriated funds, amounts due from debtors for reimbursements earned or for appropriation refunds due.

*DAAT*

(2) Accounts receivable represent amounts due the company for goods shipped or services rendered, but for which the company has not yet been paid.

*NES-02*

## ACCRUAL ACCOUNTING

The accrual basis of accounting recognizes important concepts, such as receivables due from customers, payables due to vendors, interest due from investments, and other "matching" concepts, as a means of providing an accurate picture of a company's financial (economic) position.

*NCMA-CA*

See also "Matching Principle."

## ACKNOWLEDGMENT

A form used to inform the buyer that the supplier has accepted the purchase order. As a result of this acknowledgment, a bilateral agreement is consummated, as long as the terms of the acknowledgment are not substantively different from those of the purchase order.

*Commercial Practices*

## ACQUISITION

(1) A process that begins with the establishment of needs and includes the description of requirements, solicitations and source selection, contract award, contract financing, contract performance, contract administration, and all technical and management functions directly related to the process of fulfilling an organization's needs by contract.

*AFIT*

(2) The process of obtaining supplies, services, or systems by contract with appropriated funds, whether the supplies, services, or systems exist or must be created.

*NCMA-SS*

(3) The acquiring by contract with appropriated funds or supplies or services (including construction) by and for the use of the federal government through purchase or lease, whether the supplies or services are already in existence or must be created, developed, demonstrated, and evaluated. Acquisition begins at the point when agency needs are established and includes the description of requirements to satisfy agency needs, solicitation, and selection of sources; award of contracts; contract financing, performance, and administration; and those technical and management functions directly related to the process of fulfilling agency needs by contract.

*FAR*

## ACQUISITION CENTRAL

Hosted by Integrated Acquisition Environment (IAE), the E-Gov Initiative that is streamlining the federal acquisition process. Acquisition Central hopes to reach out to help every member of the acquisition community by providing one Web site for all things acquisition. From here, you can learn about regulations, systems, resources, opportunities, and training.

*http://acquisition.gov/*

## ACQUISITION COST

(1) In the context of Economic Order Quantity (EO.Q) analysis, the acquisition cost includes all costs associated with generating and processing an order and its related paperwork. In a broader management sense, the acquisition cost is the sum of the ordering, transporting, handling, and all inventory holding costs associated with the acquisition of a material.

*Commercial Practices*

(2) The money invested up front to bring in new customers.

*Garrett*

## ACQUISITION ENVIRONMENT

Internal and external factors that have an effect on and help shape acquisition programs. Often, those factors work at opposite extremes and contradict each other. They include political forces, policies, regulations, reactions to unanticipated requirements, and emergencies.

*DAAT*

## ACQUISITION GOALS

See "Goals of the Acquisition Process."

## ACQUISITION PLAN

A plan for an acquisition that serves as the basis for initiating the individual contracting actions necessary to acquire a system or support a program.

*FAI*

## ACQUISITION PLANNING

The process by which efforts of all personnel responsible for an acquisition are coordinated and integrated through a comprehensive plan for fulfilling the agency need in a timely manner at a reasonable cost. It includes developing the overall strategy for managing the acquisition.

*FAR*

## ACQUISITION PROGRAM

A directed effort funded through either procurement appropriation, or a research, development, test, and evaluation appropriation with the goal of providing a new or improved capability for a validated need. An acquisition program may include either development or procurement, or modifications of systems, subsystems, equipment, or components, as well as supporting equipment, systems, projects, and studies.

*DSMC*

## ACQUISITION REFORM NETWORK (ARNet)

ARNet was created as a result of Vice President Al Gore's National Performance Review (NPR) to "foster and propagate measurable breakthrough improvements in the way the government obtains goods and services."

*NES-98*

*Sixth edition revision:* ARNet is migrating all of the information within **Acqnet.gov**

and **Arnet.gov** to Acquisition Central.
Ref: **www.acqnet.gov/.**

## ACQUISITION RISK

The chance that some element of an
acquisition program produces an
unintended result with an adverse effect
on system effectiveness, suitability
cost, or availability for deployment.

*DSMC*

## ACQUISITION STRATEGY

(1) The conceptual framework for
conducting systems acquisition. It
encompasses the broad concepts and
objectives that direct and control the
overall development, production, and
deployment of a system. Required by
OMB Circular A-109 and government
department directives for virtually all
programs.

*DSMC*

(2) A business and technical management approach designed to achieve
program objectives within the resource
constraints imposed. It is the framework
for planning, directing, contracting for,
and managing a program. It provides
a master schedule for research,
development, test, production, fielding,
modification, postproduction management, and other activities essential for
success.

*DAAT*

## ACQUISITION STREAMLINING

Any action that results in more efficient
and effective use of resources to
develop, produce, and deploy quality
systems and products. This action
includes ensuring that only cost-effective
requirements are included, at the
most appropriate time, in system and
equipment solicitations and contracts.

*DSMC*

## ACQUISITION TEAM

The Acquisition Team consists of all
participants in government acquisition,
including not only the representatives
of technical, supply, and procurement
communities but also the customers
they serve and the contractors who
provide the products and services. The
role of each member of the Acquisition
Team is to exercise personal initiative
and sound business judgment in
providing the best value product or
service to meet the customer's needs.
In exercising initiative, government
members of the Acquisition Team may
assume if a specific strategy, practice,
policy, or procedure is in the best
interests of the government and is not
addressed in the FAR, nor prohibited
by law (statute or case law), executive
order, or other regulation, then the
strategy, practice, policy, or procedure
is a permissible exercise of authority.

*FAR*

## ACTION PLAN

The steps a team develops to implement a solution or the actions needed to make continued progress toward a solution.

*BOE II*

## ACTIVE CONTRACT

Any contract that has been awarded and on which any element of contractor performance, payment, or admin-istrative closing action is outstanding.

*AFIT*

## ACTIVITY ACCOUNTING

See "Responsibility Accounting."

## ACT OF GOD

An inevitable, accidental, or extraordinary event that cannot be foreseen and guarded against, such as lightning, a tornado, or an earthquake.

*Garrett*

## ACTUAL AUTHORITY

The power that the principal intentionally confers on the agent or allows the agent to believe he or she possesses.

*Garrett*

See also "Agent Authority."

## ACTUAL COST

A cost sustained in fact, on the basis of costs incurred, as distinguished from a forecasted or estimated cost.

*DAAT*

See also "Actual Cost of Work Performed (ACWP)."

## ACTUAL COST BASIS

A means of pricing equitable adjustments that relies on direct costing, whereby the contractor [seller] tracks all the actual direct costs that are incurred as a result of the change. This method requires that (a) the pricing action occurs *after* the work has been completed (retrospectively), and that (b) the contractor [seller] segregates the actual costs. It is rare that both of these factors will be met completely.

*W-ATCC*

See also "Jury Verdict Basis," "Modified Total Cost Basis," and "Total Cost Basis."

## ACTUAL COST OF WORK PERFORMED (ACWP)

(1) The program's total incurred cost, which is based on summation from the accounting system.

*NES-93*

(2) The costs incurred and recorded in accomplishing the work performed within a given time period.

*DAAT*

Compare "Budgeted Cost of Work Performed (BCWP)" and "Budgeted Cost of Work Scheduled (BCWS)."

**AD VALOREM** (According to Value)
A term usually applied to a customs duty charged on the value only of goods that are dutiable, irrespective of quality, weight, or any other considerations. The ad valorem rates of duty are

expressed in percentages of the value of the goods, usually ascertained from the invoice.

*Commercial Practices*

## ADJUSTED CEILING

A negotiated adjustment to the ceiling price that is for changes and that reflects a change in the negotiated maximum liability of the government.

*AFIT*

See also "Negotiated Ceiling."

## ADJUSTED TARGET

Accumulated price resulting from changes to the basic contract for in-program change, change in scope, and/or terminations reflecting the current negotiated target price for work authorized.

*AFIT*

## ADMINISTRATIVE APPEAL AUTHORITY

With receipt of an appeal, the official designated in paragraph 9.a. of the Circular A-76 or the designee assigns an official(s) to serve on an A-76 Administrative Appeal Authority for that appeal. The individual(s) selected must be (a) independent of the activity under review or (b) at least two organizational levels above the official who certified the Government's Management Plan and Most Efficient Organization (MEO). The appeal authority reviews appeals to ensure that all costs are properly accounted for in accordance with the principles and procedures of this supplemental handbook. The authority shall also ensure that all participants have full and equal access to the decision process.

*OMB A-76*

## ADMINISTRATIVE CHANGE

A unilateral contract change, in writing, that does not affect the substantive rights of the parties, such as a change in the paying office or the appropriation data.

*FAR*

## ADMINISTRATIVE CONTRACTING OFFICER (ACO)

The government contracting officer, often at an installation other than the one making the contract, who is authorized to perform post-award contract administration duties, monitor contractor's performance, and perform post-award contractual functions delegated by the purchasing office.

*DSMC, OPM*

## ADMINISTRATIVE COSTS

General overhead expenses incident to the issue, sale, and transfer of material.

*AFIT*

## ADMINISTRATIVE LEAD TIME

The time interval between initiation of procurement action and letting [award] of contract or placing of order.

*AFIT*

## ADMINISTERED PRICE

A price determined by the conscious price policy of a seller rather than by the competitive forces of the marketplace.

*Commercial Practices*

## ADVANCE ACQUISITION CONTRACT (AAC)

A preliminary contract committing the contractor to proceed with an effort, including planning and engineering, placement of orders for material, and other production efforts necessary to protect the required delivery schedule for the contract end items cited in the contract. Used when the lead time is too long to allow waiting for funds in the fiscal year for which the end items are to be procured. Long lead funds are specifically appropriated for this type of effort. The definitive contract is negotiated at a later date and supersedes the AAC.

*Navy*

## ADVANCE AGREEMENT

An agreement between the contractor and the government regarding the treatment of specified costs negotiated either before or during contract performance but preferably before the cost covered by the agreement is incurred.

*PW*

## ADVANCE ARRANGEMENT

An advance agreement required for the movement of certain commodities by air carrier. Gold and other precious metals, live animals, and other classes of shipments may require such arrangement.

*Commercial Practices*

## ADVANCE BUY

(1) Procurement to provide for components that require a longer lead time than the system of which they are a part.

*AFIT*

(2) Also called forward buying, it is the commitment of purchases in anticipation of future requirements beyond current lead times. Organizations may buy ahead as a matter of strategy or because of anticipated shortages, strikes, or price increases.

*Commercial Practices*

## ADVANCE PAYMENT

An advance of money made by the government to a contractor prior to, in anticipation of, and for the purpose of performance under a contract.

*OPM*

See also "Contractor Financing."

## ADVANCE PAYMENT BOND

This bond secures fulfillment of the contractor's obligations under an advance payment provision.

*FAR*

## ADVANCE PROCUREMENT PLAN

A plan of procurement accomplishment showing the method of procurement, the general timetable, and the expected price.

*OPM*

## ADVANCED CHARGE

The amount of freight or other charge on a shipment advanced by one transportation to another, or to the shipper, to be collected from the consignee.

*Commercial Practices*

## ADVANCED DEVELOPMENT

Projects that have advanced to a point where development of experimental hardware for technical or operational testing is required prior to determination of whether those items should be designed or engineered for eventual use.

*AFIT*

## ADVISORY AND ASSISTANCE SERVICES

Means those services provided under contract by nongovernmental sources to support or improve organizational policy development, decision-making, management and administration, program and/or project management and administration, or R&D activities. It can also mean the furnishing of professional advice or assistance rendered to improve the effectiveness of federal management processes or procedures (including those of an engineering and technical nature). In rendering the foregoing services, outputs may take the form of information, advice, opinions, alternatives, analyses, evaluations, recommendations, training, and the day-to-day aid of support personnel needed for the successful performance of ongoing federal operations. All advisory and assistance services are classified in one of the following definitional subdivisions:

(1) Management and professional support services (i.e., contractual services that provide assistance, advice, or training for the efficient and effective management and operation of organizations, activities, including management and support services for R&D activities, or systems). The services are normally closely related to the basic responsibilities and mission of the agency originating the requirement for the acquisition of services by contract. Included are efforts that support or contribute to improved organization of program management, logistics management, project monitoring and reporting, data collection, budgeting, accounting, performance auditing, and administrative technical support for conferences and training programs.

(2) Studies, analyses, and evaluations (i.e., contracted services that provide organized, analytical assessments/evaluations in support of policy development, decision-making, management, or administration). Included are studies in support of R&D activities. Also included are acquisi-

tions of models, methodologies, and related software supporting studies, analyses, or evaluations.

(3) Engineering and technical services (i.e., contractual services used to support the program office during the acquisition cycle by providing such services as systems engineering and technical direction to ensure the effective operation and maintenance of a weapon system or major system as defined in OMB Circular No. A-109 or to provide direct support of a weapon system that is essential to research, development, production, operation, or maintenance of the system).

*FAR*

## ADVISORY PANEL ON STREAMLINING AND CODIFYING ACQUISITION LAWS
See "Section 800 Panel."

## AFFIDAVIT
A written statement sworn to and acknowledged by a notary.

*Commercial Practices*

## AFFECTED PARTIES
Federal employees and existing federal contractors who will or could be affected by a decision to waive a cost comparison or who have submitted bids to convert to or from in-house, contract, or Interservice Support Agreement (ISSA) performance, as a result of a cost comparison, and their representatives are affected parties. Agencies or parts of agencies that have submitted formal bids or offers, in order to compete for the right to provide services through ISSAs, are also considered Affected Parties.

*OMB A-76*

## AFFILIATES
Associated business concerns or individuals if, directly or indirectly, (a) either one controls or can control the other, or (b) a third party controls or can control both.

*FAR*

## AFFIRMATIVE ACTION
A provision of the Equal Opportunity Act of 1972 that requires all firms to take affirmative action to move toward achieving a workforce that accurately reflects the composition of the community. A firm must compare its employment, by department and by job level, with data on the availability of talent in the relevant labor market.

*Commercial Practices*

## AFFIRMATIVE ACTION PLAN
A plan submitted with a bid, under which the bidder agrees to use its best efforts to employ certain percentages of minority workers.

*GUIDE*

## AGENCY

(1) A relationship whereby the principal authorizes another (the agent) to act for and on behalf of the principal and to bind the principal in contract.

*FBL*

(2) The term "agency" means any executive department, military department, government corporation, government controlled corporation, or other establishment in the executive branch of the federal government, or any independent regulatory agency. Within the Executive Office of the President, the term includes only the Office of Management and Budget (OMB) and the Office of Administration.

*OMB A-130*

(3) A relationship that exists when there is a delegation of authority to perform all acts connected within a particular trade, business, or company. It gives authority to the agent to act in all matters relating to the business of the principal.

*Garrett*

See also "Agent Authority."

## AGENCY FOR INTERNATIONAL DEVELOPMENT (AID)

A division of the U.S. Department of State that provides grants and loans to developing countries for development and foreign policy reasons.

*NES-94*

## AGENCY-PECULIAR PROPERTY

A property category that encompasses government-owned property that is peculiar to the mission of one agency (i.e., military hardware, such as an aircraft carrier, or space equipment, such as a space shuttle).

*W-GPB*

## AGENT

An employee (usually a contract manager) empowered to bind his or her organization legally in contract negotiations.

*Garrett*

## AGENT AUTHORITY

The power delegated by a principal to his or her agent; a right to exercise power. *Actual authority:* Authority that the principal intentionally confers on the agent or allows the agent to believe himself or herself to possess. *Apparent authority:* The principal knowingly permits the agent to exercise authority, though not actually granted. *Express authority:* Authority delegated to an agent intentionally, distinctly, plainly expressed orally, or in writing. *Implied authority:* Authority implied from the principal's conduct; it includes only such acts as are incident and necessary to the exercise of the authority expressly granted.

*BLD*

See also "Agency."

## AGING SCHEDULE

A report of the status of invoices that are outstanding. Used in collection activities.

*Cohen*

## AIRWAY BILL

The document used for the shipment of air freight by national and international air carriers that states the commodities shipped, shipping instructions, shipping costs, etc.

*Commercial Practices*

## ALLOCABLE COST

(1) A cost whose relative benefits make it assignable or chargeable to one or more of the cost objectives agreed to between contractual parties.

*OPM*

(2) A cost is allocable to a government contract if it (a) is incurred specifically for the contract; (b) benefits both the contract and other work, and can be distributed to them in reasonable proportion to the benefits received; or (c) is necessary to the overall operation of the business, although a direct relationship to any particular cost objective cannot be shown.

## ALLOCATE

Assignment of a cost item, or group of cost items, to one or more cost objectives for both direct and indirect costs.

*FAR*

## ALLOWABLE COST

A cost that is reasonable, allocable, within accepted standards, or otherwise conforms to generally accepted accounting principles (GAAP), specific limitations or exclusions, or agreed-to terms between contractual parties.

*OPM*

## ALPHA CONTRACTING

Alpha contracting converts the traditionally consecutive contracting process into a concurrent exchange of information and agreements. Team members work together simultaneously to make quicker decisions. Alpha contracting establishes a team consisting of contracting, program, and audit personnel; the user; and the contractor and its principal subcontractors. Together, this team develops the scope of work and other contract requirements, which form a baseline from which the team can jointly develop the technical and cost details that are the basis of the contract agreement.

*NES-00*

## ALTERNATE BID

One of two or more bids on the same item, submitted on different bases by the same bidder, as provided by the invitation to bid.

*AFIT*

## ALTERNATE ITEM

An item selected by the responsible engineering activity in lieu of the forecast item.

*AFIT*

## ALTERNATIVE DISPUTE RESOLUTION (ADR)

(1) Any procedure that is used, in lieu of litigation, to resolve issues in controversy, including but not limited to, settlement negotiations, conciliation, facilitation, mediation, fact-finding, mini-trials, and arbitration.

*Garrett*

(2) ADR means any type of procedure or combination of procedures voluntarily used to resolve issues in controversy. Those procedures may include, but are not limited to, conciliation, facilitation, mediation, fact-finding, mini-trials, arbitration, and use of ombudsmen.

*FAR*

## AMENDMENT

A change (correction, deletion, or addition) to any information contained in an Invitation for Bid (IFB) or Request for Proposal (RFP) (or previous amendment thereto). The amendment becomes part of the solicitation and any resulting contract.

*FAI*

See also "Contract Modification."

## AMORTIZATION

(1) The gradual reduction, redemption, or liquidation of the balance of an account according to a specified schedule of time and amounts.

*AFIT*

(2) Process of spreading the cost of an intangible asset over the expected useful life of the asset.

*Garrett*

## ANSI X12

A set of standards promulgated by the American National Standards Institute (ANSI) for use in formatting and handling purchasing-related documents transmitted by electronic data interchange (EDI).

*Commercial Practices*

## ANTICIPATED INVENTORY

Anticipated stocks are accumulated for a well-defined future need. They differ from buffer (safety) stocks in that they are committed in the face of certainty.

*Commercial Practices*

## ANTICIPATED REIMBURSEMENT

The amount of reimbursements expected to be earned and added to appropriation or other funding authority as a source of funds in order to cover obligations incurred in performance of work, services, procurement of material for others, or material delivered from stock.

*AFIT*

## ANTICIPATORY PROFIT

Profits payable for work not performed. This payment is viewed as a reasonable sanction to be imposed upon defaulters in ordinary contractual relationships. The Termination for Convenience clause established for government contracts bars payment of anticipatory profit.

*Sherman*

See also "Convenience Termination."

## ANTICIPATORY REPUDIATION

When the contractor (supplier), without justification, makes a positive statement to the government (buyer) that it will not perform its contractual duties.

*BLD*

## ANTIDEFICIENCY ACT

An Act prohibiting the obligation of government money in advance of an appropriation or in excess of the amount of an available appropriation.

*DOD*

(2) The salient features of this Act include prohibitions against authorizing or incurring obligations or expenditures in excess of amounts apportioned by the Office of Management and Budget (OMB) or in excess of amounts permitted by agency regulations; and establishment of procedures for determining the responsibility for violations and for reporting violations to the President, through OMB and to the Congress.

*DAAT*

## ANTIKICKBACK ACT

Legislation designed to deter subcontractors from making payments to influence the award of subcontracts, 41 U.S.C. 51–54.

*FAR*

Also known as "Copeland Antikickback Act."

## ANTITRUST ACTS

Federal and state statutes to protect trade and commerce from unlawful restraints, price discrimination, price fixing, and monopolies. Most states have mini-antitrust acts patterned on the federal acts. The principal federal antitrust acts are the Sherman Act (1890), the Clayton Act (1914), the Federal Trade Commission Act (1914), and the Robinson-Patman Act (1936).

*BLD*

## ANTITRUST VIOLATIONS

Anticompetitive practices, such as collusive bidding, follow-the-leader pricing, rotated low bids, and collusive price estimating systems, are antitrust violations.

*FAR*

## APPARENT AUTHORITY

See "Agent Authority."

## APPEAL

Resort to a superior (i.e., appellate) court to review the decision of an inferior (i.e., trial) court or administrative agency.

*BLD*

## APPEAL NOTICE

A notice to a board of contract appeals that a contracting officer's final decision will be appealed.

*GUIDE*

## APPORTIONMENT

The Office of Management and Budget (OMB) distributes funds to federal agencies for obligation. An agency may not obligate more funds than it receives.

*DLA*

## APPROPRIATION

An authorization by an act of Congress that permits federal agencies to incur obligations and to make payments from the Treasury. An appropriation usually follows enactment of authorizing legislation. An appropriation act is the most common means of providing budget authority (BA).

*DAAT*

See "Budget Authority." Appropriations do not represent cash actually set aside in the Treasury; they represent limitations of amounts that agencies may obligate during a specified time period.

## APPROPRIATION BILL

(1) Passed by Congress and signed by the president, this bill tells an agency how much it can spend on a program. This law actually gives the agency the funds to pay the bills.

*DLA*

(2) After an appropriation is enacted by Congress, the Office of Management and Budget (OMB) divides those appropriated funds on a quarterly basis to the various executive organizations through a process called apportionment. Departments and agencies then allocate funds throughout their respective organizations.

*TIPS(2-6)*

## ARBITRAGE

A financial term meaning the simultaneous buying of a security, commodity, or currency in one market while selling the same item in another market. In international currency transactions, one can use arbitrage to make a profit from simultaneous buy and sell transactions for one currency or buy simultaneous transactions in more than one currency. The key to arbitrage is taking advantage of temporary aberrations in the market.

*Commercial Practices*

## ARBITRATION

(1) A nonjudicial method for settling matters of disputes between parties.

*Cohen*

(2) Procedure whereby a dispute is referred to one or more impartial persons (selected by the disputing parties) for a final and binding determination.

*GUIDE*

(3) To settle a dispute, an appointed arbitrator (third person) comes in to help the parties make an out-of-court decision. This arbitration saves the time and expense of litigation.

*FBL*

(4) A means of setting disputes between parties with an objective outside party acting as a fact-finder and a primary decision-maker.

*Commercial Practices*

### ARBITRATOR
A third person chosen to decide a dispute between two other persons.

*FBL*

### ARMED SERVICES BOARD OF CONTRACT APPEALS (ASBCA)
Board established to act as the authorized representative of the Secretary of Defense (SECDEF) or Department Secretaries in deciding claims under the disputes clause of government contracts.

*DAAT*

### ARMED SERVICES PROCUREMENT ACT
General federal statute enacted in 1947 that governs contracting by the Department of Defense (DOD) and its military services.

*GUIDE*

### ARMED SERVICES PROCUREMENT REGULATION (ASPR)
Set of procurement regulations issued in 1949 that once governed procurement by military agencies and later (in 1978) became known as the Defense Acquisition Regulation (DAR).

*GUIDE*

### AS IS
A contract phrase referring to the condition of property to be sold or leased; generally pertains to a disclaimor of liability. Property sold in as-is condition is generally not guaranteed.

*Garrett*

### ASSEMBLAGE
A collection of items that is designed to accomplish one general function and is identified and issued as a single item.

*AFIT*

### ASSETS
Property of all kinds (real and personal, tangible and intangible), including, among other things, for certain purposes, patents, and causes of action that belong to any person (including a corporation and the estate of a decedent). The entire property of a person, association, corporation, or estate that is applicable or subject to the payment of his or her debts.

*BLD*

## ASSIGN

To convey or transfer to another, as to assign property, rights, or interests to another.

*Garrett*

## ASSIGNMENT

(1) A transfer of rights (usually contract rights) from an assignor to an assignee.

*FBL*

(2) A transference of a property right (such as a contact or a purchase order) or title to another party. In shipping, it is commonly used with a bill of lading, which involves transfer of rights, title, and interest for the purpose of endorsement. Such endorsement gives, to the party named, the title to the property covered by the bill of lading.

*Commercial Practices*

## ASSIST AUDIT

An audit performed by one audit office at the request of another audit office; usually, an adjunct to or an integral part of an audit being performed by the requestor.

*OPM*

## ATTACHMENT

A legal proceeding accompanying an act in court by which a plaintiff may acquire a lien on a defendant's property as a security for the payment of any judgment which the plaintiff may obtain.

*Commercial Practices*

## ATTRIBUTE SCREENING

A methodology for ensuring that technical or specification requirements and customer expectations are clearly defined, described, and reflected in the product. The process to be followed is to tabulate the functional and physical attributes, including inputs resulting from customer specification documents, government regulations, internal reviews, and industry standards. Next, the attributes are refined as to requirements and attendant priorities (the must-haves, the nice-to-haves, and the can-do-withouts). This process is repeated until the effect of the requirement is clear to all parties. At the end of the procedure, an accurate design definition and an understanding of the customer requirements and priorities should be evident.

*W-GSD*

## ATTRITION

The loss of a resource resulting from natural causes in the normal course of events, such as a turnover of employees or spoilage and obsolescence of material.

*DOD-MMH*

## AUDIOVISUAL PRODUCTION

A unified presentation, developed according to a plan or script, containing visual imagery, sound, or both, and used to convey information.

*OMB A-130*

## AUDIT

The systematic examination of records and documents and/or the securing of other evidence by confirmation, physical inspection, or otherwise, for one or more of the following purposes: (a) determining the propriety or legality of proposed or completed transactions; ascertaining whether all transactions have been recorded and are reflected accurately in accounts; (b) determining the existence of recorded assets and inclusiveness of recorded liabilities; (c) determining the accuracy of financial or statistical statements or reports, plus the fairness of the facts they represent; (d) determining the degree of compliance with established policies and procedures in terms of financial transactions and business management; and (e) appraising an account system and making recommendations concerning it.

*OPM*

See also "Desk Audit."

## AUDITOR

A professional accountant acting as a principal advisor to contracting officers on contractor accounting and contract audit matters.

*OPM*

## AUTHORITY

See "Agent Authority."

## AUTHORIZATION

(1) Funds for programs are authorized by an "authorization act" before the appropriation act is passed.

*NC-F*

(2) An act of Congress that permits a federal program or activity to begin or continue from year to year. It sets limits on funds that can be appropriated but does not grant funding, which must be provided by a separate congressional appropriation.

*DAAI*

## AUTHORIZATION BILL

(1) A bill authorizing the expenditure of public funds.

*BLD*

(2) This bill provides an agency with the legal authority to operate. It recommends policy guidelines and funding levels and must be passed by Congress and signed by the president, but it does not actually provide any money.

*DLA*

(3) Congress approves federal programs through passage of an authorization bill, which permits an expenditure of money for specific purposes. Congress subsequently appropriates funds out of the Treasury for those purposes.

*TIPS(2-6)*

## AUTHORIZED WORK

That effort which has been definitized and is on contract, plus that which definitized contract costs have not been agreed to but for which written authorization has been received.

*DAAT*

## AUTOMATED CLEARING HOUSE (ACH)

A nationwide electronic funds transfer (EFT) system used by financial institutions, corporations, and consumers. It serves as a centralized distribution and settlement point for wire transfers and other electronic exchanges. The Federal Reserve serves as the ACH for the Department of Treasury. The National Automated Clearing House Association (NACHA) is the regulatory body for the entire ACH system.

*NES–98*

## AUTOMATIC DATA PROCESSING (ADP)

Data processing performed by a system of electronic or electrical machines so interconnected and interacting as to reduce to a minimum the need for human assistance or intervention.

*AFIT*

## AUTOMATIC DATA PROCESSING EQUIPMENT (ADPE)

See "Information Technology."

## AUXILIARY TECHNIQUES

A price analysis technique used to support results from primary or secondary comparisons. Example auxiliary techniques include value analysis and visual analysis. Value analysis answers this question: "What is the item worth?" Visual analysis is an estimating technique that uses visual inspection of an item to determine a worth.

*W-ICPA*

Compare "Primary Comparison" and "Secondary Comparison."
See also "Value Analysis."

## AVERAGE PROCUREMENT LEAD TIME

The average time elapsing between the initiation of procurement action and the receipt into the system of material purchased as a result of such action.

*AFIT*

## AVOIDABLE COSTS

Those costs that will not continue if an ongoing operation is changed or deleted. Avoidable costs include department salaries and other costs that could be avoided by not operating the specific department.

*MGMT*

## AWARD

(1) Notification to bidder of acceptance of a bid [or proposal].

*AFIT*

(2) The procurement decision to buy a supply or service from a specific concern on specified terms, including dollar amount.

*SPP*

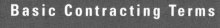

## BACKDOOR SELLING
Bypassing of the purchasing department by a salesperson who goes directly to the department or end user of the product being purchased.

*Commercial Practices*

## BACK ORDER
Items that have been ordered but that cannot be shipped because of a stockout or some other reason. This order is widely used as a measure of supplier performance and customer service (percentage of back orders, number of occurrences, number of back-order days, etc.).

*Commercial Practices*

## BAILEE
In the law of contracts, one to whom goods are bailed; the party to whom personal property is delivered under a contract of bailment. A species of agent to whom something movable is committed in trust for another.

*BLD*

## BAILMENT
The temporary transfer of possession of personal property without a change of ownership for a specific purpose and with the intent that possession will revert to the owner at a later date.

*FBL*

*Example*: The lending of government-owned property to a contractor for the performance of a contract.

*OPM*

## BANK(ER'S) ACCEPTANCE
An instrument used in financing foreign trade, making possible the payment of cash to an exporter covering all or part of the amount of a shipment made by that exporter.

*Commercial Practices*

## BAR CODE
A pattern of alternating parallel bars and spaces representing numbers and other characters that are machine readable. The major advantages of using bar coding technology in receiving and store operations are the reductions in error rate and improved entry speed and count accuracy.

*Commercial Practices*

## BARTERING

The original form of trade, it involves the exchange of one product for another. Bartering is used when there is a shortage of cash, when financial conditions do not support a cash transaction, or when currency is protected through legislation in order to retain value.

*NES-94*

## BASED-ON PRICE

A price derived from established catalog or market prices of commercial items sold in substantial quantities to the general public. The item being purchased must be sufficiently similar to the commercial item to permit the difference between the prices of the items to be identified and justified without resort to cost analysis.

*OPM*

## BASE PROFIT

The money that a company is paid by a customer and that exceeds the company's cost.

*Garrett*

## BASELINING

A process whereby all managers concerned collectively agree on the specific description of the program, requirements, and funding, and make a commitment to manage the program along those guidelines.

*DSMC*

## BASE-STOCK SYSTEM

In its simplest form, a base-stock system is an inventory system in which a replenishment order is issued each time a withdrawal is made, and the order quantity is equal to the amount of the withdrawal. This type of system is commonly referred to as a par-stock system (bringing stock back to par level).

*Commercial Practices*

## BASIC ORDERING AGREEMENT (BOA)

(1) An instrument of understanding (not a contract) executed between a procuring activity (buyer) and a contractor (seller) setting forth negotiated contract clauses applicable to future procurements entered into between the parties during the term of the agreement. It includes as specific as possible a description of the supplies or services and a description of the method for determination of prices.

*DSMC*

(2) A BOA contains all applicable clauses and must specify when an order actually becomes a binding contract. Depending on the circumstances, a contract could be established upon the issuance of an order, upon the contractor's failure to reject the order within a specified time, or upon actual acceptance of the order by the contractor through performance (e.g., shipping the goods) or formal acceptance.

*W-CCC*

Compare "Blanket Purchase Agreement (BPA)."

## BAYH AMENDMENT

This Act (P.L. 92-570) requires that no funds be spent for any contract or agreement with any foreign corporation, organization, person, or other entity for the performance of research and development (R&D) in connection with any weapons system or other military equipment for the Department of Defense (DOD) when there is a U.S. corporation, organization, person, or other entity equally competent to carry out such R&D at a lower cost.

*W-CC*

## BAYH-DOLE TRADEMARK AMENDMENTS ACT

Amended the Stevenson-Wydler Act in order to further assist the process of technology transfer. This Act (P.L. 96-517) allows small businesses and nonprofit organizations to retain title to inventions under government contracts or grants.

*TIPS(1-14)*

## BENCHMARK

A standard or point of reference used in measuring or judging quality, value, performance, price, etc. Benchmarks of purchasing performance such as purchasing operating expense as a percentage of company sales dollars gives purchasing professionals a reference point that can be used to evaluate their own firm's performance.

*Commercial Practices*

## BENCHMARKING

The concept of benchmarking in purchasing has been pioneered by the Center for Advanced Purchasing Studies (CAPS), and consists of collecting performance data from firms in target industries. The data are analyzed systematically and are calculated so that purchasing performance benchmarks can be developed on an inductry basis.

*Commercial Practices*

## BEST BUY

A term used to imply that a purchase represents an overall combination of quality, price, and various elements of required service that in total are optimal relative to the firm's needs.

*Commercial Practices*

## BEST VALUE

(1) The essential principle of best value is to obtain the best trade-off between competing factors for a particular purchase requirement. The keys to successful best-value contracting are (a) consideration of life-cycle costs, and (b) marginal analysis, [i.e., the use of quantitative as well as qualitative techniques to measure price and technical performance trade-off between various proposals]. The best value concept applies to acquisitions where price or price-related factors

are not the primary determinant of who receives the contract award.

*TIPS(3-5)*

(2) Best value means the expected outcome of an acquisition that, in the government's estimation, provides the greatest overall benefit in response to the requirement.

*FAR*

(3) The most advantageous trade-off between price and performance for the government. Best value is determined through a process that compares strengths, weaknesses, risk, price, and performance, in accordance with selection criteria, to select the most advantageous value to the government.

*DAAT*

(4) The best trade-off between competing factors for a particular purchase requirement. The key to successful best-value contracting is consideration of life-cycle cost, including the use of quantitative as well as qualitative techniques to measure price and technical performance trade-offs between various proposals. The best-value concept applies to acquisitions in which price or price-related factors are not the primary determinant of who receives the contract award.

*Garrett*

## BID

(1) An offer in response to an Invitation for Bids (IFB).

*BLD*

(2) In purchasing, a bid can be an offer to sell or an offer to buy. In public sector purchasing, a bid is the offer in the sealed-bid process (as opposed to other than sealed-bid procurement, where the offer may be referred to as a proposal or a quotation). See also "Offer."

## BID AND PROPOSAL COSTS

Costs incurred in preparing, submitting, and supporting bids and proposals (whether or not solicited) on potential government or nongovernment contracts.

*OPM*

## BID BOND

In government contract administration, an insurance document in which a third party agrees to pay a specific amount of money if the bonded (insured) bidder fails to sign a contract as bid and accepted by the government.

*P&L*

## BID DEVELOPMENT

All of the work activities required to design and price the product and service solution and to accurately articulate this development in a proposal for a customer.

*Garrett*

## BID GUARANTEE

A form of security accompanying a bid or proposal as assurance that the bidder will not withdraw its bid during the specified time period, will execute a written contract, and will furnish such bonds as may be required.

*AFIT*

## BID OPENING

The public announcement of all the bids submitted in response to an Invitation for Bids (IFB).

*McVay*

## BID PHASE

The period of time a seller of goods or services or both uses to develop a bid or proposal, to conduct internal bid reviews, and to obtain stakeholder approval to submit a bid or proposal.

*Garrett*

## BID PROTEST

See "Protest."

## BID SAMPLE

A sample to be furnished by a bidder to show the characteristics of the product offered in the bid.

*FAR*

## BIDDER

One who makes a bid.

*BLD*

## BIDDERS' CONFERENCE

See "Pre-bid Conference."

## BIDDERS' LIST

A list, which is maintained by the procurement office, of contractors and suppliers that have expressed interest in furnishing a specific supply or service to the government.

*McVay*

Also known as "Bidders' Mailing List."

## BILATERAL CONTRACT

A contract formed by the exchange of promises in which the promise of one party is consideration supporting the promise of the other. Contrast to "Unilateral Contract," which is formed by the exchange of a promise for an act.

*BLD*

## BILL OF LADING

(1) A document evidencing receipt of goods for shipment issued by a person engaged in the business of transporting for forwarding goods.

*BLD*

(2) A carrier's contractual agreement to transport goods from one place to another and to deliver them to a designated person or location for compensation under the terms stated in the agreement.

*SPP*

## BILL OF MATERIALS (BOM)

A descriptive and quantitative listing of materials, supplies, parts, and components required to produce a designated, complete end-item.

*OPM*

## BILL OF SALE

A written document formally transferring ownership of personal property specified in the document from the supplier to the purchaser.

*Commercial Practices*

## BILLING RATE

A billing rate is an indirect cost rate (a) established temporarily for interim reimbursement of incurred indirect costs, and (b) adjusted as necessary pending establishment of final indirect cost rates.

*FAR*

## BLAIR HOUSE PAPERS

These papers provide a road map for federal workers to continue to create a government that works better and costs less. Fifteen guidelines under their three major objectives:

- Deliver great service.
- Foster partnership and community solutions.
- Reinvent to get the job done with less.

*CM-4/98*

## BLANK CHECK PURCHASE ORDER

An ordering technique that includes a bank draft as the bottom portion of the purchase order form. When the order is shipped, the supplier enters the amount due for payment on the draft and sends it to the firm's bank for deposit. Many firms that use this approach for numerous small purchases refer to it as a purchase order draft system.

*Commercial Practices*

## BLANKET ORDER

A term commitment (usually one year or more) to a supplier for certain goods or services over a predetermined period of time at predetermined prices, most-favored customer prices, or prices to be revised as a result of market or other conditions. This practice is aimed at reducing the number of small orders, thus using short-term releases to satisfy demand requirements.

*Commercial Practices*

## BLANKET PURCHASE AGREEMENT (BPA)

(1) A method for the government to fill purchase requirements for related supplies, material, equipment, or services by establishing accounts with established sources of supply. It includes certain conditions and provisions that have been negotiated and agreed to in advance, and it allows the government to make frequent purchases or calls, verbally

or in writing, and to receive one monthly bill for all supplies or services purchased.

*DSMC*

(2) A BPA is not a contract; it is viewed as a type of "charge account" with certain qualified vendors. It serves as the baseline for future transactions between the parties. An individual BPA is considered complete when the amount purchased under it equals the total dollar limitation, if any, or when the stated time limitation (period of performance) expires.

*W-CCC*

(3) Regulations limit the use of BPAs to small purchases of items or services needed to fill anticipated recurring needs.

*W-BPA*

Compare "Basic Ordering Agreement (BOA)."

## BOARD OF CONTRACT APPEALS
A designated administrative tribunal within an executive agency that is authorized to hear, examine, and decide on written requests asking for a change (an appeal) of a contracting officer's (CO's) decision, and related to a contract made by that agency.

*L&P*

## BOILERPLATE
The name used for printed terms and conditions that are frequently found on the back of purchase order (PO) forms in contracts, usually attached as "General Provisions."

*Cohen*

## BOND
(1) A written instrument executed by a bidder or contractor [supplier] (the "principal") and a second party (the "surety" or "sureties") to ensure fulfillment of the principal's obligations to a third party (the "obligee" or "government"), which is identified in the bond. If the principal's obligations are not met, the bond ensures payment, to the extent stipulated, of any loss sustained by the obligee.

*FAR*

See also "Advance Payment Bond," "Bid Bond," "Performance Bond," and "Payment Bond."

(2) A written instrument executed by a seller and a second party (the surety or sureties) to ensure fulfillment of the principal's obligations to a third party (the obligee or buyer) identified in the bond. If the principal's obligations are not met, the bond ensures payment, to the extent stipulated, of any loss sustained by the obligee.

*Garrett*

## BOOK VALUE
An accounting term for the value of assets as carried on the books, that is, cost less reserve for depreciation.

*BLD*

## BOYLE RULE
See "Government Contractor Defense."

## BRAINSTORMING
An idea-gathering technique that uses group interaction to generate many ideas in a short time period.

## BRAND NAME DESCRIPTION
A purchase description that identifies a product by its brand name and model or part number, or other appropriate nomenclature by which the product is offered for sale.

*FAR*

Also known as "Brand Name or Equal."

## BREACH OF CONTRACT
The failure, without legal excuse, to perform any promise that forms the whole or part of a contract. Anticipatory breach occurs when the promisor, without justification and before he or she has committed a breach, makes a positive statement to the promisee indicating he or she will not or cannot perform his or her contractual duties.

*BLD*

## BREACH OF WARRANTY
This breach occurs when the material or product fails to meet the quality or other specification warranted by the supplier.

*Commercial Practices*

## BREAK BULK
The splitting of one consolidated or large-volume shipment into smaller ones for ultimate delivery to consignees. This term also is used commonly to describe the process of splitting up case quantities and selling by each.

*Commercial Practices*

## BREAKEVEN ANALYSIS
(1) The managers of profit-seeking organizations usually study the relationship of revenue [sales], expenses [costs], and net income [net profit]. This study is commonly called "Cost-Volume-Profit Analysis." The study of cost-volume-profit relationships is often called "Break-even Analysis." This term is a misnomer, because the breakeven point is often incidental to the plan-ning decision at hand.

*MGMT*

(2) Breakeven analysis determines the point at which total revenues are exactly equal to total fixed and variable costs.

*NES-02*

## BREAKEVEN POINT
That level of operations where total costs equal total revenue.

*NCMA-CA*

## BREAKOUT
(1) The review of a major weapons system to determine if a particular component may be purchased as a separate item instead of buying it from

the weapons system manufacturer. This subsystem would then be provided in the weapons system contract as government-furnished equipment (GFE), rather than contractor-furnished equipment (CFE).

*Navy*

(2) Execution of acquisition strategy to convert some parts or system components from contractor-furnished to government-furnished. Rather than having the prime contractor provide from its sources, the government procures items directly and provides them to the prime contractor.

*DAAT*

## BRIBE BROKER

An intermediary who, for a fee, brings a buyer and seller together. Normally, a broker provides some additional service to the purchaser. The broker has no ownership of the goods being sold, with the payment and credit transactions remaining the responsibility of the buyer and seller.

*Commercial Practices*

## BROKER

A third party authorized to negotiate with potential vendors for the purchaser, but not authorized to commit the purchaser to the transaction via a contractual document.

*Cohen*

## BUDGET

(1) A plan of action expressed in figures.

*NCMA-CA*

(2) A comprehensive financial plan for the federal government, encompassing the totality of federal receipts and outlays (expenditures). Budget documents routinely include the on-budget and off-budget amounts and combine them to derive a total of federal fiscal activity, with a focus on combined totals. Also a plan of operations for a fiscal period in terms of estimated costs, obligations, and expenditures; a source of funds for financing, including anticipated reimbursements and other resources; and a history and set of workload data for the projected program and activities.

*DAAT*

## BUDGET AT COMPLETION (BAC)

The budget, or planned value, at the end of the project.

*Verzuh*

## BUDGET AUTHORITY

Authority provided by law to enter into obligations that will result in outlays of federal funds. Budget authority may be classified by the period of availability (one-year, multiyear, no-year), by the timing of congressional action (current or permanent), or by the manner of determining the amount available (definite or indefinite).

*www.senate.gov/reference/glossary*

## BUDGET RESOLUTION

Congressional budget committees come up with this legislation, basically an outline that determines ceilings for the budget authority and outlays for spending. Not legally binding.

*DLA*

## BUDGET VARIANCE

The difference between the amount incurred and the budget figure.

*NCMA-CA*

## BUDGETED COST OF WORK PERFORMED (BCWP)

(1) The sum of the budgets for completed work packages and completed portions of open work packages.

*AFIT*

(2) A measurement of the work completed [in Earned Value Management (EVM) terminology]. BCWP is the value of work performed, or "earned," when compared to the original plan, that is, the Budgeted Cost of Work Scheduled (BCWS). The BCWP is called the Earned Value.

*DAAT*

Also called Earned Value (EV). Compare "Actual Cost of Work Performed (ACWP)" and Budgeted Cost for Work Scheduled (BCWS)."

## BUDGETED COST OF WORK SCHEDULED (BCWS)

(1) The sum of the budgets for all work packages and planning packages scheduled to be accomplished, (including in-process work packages).

*AFIT*

(2) The sum of the budgets for all work (work packages, planning packages, etc.) scheduled to be accomplished (including in-process work packages), plus the amount of Level of Effort (LOE) and apportioned effort scheduled to be accomplished within a given time period.

Also called Planned Value (PV) or Performance Measurement Baseline (PMB).

Compare "Actual Cost of Work Performed (ACWP)" and "Budgeted Cost for Work Performed (BCWP)."

## BusinessLINC

Business Learning, Information, Networking and Collaboration that encourages large firms to share their expertise and resources with small disadvantaged companies by acting as mentors.

*CM-3/99*

## BULK FUNDING

A system whereby a contracting officer (CO) receives authorization from a fiscal and accounting officer to obligate funds on purchase documents against a specified lump sum of funds reserved for the purpose and for a specified period of time, rather than obtaining individual obligational authority on each purchase document.

*FAR*

## BUNDLING, CONTRACT
Contract bundling is the practice of combining requirements into one "umbrella" solicitation, with the result that the offeror must be able to perform increasingly larger contracts covering multiple and diverse elements of performance.

*TIPS(5-1)*

## BURDEN
Also known as "Overhead." See "Overhead."

## BURDEN CENTER
See "Cost Center."

## BURN RATE
The monthly rate at which a contractor's funds are expended during the period of the contract.

*DAAT*

## BUSINESS MANAGER
The acquisition professional as a business manager will need skills in fostering good government–industry relations; implementing and administering a strong training program; achieving computer literacy; using electronic commerce to the maximum extent possible; and understanding interaction between the program or project office and the procurement, finance, and technical personnel.

*NES-00*

## BUSINESS OPPORTUNITY DEVELOPMENT REFORM ACT
See "Small Business Competitiveness Demonstration Program (SBCDP)."

## BUY AMERICAN ACT
A federal policy stating that manufactured materials, supplies, or articles acquired for public use shall be substantially constituted from domestically mined or manufactured materials; products are considered to be not of domestic origin if the cost of foreign products used in them accounts for 50 percent of the total cost.

*DOD*

## BUYBACK
A type of countertrade that occurs when a firm builds a plant in a foreign country, or supplies technology, equipment, training, or other services, and agrees to take a certain portion of the plant's output as partial payment for the investment.

*Commercial Practices*

## BUYER
(1) A professional buying specialist. Buyers typically specialize in a given group of materials or commodities and are responsible for market analysis, purchase planning; coordination with users; supplier qualification; and selection, order placement, and follow-up activities.

*Commercial Practices*

(2) The party contracting for goods or services or both with one or more sellers.

*Garrett*

## BUYER'S MARKET
A competitive market condition (supply exceeds demand) that exists when goods or services or both can be secured easily, and when the economic forces of business tend to cause prices to be close to the purchaser's estimate of value.

*Commercial Practices*

## BUY-IN
The knowing submission of an offer below anticipated cost, with the expectation of increasing the contract amount after award, or receiving follow-on contracts at artificially high prices.

*FAR*

## BYRD AMENDMENT
A common name for P.L. 101-121, Section 219, which instructed the Office of Management and Budget (OMB) to issue governmentwide guidance restricting the use of public funds to pay for lobbying. The guidelines define lobbying as influencing or attempting to influence any agency employee, member of Congress, or congressional staff member in connection with the award, renewal extension, or modification of any federal contract. Companies must file compliance certifications disclosing any outside personnel it hires, or expects to hire, with private funds.

*TIPS(1-6)*

## CANCELLATION
The withdrawal of the requirement to purchase goods or services or both by the buyer.

*Garrett*

## CAPITAL
An economist uses this term to mean all the human-constructed aids used in production. Sometimes called "Investment Goods," capital consists of machinery, tools, buildings, transportation and distribution facilities, and inventories of unfinished goods. A basic characteristic of capital goods is that they are used to produce other goods.

*ECON*

## CAPITAL ASSETS
The land, structures, equipment, intellectual property (e.g., software), and information technology (including IT service contracts) that is used by the federal government and that has an estimated useful life of two years or more. Capital assets do not include items acquired for resale in the ordinary course of operations or items that are acquired for physical consumption, such as operating materials and supplies.

Capital assets may be acquired in different ways: through purchase, construction, or manufacturing; through a lease-purchase or other capital lease (regardless of whether title has passed to the federal government); through an operating lease for an asset with an estimated useful life of two years or more; or through exchange.

*OMB A-11*

## CAPITAL BUDGETING
Capital budgeting is the process of evaluating and selecting long-term investment projects.

*NES-02*

## CAPITAL, COST OF
Under the net-present-value method, a manager determines some minimum desired rate of return. The minimum rate is often called "Cost of Capital." All expected future cash flows are discounted to the present, using this minimum desired rate. If the result is zero or positive, the project is desirable, and if negative, it is undesirable.

*MGMT*

## CAPITAL EQUIPMENT

For accounting purposes, most firms classify capital equipment as noncurrent assets, which are capitalized and depreciated over the course of their economic lives. The purchase of a particular piece of capital equipment typically occurs only once every five to 10 years or so. A unique feature of most capital equipment purchases is the lead time requirements. Manufacturing lead time is usually a matter of months or years. An expenditure of funds for capital equipment is an investment. If purchased wisely and operated efficiently, capital equipment generates profit for its owner. The purchase of most major equipment involves the expenditure of a substantial sum of money.

*DBL*

## CAPITAL PROGRAMMING

Means an integrated process within an agency for planning, budgeting, procurement, and management of the agency's portfolio of capital assets to achieve agency strategic goals and objectives with the lowest life-cycle cost and least risk.

*OMB A-11*

## CAPITAL PROJECT (INVESTMENT)

Means the acquisition of a capital asset and the management of that asset through its life cycle after the initial acquisition. Capital projects (investments) may consist of several useful segments.

*OMB A-11*

## CAPTURE MANAGEMENT

The art and science of winning more business.

*Garrett*

## CAPTURE MANAGEMENT LIFE CYCLE

The art and science of winning more business throughout the entire business cycle.

*Garrett*

## CAPTURE PROJECT PLAN

A document or game plan of who needs to do what, when, where, how often, and how much to win business.

*Garrett*

## CARDINAL CHANGE

(1) A major change to a contract that is made outside the scope of the contract and is, therefore, unenforceable by the government.

*McVay*

(2) Contract change having the effect of making the work as performed not essentially the same work as the parties bargained for when the contract was awarded, and thus constituting a breach of contract by the government.

*GUIDE*

## CASH FLOW
(1) The cash generated from the property. It is different from net income; cash flow looks at the amount left after all payments are made, whether they are tax deductible or not. Also defined as cash receipts minus disbursements from a given asset, or group of assets, for a given period.

*BLD*

(2) The net effect of cash receipts and disbursements.

*NCMA-CA*

## CAUSE AND EFFECT DIAGRAM
A structured form of brainstorming that graphically shows the relationship of causes and subcauses to an identified effect (problem).

*DGCQI*

See also "Fishbone Diagram."

## CAVEAT EMPTOR
Let the buyer beware. The purchase is at the buyer's risk.

*Commercial Practices*

## CEILING
See "Adjusted Ceiling" and "Negotiated Ceiling."

## CENTRAL PROCUREMENT ACTIVITY
A level of government contracting activity in which assignments are performed by formal contracting and involve procurements up to major components of agency critical programs and facilities, and the equipment to support those programs. Also includes coordinated interdepartmental, and governmentwide commodity assignments, as well as area-wide support responsibilities.

*OPM*

## CENTRALIZATION OF PURCHASING
Centralization exists when the entire purchasing function is made the responsibility of a single person, who is held accountable by top management for proper performance of purchasing activities. When functioning properly, centralized purchasing produces the following benefits: (a) duplication is minimized, (b) volume discounts are possible, (c) transportation savings can be realized, (d) purchasing specialists can buy more efficiently because of their expertise, (e) suppliers can offer better prices because their administrative costs are reduced, (f) more effective inventory control is possible, (g) fewer orders are processed for the same quantity of goods, and (h) management control is facilitated.

*DBL*

Compare "Decentralization of Purchasing."

## CERTIFICATE OF APPOINTMENT
The document that empowers a person to act on the behalf of the

government as a contracting officer.

*McVay*

See also "Warrant."

## CERTIFICATE OF COMPETENCY

The certificate issued by the Small Business Administration (SBA) stating that the holder is responsible (with respect to all elements of responsibility) for the purpose of receiving and performing a specific government contract.

*FAR*

## CERTIFICATE OF CURRENT COST OR PRICING DATA

(1) A document submitted by the contractor attesting that the cost or pricing data provided to the government were accurate, complete, and current as of the date negotiations were completed.

*McVay*

(2) Prescribed certificate required to be executed by contractors that must submit certified cost or pricing data under the Truth in Negotiations Act (TINA).

*GUIDE*

## CERTIFICATION OF A CLAIM

The requirement, under the Contract Disputes Act (CDA), that contract claims more than $100,000 be accompanied by a statement that simultaneously asserts that the claim is made in good faith, that supporting data are accurate and complete, and that the amount requested reflects the contract adjustment believed due. (Certification threshold revised in sixth edition.)

*GUIDE*

## CHANGE IN SCOPE

Change to approved program requirements or specifications after negotiation of a basic contract. It may result in an increase or decrease.

*AFIT*

## CHANGE ORDER

A written order signed by the contracting officer or buyer, authorized by contract clause, to modify contractual requirements within the scope of the contract.

*OPM*

Compare "Constructive Change."

## CHANGE PROPOSAL

See "Engineering Change Proposal (ECP)" and "Equitable Adjustment."

## CHANGES CLAUSE

A standard clause in government contracts. There are several versions corresponding to the specific type of contract, but all have certain common characteristics. The clause, which is mandatory for most government contracts, provides a contractual grant of authority to the government by its supplier. It gives the government the right to alter unilaterally specific matters affecting the performance of the contract.

*Sherman*

## CHIEF ACQUISITION OFFICERS COUNCIL

The Chief Acquisition Officers Council (the Council) is established pursuant to Section 16 of the Office of Federal Procurement Policy (OFPP) Act, as amended, 41 U.S.C. 403, et seq.

The Council consists of a diverse group of acquisition professionals that is in the executive branch and that was established to provide a senior level forum for monitoring and improving the federal acquisition system. The Council promotes effective business practices that ensure the timely delivery of best-value products and services to the agencies; achieve public policy objectives; and further integrity, fairness, competition, and openness in the federal acquisition system. The Council works closely with the Administrator, OFPP, and the Federal Acquisition Regulatory Council to promote the business practices in the acquisition system. The Council is focused on promoting the president's management agenda in all aspects of the acquisition system. The Council also promotes the president's specific acquisition-related initiatives and policies.

*IAE*

## CHIEF FINANCIAL OFFICERS ACT (1990)

The Act calls for (a) integration of accounting and budgeting information so that principles used in accounting for program costs are consistent with those used in developing budgets, (b) the systematic measurement of performance at the agency level to identify cost trends and other types of performance indicators, and (c) the preparation and audit of financial statements on a uniform, consistent basis and subsequent communication of results to financial decision-makers.

*CM-1/99*

## CHIEF INFORMATION OFFICER COUNCIL

The Chief Information Officers (CIO) Council was established by Executive Order 13011, Federal Information Technology, on July 16, 1996. A charter for the Council was adopted on February 20, 1997, and later codified by the E-Government Act of 2002. The CIO Council serves as the principal interagency forum for improving practices in the design, modernization, use, sharing, and performance of federal government agency information resources. The Council's role includes (a) developing recommendations for information technology management policies, procedures, and standards; (b) identifying opportunities to share information resources; and (c) assessing and addressing the needs of the federal government's IT workforce.

*IAE*

## CHRISTIAN DOCTRINE

On the basis of an actual court case, a principle that maintains that if a significant clause is required to be included in a government contract, the contract will be read to include it, even though the clause is not physically incorporated in the document.

*NC-F*

## CIVILIAN AGENCY ACQUISITION COUNCIL (CAAC)

A group composed of members from federal civilian agencies that has joint responsibility with the Defense Acquisition Regulatory Council (DARC) for revision of the Federal Acquisition Regulation (FAR).

*GUIDE*

See also "Defense Acquisition Regulatory Council."

## CLAIM

(1) A written demand or written assertion by one of the contracting parties seeking, as a matter of right, the payment of money in a sum certain, the adjustment or interpretation of the contract terms, or other relief arising under or relating to the contract. A claim arising under a contract, unlike a claim relating to that contract, is a claim that can be resolved under a contract clause that provides for the relief sought by the claimant. A voucher, invoice, or other routine request for payment that is not in dispute when submitted is not a claim. The submission is not a claim. The submission may be converted to a claim, by written notice to the contracting officer (CO).

*FAR*

(2) A demand by one party to contract for something from another party, usually but not necessarily for more money or more time. Claims are usually based on an argument that the party making the demand is entitled to an adjustment by virtue of the contract terms or some violation of those terms by the other party. The word does not imply any disagreement between the parties, although claims often lead to disagreements.

*Garrett*

See also "Contract Claim" and "Termination Claim."

## CLAIM CERTIFICATION

See "Certification of a Claim."

## CLAIMS COURT

See "United States Claims Court" and "United States Court of Claims."

## CLARIFICATION

A communication in negotiations for the sole purpose of eliminating minor irregularities, informalities, or apparent clerical mistakes in a proposal.

*FAR*

## CLARIFICATION REQUEST (CR)

Written communication that is issued by the source selection evaluation board through the contracting officer (CO) for the purpose of eliminating minor irregularities, informalities, or apparent clerical mistakes and does not give the offeror an opportunity to revise or modify its proposal.

*W-HAP*

See also "Deficiency Report."

## CLAUSE

A term or condition used in both contracts and solicitations, and applying after contract award or both before and after award. Clauses state the rights and obligations of the parties to a contract.

*FAI*

## CLAYTON ACT

A federal law (15 U.S.C.A. 12-27) enacted in 1914 as an amendment to the Sherman Antitrust Act dealing with antitrust regulations and unfair trade practices. The Act prohibits price discrimination, tying and exclusive dealing contracts, mergers, and interlocking directorates, where the effect may be substantially to lessen competition or tend to create a monopoly in any line of commerce.

*BLD*

See also "Robinson-Patman Act" and "Sherman Antitrust Act."

## CLEAN AIR ACT (1955) (Amend. 1990) (CAA)

The Act was designed to accelerate, expand, and intensify efforts against air pollution in the United States. The Act requires the Environmental Protection Agency (EPA) to identify each substance that it believes causes or contributes to air pollution. Further, the EPA must identify each substance, whether from numerous or diverse sources, that it reasonably believes endangers public health or welfare.

*NES-94*

## CLEAN WATER ACT (1972) (Amend. 1987) (CWA)

The Act regulates, among other things, the discharge of pollutants into navigable waters. The CWA redirected the regulatory focus of water pollution control from water quality standards to limits (called "effluent limits") on the concentrations of chemicals in the water quality.

*NES-94*

## CLINGER-COHEN ACT

See "Federal Acquisition Reform Act 1996."

## CLOSED CONTRACT

A contract on which all contractor and government obligations and administrative actions have been completed.

*AFIT*

## CLOSEOUT

The process of declaring that the obligations under a contract have been satisfied and that a procurement file is both physically and administratively complete. A closeout can occur when (a) the contractor's supplies or services have been accepted and paid for, and (b) all documentation on the procurement is finalized and properly assembled.

*SPP*

See also "Quick Closeout" and "Record Retention."

## CLOSING DATE

The last day on which proposals or quotations will be accepted.

*NCMA-SB*

## CODE OF FEDERAL REGULATIONS (CFR)

Official codification of United States administrative regulations.

*GUIDE*

The Federal Acquisition Regulation (FAR) is Title 48 of the CFR and is thus part of the CFR.

## CO-DEVELOPMENT

A joint development project between the U.S. government and a foreign government to satisfy a common requirement.

*MSA*

## COLLATERAL BENEFIT

The degree to which pursuit of an opportunity will improve the existing skill level or develop new skills that will positively affect other or future business opportunities.

*Garrett*

## COLLECTIVE BARGAINING AGREEMENT (CBA)

(1) Agreement that regulates terms and conditions of employment between an employer and a labor union.

*BLD2*

(2) Under Section 4(c), the Service Contract Act (41 U.S.C. 351–357) generally requires a contractor to pay the wages negotiated by its predecessor contractor under a collective bargaining agreement.

*W-ESCA*

## COLLUSION

Any understanding or agreement, expressed, implied, formal, or informal, among bidders or competitors concerning bids or proposals for the sale of products or services; disclosure of a bid or proposal by a bidder to any other bidder or competitor prior to the official opening of all bids or proposals; any attempt to induce a competitor not to submit a bid or proposal.

*BCG*

## COLOR OF MONEY

A term used to describe the type of procurement money used for a particular item. Different kinds of appropriated funds must be used for various procurements (e.g., Research, Development, Test, and Evaluation [RDT&E]; Operations and Maintenance [O&M]; and Foreign Military Sales [FMS]).

*Navy*

## COMMERCIAL AND GOVERNMENT ENTITY (CAGE) CODE

An identification code that provides a government agency the following information about a firm: name, address, socioeconomic data, and type of business (i.e., manufacturer or regular dealer). A firm needs only one code.

*Foglia*

## COMMERCIAL ACTIVITY

A commercial activity is the process resulting in a product or service that is or could be obtained from a private sector source. Agency missions may be accomplished through commercial facilities and resources, government facilities and resources or mixes thereof, depending upon the product, service, type of mission, and equipment required.

*OMB A-76*

## COMMERCIAL COMPONENT

Any component that is a commercial item.

*NES-97*

## COMMERCIAL ITEM

An item, including both supplies and services, of a class or kind that is regularly used for other than government purposes and is sold or traded in the course of conducting normal business operations.

*OPM*

See also "Nondevelopmental Item (NDI)" and "Off-the-Shelf."

## COMMERCIAL-OFF-THE-SHELF (COTS)

See "Off the Shelf."

## COMMERCIAL SALE

A sale of defense articles or defense services that is made under a Department of State issued license by U.S. industry directly to a foreign buyer, and that is not administered by Department of Defense (DOD) through foreign military sales (FMS) procedures. Also referred to as a direct commercial sale.

*MSA*

## COMMERCIAL SOURCE

A commercial source is any business or other concern that is eligible for contract award in accordance with Federal Acquisition Regulations (FAR).

*OMB A-76*

## COMMERCIAL-TYPE ITEMS

Any items, including those expended or consumed in use, which, in addition to military use, are used and traded in normal civilian enterprise, and which are, or can be, imported or exported through normal international trade channels.

*MSA*

## COMMISSION ON GOVERNMENT PROCUREMENT (COGP)

In 1969, P.L. 91-129 established the Commission. The COGP was a group of 12 members, representing Congress, the executive branch, and the public. The Comptroller General was made a statutory member. The COGP report released in December 1972 contained 149 recommendations for improvements of the federal procurement process. Among the recommendations were establishment of an independent, centralized office for governmentwide procurement policy matters, a federal procurement institute for the uniform training and development of government procurement personnel, and a single uniform procurement system for all government agencies.

*Culver*

## COMMITTEE FOR PURCHASE FROM PEOPLE WHO ARE BLIND OR SEVERELY DISABLED

The Javits-Wagner-O'Day (JWOD) Act (P.L. 92-28) requires that the government buy some of its supplies and services from nonprofit agencies that employ Americans who are blind or have other severe limitations. The committee is an independent federal agency admin-istered by a presidentially appointed committee. Originally called "Committee for Purchase from the Blind and Other Severely Handicapped (CPBOSH)," the committee was renamed "Committee for Purchase from People Who Are Blind or Severely Disabled" in 1992. The committee has designated two central nonprofit agencies—the National Industries for the Blind (NIB) and the National Industries for the Severely Handicapped (NISH)—to serve as liaisons. NIB and NISH are independent private organizations that adhere to committee regulations in carrying out functions associated with the JWOD program.

*W-PSP*

See also "Javits-Wagner-O'Day Act" and "Required Sources of Supplies and Services."

## COMMITTEE FOR PURCHASE FROM THE BLIND AND OTHER SEVERELY HANDICAPPED (CPBOSH)

See "Committee for Purchase from People Who Are Blind or Severely Disabled."

## COMMON COST
See "Joint Cost."

## COMMON LAW
Written or unwritten laws that have evolved through custom and usage (from English common law) without written legislation.

*FBL*

## COMMONALITY

A quality applying to material or systems possessing like and interchangeable characteristics enabling each to be used or operated and maintained by personnel trained on the others without additional specialized training. Also, having interchangeable repair parts or components, and applying to consumable items interchangeably equivalent without adjustment.

*DSMC*

## COMPARATIVE ANALYSIS

A type of secondary comparison used in performing price analysis. Comparative analysis may be accomplished by a comparison of previous contract prices with a current quotation for the same or similar items. Factors that affect the comparability of previous and current prices include the following: age of data, inflation, quantity requirements, delivery requirements, geographic region, extent of competition, and technology changes.

*W-ICPA*

See also "Secondary Comparison."

## COMPENSABLE DELAYS

(1) A delay for which the government is contractually responsible that excuses the contractor's failure to perform and is compensable. Suspension of Work (FAR 52.212-12), Stop Work (FAR 52.212-13), and Government Delay of Work (FAR 52.212-15) are examples of compensable delays.

*FAR*

(2) A delay for which the buyer is contractually responsible and that excuses the seller's failure to perform and is compensable.

*Garrett*

## COMPENSATION CLAUSE

Also sometimes called "Payment." This clause sets out the amount payable under the contract, supporting data required to be furnished with invoices, and other payment terms, such as time for payment and retention. Depending on the complexity of the contract, those areas may be individually addressed in separate clauses.

*Cohen*

## COMPENSATORY DAMAGES

Damages that will compensate the injured party for the loss sustained and nothing more. They are awarded by the court as the measure of actual loss, and not as punishment for outrageous conduct or to deter future transgressions. Compensatory damages are often referred to as "actual damages."

*Garrett*

## COMPETITION

Part of an acquisition strategy whereby more than one contractor is sought to bid on performing a service or function, with the winner being selected on the basis of criteria established by the activity for whom the work is to be performed.

*DSMC*

## COMPETITION ADVOCATE

A position established by the Competition in Contracting Act (CICA) of 1984. Each agency is required to have a competition advocate who, in turn, designates a competition advocate for each procuring activity of the agency. The competition advocate is responsible for promoting full and open competition and for challenging any barriers to such competition.

*Navy*

## COMPETITION IN CONTRACTING ACT (CICA)

A 1984 congressional act designed to foster competition and promote cost savings; requires the use of advance procurement planning and market research, as well as the use of commercial products whenever practicable.

*FAR*

## COMPETITIVE INTELLIGENCE

Information that is about competitors or competitive teams and that is specific to an opportunity.

*Garrett*

## COMPETITIVE NEGOTIATION

(1) A procurement involving (a) a request for proposal (RFP) that states the government's requirements and criteria for evaluation, (b) the submission of timely proposals by a maximum number of offerors, (c) discussions with those offerors found to be within the competitive range, and (d) award

of a contract to the one offeror whose offer, price, and other consideration factors are most advantageous to the government.

*OPM*

## COMPETITIVE BIDDING

A common method of source selection; the offer of prices and specified elements of performance by firms competing for a contract. Major public sector purchases commonly are requested to be on a sealed bid basis, with the law requiring that the award be made to the lowest responsive and responsible bidder. In industrial purchasing, preliminary bids are sometimes solicited with the stated intention of selecting those firms with whom negotiations subsequently will be conducted to arrive at a final sourcing decision.

*Commercial Practices*

## COMPETITIVE PROPOSALS

A competitive procurement practice in government purchasing that (a) is initiated by a request for proposal evaluation; (b) contemplates the submission of timely proposals by the maximum number of possible suppliers; (c) usually provides discussion with those suppliers found to be within the competitive range; and (d) concludes with the award of a contract to the one supplier whose proposal is most advantageous to the government, considering price and the other factors included in the solicitation.

*Commercial Practices*

## COMPETITIVE RANGE

A range of acceptable standards, determined by the contracting officer (CO) on the basis of price, cost, or technical factors; the CO must conduct written or oral discussions with all responsible offerors that submit proposals within this range.

*OPM*

## COMPETITIVE TIME

See "Uncompensated Overtime."

## COMPLIANCE MANAGEMENT

A means of obtaining what the purchase order required, within the terms and conditions of the purchase, as agreed upon by buyer and vendor.

*W-GSD*

## COMPLIANCE PROGRAM

A program that establishes and maintains a system to ensure that the company complies with government contract requirements and applicable government procurement laws and regulations. The Federal Sentencing Guidelines contain seven criteria that such a program must satisfy.

*TIPS(4-5)*

See also "Federal Sentencing Guidelines."

## COMPONENT BREAKOUT

An acquisition strategy to convert some items, usually parts or self-contained elements of a complete operating equipment end item, from contractor-furnished to government-procured items.

*P&L*

## COMPREHENSIVE ENVIRONMENTAL RESPONSE, COMPENSATION, AND LIABILITY ACT (1986) (CERCLA)

Regulates environmental cleanup when wastes have been dumped or spilled in the environment. Also known as "Superfund," the Act focuses on the cleanup of hazardous waste by (a) establishing an information-gathering and analysis system to characterize site contamination, to assess risks, and to develop cleanup actions; (b) providing for a national inventory of inactive hazardous waste sites; and (c) establishing a program designated to respond to the dangers of spills from such sites.

*NES-94*

## COMPTROLLER GENERAL

The head of the General Accountability Office (GAO).

*TIPS(3-4)*

## COMPUTER-AIDED ACQUISITION AND LOGISTICS SUPPORT (CALS)

A Department of Defense (DOD) initiative that mandates electronic interchange between contractors and government agencies of technical information, documents, and support information, including cost and schedule details, using Electronic Data Interchange (EDI).

*EDIW(1-11)*

## COMPUTER-AIDED DESIGN/COMPUTER-AIDED MANUFACTURING (CAD/CAM)

(1) CAD/CAM systems are a computerized means of providing standardization in the predesign stage in order to facilitate data transfer between CAD systems of different manufacturers and for transfers between CAD and CAM systems.

*DBL*

(2) CAD/CAM represents a new wave of Electronic Data Interchange (EDI) technology that helps improve the speed and quality of manufacturing processes. For example, two engineering teams located miles apart cooperate on a design by moving the needed drawings back and forth electronically, altering schematics on their computer screens. Together, they design an intricate part that can be efficiently manufactured to satisfy the customer's requirements.

*EDIW(2-1)*

## CONCERTED REFUSALS TO DEAL

Agreements or understandings by which two or more companies jointly refuse to do business with a specific third party.

*BCG*

## CONCURRENT INSPECTION

Judgment of product or procedural acceptability conducted concurrently by the contractor's inspection personnel and the government's quality assurance personnel.

*AFIT*

## CONDITION PRECEDENT

A condition that activates a term in a contract.

*Garrett*

## CONDITION SUBSEQUENT

A condition that suspends a term in a contract.

*Garrett*

## CONFIGURATION

A collection of an item's descriptive and governing characteristics that can be expressed in functional terms (what performance the item is expected to achieve) and in physical terms (what the item should look like and consist of when it is built).

*DSMC*

## CONFIGURATION MANAGEMENT

(1) A procedure for applying technical and administrative direction and surveillance to identify and document the functional and physical characteristics of an item or system; to control any changes to such characteristics; and to record and report the change, process, and implementation status. The configuration management process must be carefully tailored to the capacity, size, scope, phase of the

life cycle, and nature and complexity of the system involved.

*DSMC*

(2) The technical and administrative direction and surveillance actions taken to identify and document the functional and physical characteristics of a configuration item (CI), to control changes to a CI and its characteristics, and to record and report change processing and implementation status. It provides a complete audit trail of decisions and design modifications.

*DAAT*

## CONFLICT OF INTEREST

Term used in connection with public officials and fiduciaries and their relationship to matters of private interest or gain to them. Ethical problems connected therewith are covered by statutes in most jurisdictions and by federal statutes on the federal level. A conflict of interest arises when an employee's personal or financial interest conflicts or appears to conflict with his or her official responsibility.

*BLD2*

See also "Organizational Conflict of Interest (OCI)."

## CONSENSUS DECISION

A decision made after all aspects of an issue, both positive and negative, have been brought out to the extent that everyone openly understands and

supports the decision and the reasons for making it.

*DGCQI*

## CONSEQUENTIAL DAMAGES

Those costs that result from a particular cause. For example, a product's failure may mean that the purchaser not only has incurred the added cost necessary to replace the product, but also has lost income that would have resulted had the product not failed. The lost income would be a consequential damage. The extent to which consequential damages may be recovered depends on the language contained in the contract and the law in a particular jurisdiction.

*Cohen*

## CONSERVATISM

An accounting convention that provides guidance for accountants where solutions to uncertain elements should be chosen on the basis that would least likely overstate assets and income. Historically, this approach has been the most pervasive one that accountants have used in preparing financial statements.

*NCMA-CA*

## CONSIDERATION

(1) Anything of value that changes hands between the parties to a contract.

*FAI*

(2) The thing of value (amount of money or acts to be done or not done) that must change hands between the parties to a contract.

*Garrett*

(3) The inducement to a contract—the cause, motive, price, or impelling influence that induces a contracting party to enter a contract.

*Garrett*

## CONSIGNEE
A person, group of persons, or organization that receives supplies and services and that is named on the bill of lading.

*SPP*

## CONSISTENCY
An accounting principle that is vital in order to provide comparable financial information to interested users from period to period. Financial statements would not provide meaningful information if the accounting treatment of financial data changed continuously over a span of time. The consistency principle is designed to achieve comparability between accounting periods. Any changes in accounting treatment that may occur should be reported and the effects of the change disclosed.

*NCMA-CA*

## CONSOLIDATED LIST OF DEBARRED, SUSPENDED, AND INELIGIBLE CONTRACTORS
A single, comprehensive listing prepared by the General Services Administration (GSA) of business firms and individuals debarred, suspended, or otherwise excluded by government agencies from receiving government contracts.

*DOD*

See also "Debarment" and "Suspension."

## CONSTANT YEAR DOLLARS
Level of costs, without inflation, in a specified base year.

*Navy*

## CONSTRAINTS
Restrictions or boundary conditions that affect overall capability, priority, and resources in system acquisition.

*DSMC*

## CONSTRUCTIVE
That which is established by the mind of the law in its act of construing facts, conduct, circumstances, or instruments. That which has not the character assigned to it in its own essential nature, but acquires such character in consequence of the way in which it is regarded by a rule or policy of law; hence, that which is inferred, implied, or made out by legal interpretation. (The word "legal" is sometimes used here in lieu of "constructive.")

*BLD*

## CONSTRUCTIVE ACCELERATION

A requirement (based on the reasonable interpretation of the words, acts, or inaction of authorized government employees) that a contractor complete its work by a date earlier than one that would reflect the time extensions to which it is entitled because of excusable delays.

*GUIDE*

## CONSTRUCTIVE CHANGE

An oral or written act or omission that is by an authorized government official and that is of such a nature that it is construed to have the same effect as a written change order.

*OPM*

Compare "Change Order."

## CONSULTANT

An individual or firm retained for the specialized expertise it possesses.

*Cohen*

## CONSULTING SERVICES

Consulting services are those services of a purely advisory nature relating to the governmental functions of agency administration and management and program management.

*FAR*

## CONTINGENCY

A possible future event or condition arising from presently known or suspected causes, the cost of outcome of which is indeterminable at the present time.

*OPM*

## CONTINGENT CONTRACT

A contract that provides for the possibility of its termination when a specified occurrence takes place or does not take place.

*Garrett*

## CONTINGENT FEE

Any commission, percentage, brokerage, or other fee that is contingent upon the success that a person or concern has in securing a government contract.

*FAR*

## CONTINUING RESOLUTION (CR)

(1) If the appropriations bill has not been signed by the beginning of the fiscal year, this legislation allows an agency to continue operating at the previous year's spending level. The resolution has a set expiration date.

*DLA*

(2) Legislation enacted by Congress to provide budget authority (BA) for specific ongoing activities in cases where the regular fiscal year (FY) appropriation has not been enacted by the beginning of the FY. A CR usually specifies a designated period and maximum rate at which the agency may incur obligations, which are

based on the rate of the prior year, the President's Budget (PB) request, or an appropriation bill passed by either or both houses of Congress. Normally, new programs cannot be started under a CR.

*DAAT*

## CONTINUOUS ACQUISITION AND LIFE-CYCLE SUPPORT (CALS)

A core strategy to share integrated digital product data through a set of standards to achieve efficiencies in business and operational mission areas.

*DAAT*

## CONTINUOUS QUALITY IMPROVEMENT

The concept that nothing is perfect and that all work processes are grounds for constant evaluation and potential improvement.

*DGCQI*

## CONTINUOUS-REVIEW SYSTEM

A popular inventory control system in which the remaining quantity of an item is reviewed either manually or by computer each time a withdrawal is made from inventory to determine whether it is time to reorder.

*Commercial Practices*

## CONTRA PROFERENTEM

Used in connection with the construction of written documents to the effect that an ambiguous provision is construed most strongly against the person who selected the language.

*BLD*

See also "Contract Interpretation."

## CONTRACT

(1) An agreement, enforceable by law, between two or more competent parties to do or not do something not prohibited by law, for legal consideration. Involves both an offer and an acceptance.

*PW*

(2) "Contract" means a mutually binding legal relationship obligating the seller to furnish the supplies or services (including construction) and the buyer to pay for them. It includes all types of commitments that obligate the government to an expenditure of appropriated funds and that, except as otherwise authorized, are in writing. In addition to bilateral instruments, contracts include (but are not limited to) awards and notices of awards; job orders or task letters issued under basic ordering agreements; letter contracts; orders, such as purchase orders, under which the contract becomes effective by written acceptance or performance; and bilateral contract modifications. Contracts do not include grants and cooperative agreements.

*FAR*

(3) A relationship between two parties, such as a buyer and seller, that is defined by an agreement about their respective rights and responsibilities.

*Garrett*

(4) A document that describes such an agreement.

*Garrett*

## CONTRACT ADMINISTRATION

(1) The oversight of a contractor's [supplier's] performance pursuant to the fulfillment of the terms, conditions, and specifications of a contract.

*OPM*

(2) Contract administration includes those inherently governmental activities performed by warranted contracting officers (COs), the contracting officer's technical representatives (COTRs), and related payment evaluation staff members. Contract administration is not to be confused with contract quality control, performance evaluation or inspection, which are defined as commercial activities by Office of Federal Procurement Policy (OFPP) Policy Letter 92-1.

*OMB A-76*

(3) The process of ensuring compliance with contractual terms and conditions during contract performance up to contract closeout or termination.

*Garrett*

## CONTRACT ADMINISTRATION OFFICE (CAO)

The activity identified in the Department of Defense (DOD) Directory of Contract Administration Services Components assigned to perform contract administration responsibilities. It is a general term and includes ARPRO (Army Plant Representative Office), AFPRO (Air Force Plant Representative Office), NAVPRO (Navy Plant Representative Office), (SUPSHIP) Supervisor of Shipbuilding, and DCAS (Defense Contract Administrative Services)

*OPM*

## CONTRACT AUDIT

The evaluation of the accuracy and propriety of contractors' cost representations and claims by the review and analysis of contractors' and subcontractors' policies, systems and controls; it includes examination of books, accounts, basic records, and operations.

*AFIT*

## CONTRACT AWARD

Takes place when contracting officer (buyer) has signed and distributed the contract to the contractor (seller).

*DSMC*

## CONTRACT BOND

A guarantee backed by cash or other security, of the faithful performance and fulfillment of the undertakings, covenants, terms, and conditions contained in a contract.

*AFIT*

## CONTRACT CHANGE PROPOSAL (CCP)
See "Engineering Change Proposal" and "Equitable Adjustment."

## CONTRACT CLAIM
Any request for relief, adjustment, or consideration by a party to the contract for an act that, in the opinion of the claimant, is not within the scope or intent of the original contract.

*OPM*

See also "Claim."

## CONTRACT CLOSEOUT
See "Closeout."

## CONTRACT COST
The aggregate dollar amount paid to the contractor (supplier).

*AFIT*

## CONTRACT DATA REQUIREMENTS LIST (CDRL)
Document used to order (buy) and require delivery of data; it tells the contractor what data to deliver, when and how such data will be accepted, where to look for instructions, etc.

*DSMC*

See also "Technical Data Package."

## CONTRACT DISPUTES ACT (CDA)
In 1978, the Contract Disputes Act (41 U.S.C. 601–613) established procedures and requirements for asserting and resolving claims by or against contractors arising under or relating to a contract subject to the Act. The Act provides for payment of interest on contractor claims in excess of $100,000, and for a civil penalty for contractor claims that are fraudulent or based on a misrepresentation of fact. (Threshold amount was revised in sixth edition.)

*FAR*

## CONTRACT FULFILLMENT
The joint buyer and seller actions taken to successfully perform and administer a contractual agreement and to meet or exceed all contractual obligations, including effective change management and timely contract closeout.

*Garrett*

## CONTRACT INTERPRETATION
The entire process of determining what the parties agreed to in their bargain. The basic objective of contract interpretation is to determine the intent of the parties. Rules calling for interpretation of the document against the drafter, and imposing a duty to seek clarification on the contractor, allocate risks of contractual ambiguities by resolving disputes in favor of the party least responsible for the ambiguity.

## NC-A

See also "Contra Proferentem" and "Four Corners Doctrine."

## CONTRACT LINE ITEM NUMBER (CLIN)

The supplies or services to be delivered under the contract as set forth in Section B of the solicitation are categorized into CLINs. The CLIN structure and description can have a significant effect on both the government and the contractor. CLINs are based on the work breakdown structure (WBS). To effectively determine exactly what the government requires and to create a means to monitor the contractor's work progress, analyze the WBS and then design the CLINs to match this structure.

*NES-90*

## CONTRACT MANAGEMENT

The art and science of managing a contractual agreement(s) throughout the contracting process.

*Garrett*

## CONTRACT MANAGEMENT REVIEW

An appraisal of the effectiveness of local offices' interpretation and application of policies, directives, and procedures, and of the capability of field activities to comply with them.

*OPM*

## CONTRACT MODIFICATION

(1) Any written alteration in the specification, delivery point, rate of delivery, contract period, price, quantity, or other provision of an existing contract, accomplished in accordance with a contract clause; the change may be unilateral or bilateral.

*OPM*

(2) Contract modification means any written change in the terms of a contract.

*FAR*

See also "Change Order" and "Supplemental Agreement."

## CONTRACT NEGOTIATION

The process of unifying different positions into a unanimous joint decision regarding the buying and selling of products or services or both.

*Garrett*

## CONTRACT NEGOTIATION PROCESS

A three-phased approach composed of planning, negotiating, and documenting a contractual agreement between two or more parties to buy or sell products or services or both.

*Garrett*

## CONTRACT PRICING PROPOSAL

The instrument required of an offeror for the submission or identification of cost or pricing data, by which an offeror submits to the government a summary of estimated (or incurred) costs suitable for detailed review and analysis.

*OPM*

See also "Proposal."

## CONTRACT REQUIREMENTS

In addition to specified performance requirements, contract requirements include those defined in the statement of work (SOW); specifications, standards and related documents; Contract Data Requirements List (CDRL); management systems; and contract terms and conditions.

*OPM*

## CONTRACT SCHEDULE

The complete statement of the requirement in the solicitation, including not only the statement of work (SOW) and specifications, but also the terms and conditions with respect to packaging and marking, inspection and acceptance, deliveries or performance, contract administration data, and other special contract requirements. The Schedule includes Sections A through H of the Uniform Contract Format.

*FAI*

See also "Uniform Contract Format."

## CONTRACT TYPE

A specific pricing arrangement used for the performance of work under the contract.

*OPM*

See also "Cost-Plus-Award-Fee (CPAF) Contract," "Cost-Plus-Fixed-Fee (CPFF) Contract," "Cost-Plus-Incentive-Fee (CPIF) Contract," "Firm-Fixed-Price (FFP) Contract," "Fixed-Price-Incentive (FPI) Contract," and "Fixed-Price Redeterminable (FPR) Contract."

## CONTRACT WORK HOURS AND SAFETY STANDARDS ACT

Requires that certain contracts contain a clause (See FAR 52.222-4) specifying that no laborer or mechanic doing any part of the work contemplated by the contract shall be required or permitted to work more than 40 hours in any workweek unless paid for all additional hours. They are paid at least one and half (1.5) times the basic rate of pay for each hour worked over 40 hours.

*FAR*

## CONTRACTED SAVINGS

Net life-cycle cost savings realized by contracting for the performance of a value engineering (VE) study or by a Value Engineering Change Proposal (VECP) submitted by a contractor.

*OMB A-131*

## CONTRACTING

(1) The entire spectrum of action associated with obtaining supplies or services, from initial description through solicitation and contract award and all phases of contract administration.

*NCMA-SS*

(2) Contracting means purchasing, renting, leasing, or otherwise obtaining supplies or services from nonfederal sources. Contracting includes description (but not determination) of supplies and services required, selection and solicitation of sources, preparation and award of contracts, and all phases of contract administration. It does not include making grants or cooperative agreements.

## CONTRACTING ACTIVITY
An element of an agency that is designated by the agency head and to which is delegated broad authority regarding acquisition functions.

*NCMA-SS*

## CONTRACTING OFFICE
An office that prepares solicitations and awards or executes a contract for supplies or services and performs post-award functions not assigned to a contract administration office.

*NCMA-SS*

## CONTRACTING OFFICER (CO)
(1) The only person with the authority to obligate government funds and enter into, administer, or terminate contracts. The term also applies to any authorized representatives of the CO acting within their limits of delegated authority.

*OPM*

(2) CO means a person with the authority to enter into, administer, or terminate contracts and to make related determinations and findings. The term includes certain authorized representatives of the CO acting within the limits of their authority as delegated by the CO. "Administrative contracting officer (ACO)" refers to a CO who is administering contracts.

*FAR*

## CONTRACTING OFFICER'S TECHNICAL REPRESENTATIVE (COTR)
A person provided to assist the CO in matters related to inspection, acceptance, and other duties; a person without specific authority acting as an extension of the CO at a specific duty station.

*OPM*

## CONTRACTING OUT
The process by which a government activity contracts with private enterprise, as opposed to performing work in-house, for commercial or industrial products or services.

*OPM*

See also "Service Contract."

## CONTRACTOR
A supplier, vendor, or manufacturer having a contract (commitment) to provide specific supplies or services.

*SPP*

## CONTRACTOR COST DATA REPORT

A contractual report that provides a consistent, disciplined, historical database for use in cost estimate and cost analysis studies.

*AFIT*

## CONTRACTOR FINANCING

The provision of capital to a contractor through equity capital, private financing, customary progress payments, guaranteed loans, unusual progress payments, or advance payments.

*OPM*

See also "Advance Payment," "Guaranteed Loans," "Liquidation," and "Progress Payment."

## CONTRACTOR-OWNED, CONTRACTOR-OPERATED (COCO)

A manufacturing facility that is owned and operated by a private contractor performing a service, under contract, for the government.

*AFIT*

## CONTRACTOR PURCHASING SYSTEM REVIEW (CPSR)

An annual government audit of contractor management systems for contractors whose sales to the government exceed, or are anticipated to exceed, $25 million during the next 12 months. (Threshold was revised in sixth edition.)

*FAR*

## CONTRACTOR RISK ASSESSMENT GUIDE (CRAG)

A Department of Defense (DOD) program that proposes to cut oversight if industry strengthens its own internal controls. Contractors that can demonstrate the implementation of internal control systems that meet CRAG control objectives will receive less direct government oversight. Control measures have been established for five identified "high-risk" areas for government contracting:

- indirect cost submissions
- labor charging
- material management and accounting systems
- estimating system
- purchasing

*TIPS(3-2)*

## CONTRACTS FOR THE INTERNATIONAL SALE OF GOODS (CISG) (1988)

CISG established uniform legal rules to govern the formation of international sales contracts and the rights and obligations of the buyer and seller. The CISG applies automatically to all contracts for the sale of goods between traders from two different countries that have both ratified the CISG. This automatic application takes place unless the parties to the contract expressly exclude all or part of the CISG or expressly stipulate precedence of a law other than the CISG.

*NES-94*

## CONTROL ACCOUNT (CA)

(1) The assignment of lower-level work segments to responsible lower-level managers provides a key control point for management purposes and cost collection. This is called the control account (CA). A CA thus represents a defined work scope (with the associated charge number or numbers) given to a single organizational unit (and single manager or team leader) for work performance.

*EVMIG*

(2) The control account is the initiation point for work authorization, work performance management, and work performance measurement. The CA identifies the plan for work task accomplishment, defines the effort required, identifies elements of cost (labor, material, etc.), and estimates the resources required to do the work. The CA is the point where the WBS tasks and organizational breakdown structure (OBS) responsibility intersect. It is defined as the point where a single functional organization or integrated product team has responsibility for work defined to a single WBS element.

*NDIA*

Also called a Cost Account.

## CONTROL ACCOUNT PLANS (CAPS)

Represent the work assigned to one responsible organizational element on one program WBS element. This is the lowest level in the structure at which the comparison of actual costs to planned budgets and earned value is required. It is also the cost collection point that identifies the cost elements with the factors contributing to cost or schedule variances or both.

*NDIA*

## CONTROL CHART

A chart showing sequential or time-related performance of a process that is used to determine when the process is operating in or out of statistical control, using control limits defined on the chart.

*DGCQI*

## CONTROL LIMITS

A statistically derived limit for a process that indicates the spread of variations attributable to chance variation in the process. Control limits are based on averages.

*DGCQI*

## CONVENIENCE TERMINATION

Right reserved to the government, under the standard Termination for Convenience of the Government clause, to bring an end to contracts that are made obsolete by technological and other developments, or that are otherwise no longer advantageous to the government.

*GUIDE*

See also "Anticipatory Profit" and "Termination."

## CONVENTIONAL ARMS TRANSFER

The transfer of nonnuclear weapons, aircraft, equipment, and military services from supplier states to recipient states. The United States has viewed arms transfers as a useful foreign policy instrument to strengthen collective defense arrangements, maintain regional military balances, secure U.S. bases, and compensate for the withdrawal of troops. U.S. arms are transferred by grants as in the Military Assistance Program (MAP), by private commercial sales, and by government-to-government sales under foreign military sales (FMS).

*MSA*

## CONVERSION FROM A CONTRACT

Conversion from a contract to in-house performance means the change of a commercial activity from performance by contract with a commercial source to performance by federal employees with government resources. It also includes the conversion of expansions or new requirements (work) or both from contract performance to in-house performance.

*OMB A-76*

## CONVERSION TO CONTRACT

A conversion to contract is the change of performance of a commercial activity from in-house performance by federal employees to performance by a commercial source.

*OMB A-76*

See also "Foreign Military Sales (FMS)."

## COOPERATIVE AGREEMENT

Cooperative agreements and grants are a means of providing federal assistance. The cooperative agreement differs from the grant because the sponsoring federal agency is involved, collaboratively, in management of the undertaking, and because cooperative agreements are often established with private enterprise organizations. Such agreements may provide for sharing the cost as well as sharing the management of the undertaking.

*Sherman3*

See also "Federal Assistance (Grants and Cooperative Agreements)" and "Grant."

## COOPERATIVE DEVELOPMENT

Any method by which governments cooperate to make better use of their collective research and development (R&D) resources to include technical information exchange, harmonizing of requirements, codevelopment, interdependent R&D, and agreement on standards. Many of these elements occur prior to appointment of the program manager or occur outside the program management environment, but their results affect programs that have multinational involvement.

*DOD-MMH*

## COOPERATIVE PURCHASING

(1) A process whereby two or more communities, counties, or other governmental jurisdictions voluntarily agree to coordinate their purchases of one or more commodities to obtain the best unit price through volume buying.

*Steinhauer*

(2) A purchasing approach used primarily by institutions, in which a group of institutions form or use a centralized buying service that purchases specified types of items for all institutional members of the group. The resulting volume buying usually produces significant cost savings for group members. Educational and Institutional Cooperative Service, Inc. (E&I), is perhaps the largest and most widely known cooperative purchasing organization.

*Commercial Practices*

## COPELAND ACT

The law that prohibits kickbacks on construction contracts financed by the government.

*McVay*

Also known as "Antikickback Act."

## COPRODUCTION, INTERNATIONAL

A program implemented by a government-to-government or commercial licensing arrangement that enables a foreign government or firm to acquire the "know-how" to manufacture or as-semble, repair, maintain, and operate, in whole or in part, a defense item.

*MSA*

## COPYRIGHT

A property right in an original work or authorship fixed in any tangible medium of expression, giving the holder the exclusive right to reproduce, adapt, distribute, perform, and display the work.

*Blacks*

## COST

Either the amount of money expended in acquiring a product or obtaining a service, or the total of acquisition costs plus all expenses related to operating and maintaining an item once acquired.

*ASPM*

## COST ACCOUNT

See "Control Account."

## COST ACCOUNTING

A system of accounting analysis and reporting on production costs of goods or services, or the operation costs of programs, activities, functions, or organizational units; it includes cost estimating, determination of cost standards that are based on engineering data, or comparison of actual and standard costs for the purpose of aiding cost control.

**OPM**

Also known as "Management Accounting" and "Managerial Accounting."

## COST ACCOUNTING STANDARDS (CAS)

Federal standards designed to provide a consistency and coherency in defense and other government contract accounting.

*FAR*

## COST ACCOUNTING STANDARDS BOARD (CASB)

Established in 1969 as an agency of the U.S. Congress to promote uniformity and consistency of cost accounting rules and regulations for government contractors. This establishment led to developing Cost Accounting Standards (CAS), which formally became a matter of policy when the Federal Acquisition Regulation (FAR) Council incorporated the 19 CAS into the FAR at Part 30. Congress discontinued funding for the CASB in 1980, whereupon the Board ceased to exist. In 1988, P.L. 100-679 permanently reauthorized the Office of Federal Procurement Policy (OFPP). In addition, the law reconstituted CASB within the OFPP. It also mandated that the CAS be mandatory for all executive agencies, not just the Department of Defense (DOD) as previously.

*NCMA-CA*

## COST ANALYSIS

The review and evaluation of a contractor's costs or pricing data, and of the judgmental factors applied in projecting from the data to the estimated costs, for the purpose of determining the degree to which the contractor's proposed costs represent what contract performance should cost, assuming reasonable economy and efficiency.

*OPM*

## COST AVOIDANCE

An action taken in the immediate time frame that will decrease costs in the future. For example, an engineering improvement that increases the mean time between failures (MTBF) and thereby decreases operation and maintenance (O&M) costs is a cost avoidance action.

*OMB A-131*

## COST CENTER

(1) The smallest unit of activity or area of responsibility for which costs are accumulated.

*NCMA-CA*

(2) Any subdivision of an organization comprising workers, equipment areas, activities, or combination of these that is established for the purpose of assigning or allocating costs. Cost centers are also used as a base for performance standards. Also known as "Burden Center" and "Cost Pool."

*DOD-MMH*

## COST COMPARISON

A cost comparison is the process whereby the estimated cost of government performance of a commercial activity is formally compared, in accordance with the principles and procedures of Circular A-76 and Supplement to the cost of performance by commercial or Interservice Support Agreement (ISSA) sources.

*OMB A-76*

## COST CONTRACT

A cost-reimbursement contract that provides no fee.

*P&L*

## COST ESTIMATING

(1) The process of forecasting a future result in terms of cost and based on information available at the time.

*ASPM*

(2) A judgment or opinion regarding the cost of an object, commodity, or service. A result or product of an estimating procedure that specifies the expected dollar cost required to perform a stipulated task or to acquire an item. A cost estimate may constitute a single value or a range of values.

*DAAT*

## COST ESTIMATING RELATIONSHIPS (CER)

A type of secondary comparison used in performing price analysis. CER are used to adjust comparisons by establishing a common denominator between different items. For example, dollars per pound, per foot, or per loaded labor hour are yardsticks for measuring a relationship between offers.

*W-ICPA*

See also "Secondary Comparison."

## COST GROWTH

A term related to the net change of an estimated or actual amount over a base figure previously established. The base must be relatable to a program, project, or contract and must be clearly identified by source, approval authority, specific items included, specific assumptions made, date, and amount.

*DAAT*

## COST OBJECTIVE

A function, organizational subdivision, contract, or other work unit for which cost data are desired and for which provision is made to accumulate and measure the cost of processes, products, jobs, capitalized projects, etc.

*FAR*

## COST OF CAPITAL

See "Capital, Cost of."

## COST OF GOODS SOLD

(1) Inventoriable costs released to the current period (an expense) as a result of the sale of goods.

*NCMA-CA*

(2) Direct costs of producing finished goods for sale.

*Garrett*

## COST OR PRICING DATA

All verifiable facts that could reasonably have a significant effect on price negotiations and are available at the time of agreement on price.

*OPM*

## COST OVERRUN

(1) A net change in contractual amount beyond that contemplated by a contract target price (fixed-price-incentive [FPI] contract), estimated cost plus fee (any cost-reimbursable contract), or fixed-price-redeterminable [FPR] price (contract), resulting from the contractor's actual costs being over target or anticipated contract costs.

*OPM*

(2) The amount by which a contractor exceeds the estimated cost or the final limitation (ceiling) or both of the contract.

*DAAT*

## COST PERFORMANCE REPORT

A monthly report procured by the government Program Manager (PM) from the contractor to obtain data from the contractor's management system. The report in standard format is used in the PM's decision-making process.

*DSMC*

## COST PERFORMANCE INDEX (CPI)

Earned value/actual cost (CPI >1.0 = under budget; CPI <1.0 = over budget.

*Verzuh*

## COST PERFORMANCE REPORT

A contractually required report, prepared by the contractor, containing information derived from the internal Earned Value Management System (EVMS). It provides a status of progress on the contract.

*OTB*

## COST-PLUS-AWARD-FEE (CPAF) CONTRACT

A cost-reimbursement type of contract with special incentive fee provisions used to provide motivation for excellence in contract performance in areas such as quality, timeliness, ingenuity, and cost-effectiveness.

*OPM*

## COST-PLUS-FIXED-FEE (CPFF) CONTRACT

A cost-reimbursement type of contract that provides for the payment of a fixed fee to the contractor. The CPFF does not vary with actual costs, but may be adjusted as a result of any subsequent changes in the work or services to be performed under the contract.

*OPM*

## COST-PLUS-INCENTIVE-FEE (CPIF) CONTRACT

A cost-reimbursement type of contract with provision for a fee that is adjusted by a formula in accordance with the relationship between total allowable costs and target costs.

*OPM*

## COST-PLUS-PERCENTAGE-OF-COST (CPPC) CONTRACT

An outlawed contract type that bases the contractor's fee on the amount of funds it expends.

*McVay*

## COST POOL

See "Cost Center."

## COST PRINCIPLES

The regulations that establish rules and policies relating to the general treatment of costs in government contracts, particularly the allowability of costs.

*GUIDE*

## COST PROPOSAL

The instrument required of an offeror for the submission or identification of cost or pricing data by which an offeror submits to the buyer a summary of estimated (or incurred) costs, which are suitable for detailed review and analysis.

*Garrett*

## COST REASONABLENESS

A cost is reasonable in nature and amount if it does not exceed that which would be incurred by a prudent person in the conduct of competitive business.

*FAR*

## COST-REIMBURSEMENT CONTRACT

(1) A form of pricing arrangement that provides for payment of allowable, allocable, and reasonable costs incurred in the performance of a contract to the extent that such costs are prescribed or permitted by the contract.

*OPM*

(2) A family of pricing arrangements or contract types that provide for payment of allowable, allocable, and reasonable costs incurred in the performance of a contract, to the extent that such costs are prescribed or permitted by the contract. These contracts establish an estimate of total cost for the purpose of obligating funds and establishing a ceiling that the contractor may not exceed without the approval of the buyer. Types of cost-reimbursement contracts include (a) cost without fee, (b) cost-sharing, (c) cost-plus-incentive fee, (d) cost-plus award fee, and (e) cost-plus-fixed fee.

*Commercial Practices*

See also "Cost-Plus-Award-Fee (CPAF) Contract," "Cost-Plus-Fixed-

Fee (CPFF) Contract," "Cost-Plus-Incentive-Fee Contract (CPIF)," and "Cost-Sharing Contract."

## COST RISK

(1) An assumption of possible monetary loss or gain in light of the job or work to be done; an element to be considered in the negotiation of a fair and reasonable price, as well as in the determination of contract type.

*OPM*

(2) The risk that a program will not meet its acquisition strategy cost objectives that were developed using Cost as an Independent Variable (CAIV) or cost objectives established by the acquisition authority.

*DAAT*

## COST SAVINGS

(1) A reduction in actual expenditures below the projected level of costs to achieve a specific objective.

*OMB A-131*

(2) An action that will result in a smaller than projected level of costs to achieve a specific objective. Incentive contracts where the contractor and government share in any difference in cost below the estimated target cost incurred by the contractor to achieve the objective of the contract is a cost savings. It differs from a cost avoidance in that a cost target has been set from which

the amount of savings can be measured. In cost avoidance, the amount is determined as the difference between two estimated cost patterns.

*DAAT*

## COST-SHARING CONTRACT

A cost-reimbursement contract in which the contractor receives no fee and is reimbursed only for an agreed-upon portion of its allowable costs.

*FAR*

## COST-TYPE CONTRACT

Also known as "Cost-Reimbursement Contract." See "Cost-Reimbursement Contract."

## COST VARIANCE (CV)

(1) The cost variance (CV) is a true measure of cost performance, because CV compares the actual cost incurred to the value of work accomplished. It eliminates the distortions inherently present in a simple comparison of actual costs to total budget, when work is being performed ahead of or behind schedule.

*NDIA*

(2) An output of the Earned Value Management System (EVMS) that measures cost overrun or underrun relative to the program performance measurement baseline. It is equal to the difference between Budgeted Cost of Work Performed (BCWP) and Actual

Cost of Work Performed (ACWP), that is, CV = BCWP – ACWP.

*DAAT*

(3) The difference between planned and actual costs for completed work. CV = earned value – actual cost. A negative result indicates over budget.

*Verzuh*

## COST-VOLUME-PROFIT ANALYSIS
See "Breakeven Analysis."

## COUNTEROFFER
(1) The nonacceptance of the government's offer to buy as presented. A counteroffer introduces a new condition, item, quantity, or quality, or it varies from the original terms in the government's offer. Counteroffers by suppliers under sealed-bid procedure are rejected. However, under negotiated procedures (including small purchases), counteroffers are permissible and may be negotiated (e.g., a purchase order is only an offer to buy, and the terms of acceptance may be negotiated).

*SPP*

(2) A counterproposal different from an offer that an offeree makes in response to the offer. In making a counteroffer, the offeree rejects the previous offer.

*FBL*

(3) An offer made in response to an original offer that changes the terms of the original.

*Garrett*

## COUNTERPURCHASE
A form of countertrade that occurs when a firm agrees to purchase a specified dollar volume of materials from a country in return for a sale made to that country.

*Commercial Practices*

## COUNTERTRADE
A requirement imposed by a country on a foreign exporter or supplier to purchase materials in the receiving country as part of the original sales transaction. Payment is made either partially or fully with goods instead of money.

*NES-94*

## COURT OF APPEALS FOR THE FEDERAL CIRCUIT
See "United States Court of Appeals for the Federal Circuit."

## COURT OF CLAIMS
See "United States Court of Claims."

## CRADLE-TO-GRAVE
Total life cycle of a given system, from concept through development, acquisition, operations phases, and final disposition.

*DAAT*

## CRITICAL DEPENDENCIES

The interrelationships existing within or among processes that are primary drivers of defects or errors in a product or service.

*DGCQI*

## CRITICAL DESIGN REVIEW (CDR)

Determines that the detail design satisfies the performance and engineering specialty requirements of the development; that the specification establishes the detail design compatibility among the item and other items of equipment facilities, computer programs, and personnel; that the detail design assesses producibility and risk areas; and that it reviews the preliminary product specifications.

*DOD-MMH*

## CRITICAL ITEM

A subsystem, component, material, or other item that could seriously jeopardize the successful completion of program requirements if not available when required during the procurement or production. Also, an item that could have an adverse impact on cost, schedule, quality, or technical performance specifications.

*DSMC*

## CRITICAL PATH METHOD (CPM)

(1) One of the best-known (along with the Program Evaluation and Review Technique, or PERT) techniques derived from the basic critical path scheduling concept. CPM was originally developed in 1955 by the DuPont and Remington Rand companies for use in coping with complex plant maintenance problems. In practice, the application of CPM/PERT generally is accomplished with a computer program. It uses network diagrams to show time and dependency relationships between the activities that make up the total project. The purpose of the technique is to keep all the "parts" arriving on schedule so that the total project can be completed as planned.

*DBL*

(2) A technique that aids understanding of the dependency of events in a project and the time required to complete them. Activities that, when delayed, have an effect on the total project schedule are critical and are said to be on the critical path.

*DAAT*

## CRITICAL PATH SCHEDULING

A tool that can be used to manage project-buying activities, construction projects, and research and development (R&D) projects, etc. The critical path approach quantifies information about uncertainties faced by the activities responsible for meeting a predetermined time schedule. The very process of analyzing these uncertainties focuses the manager's attention on the most critical series of activities in the total project— those that constitute the critical path.

A variety of specific techniques have been derived from the basic critical path scheduling concept. The best known of these are "Critical Path Method (CPM)" and "Program Evaluation and Review Technique (PERT)."

*DBL*

## CRITICAL SUBCONTRACT
A subcontract, the failure of which seriously jeopardizes the successful completion of a program within cost, schedule, quality, and/or technical performance specifications.

*DSMC*

## CRITICAL SUCCESS FACTORS
Indicators developed by a customer that specify the defect-fee character of a product or service.

*DGCQI*

## CRITICAL-VALUE ANALYSIS
A modification of the ABC **(see page 25)** analysis concept in which the subjective value of criticalness, as opposed to the actual dollar value, is assigned to each inventory item.

*Commercial Practices*

## CUMULATIVE DISCOUNT
A variation of quantity discount that is based on the quantity purchased over a specified period of time, rather than computed on the size of a single order placed at one time. This type of discount is commonly offered by suppliers as an incentive to a purchasing firm for continued or increased patronage.

*Commercial Practices*

## CURE NOTICE
A notice sent by the contracting officer (CO) stating that the contractor will be subject to a default termination unless it corrects a specific contract noncompliance or makes necessary progress to meet the delivery schedule.

*NES-89*

See also "Default Termination."

## CURRENT YEAR DOLLARS
Level of cost, with inflation, in the year that the actual cost will be incurred.

*Navy*

Also known as "Then-year Dollars."

## CUSTOMER
Anyone for whom an organization provides goods or services.

*DGCQI*

## CYCLE COUNT
(or Continuous Inventory)
A physical stock-checking system in which the inventory is divided into 52 equal groups, one of which is physically counted each week. Thus, the physical inventory operation goes on continuously without interrupting operations or storeroom activities.

*Commercial Practices*

## CYCLE STOCK

The active portion of an inventory
(i.e., the part of inventory that is
depleted through regular withdrawals
or use and that is replenished through
repetitive orders).

*Commercial Practices*

## CYCLE TIME

In a purchasing context, the replenishment cycle represents the period of
time required to order and to make
available the required stock (e.g., the
time between receipt of the requisition
and delivery of the material to the
requisitioner).

*Commercial Practices*

## DAMAGES

In a purchasing context, damages are compensation of a specific value, which is determined by a court, to be paid for loss or injury suffered by one party to a contract as a result of the other contractual party's breach of the contract.

*Commercial Practices*

## DATABASE MANAGEMENT SYSTEM (DBMS)

Term used to describe software that organizes, catalogs, locates, retrieves, and maintains data in a database.

*F&F*

## DATA DOCUMENTATION COSTS

Costs of converting source data to the documents prescribed in the contract for delivery to the government.

*AFIT*

## DATA REQUIREMENTS REVIEW BOARD

A board appointed by a responsible manager to assist and advise in the determination of data requirements.

*AFIT*

## DATA RIGHTS CLAUSE

The data rights issue involves the complicated question of who owns the rights to data developed under a contract. The answer lies in the contract provisions that have been negotiated between the parties. Three means of protecting data are commonly used in the commercial world: (a) trade secret status, (b) copyright protection, and (c) patent provisions. Federal government contracting has four types of rights that the government can obtain for use of data developed under federal contracts: unlimited rights, limited rights, restricted rights (which apply only to computer software), and government purpose license rights.

*NES-92*

## DATA SHEET

See "Financial Accounting Data Sheet."

## DAVIS-BACON ACT

A statute that requires all laborers and mechanics employed on federally funded construction, alteration, or repair contracts to be paid the locally prevailing wage rate (as determined by the Secretary of Labor).

*McVay*

## DEBARMENT

Action taken by a debarring official to exclude a contractor from government contracting and subcontracting for a reasonable, specified period. The following are some causes for debarment per Federal Acquisition Regulation (FAR) 9.406-2: conviction of or civil judgment for any offense indicating a lack of business integrity (fraud, antitrust violations, theft, bribery, etc.); violation of the terms of a government contract so serious as to justify debarment; violations of the Drug-Free Workplace Act of 1988; or any other cause of so serious or compelling a nature that it affects the present responsibility of a government contractor or subcontractor.

*FAR*

Compare "Suspension."
See also "Consolidated List of Debarred, Suspended, and Ineligible Contractors."

## DEBRIEF(ING)

(1) An explanation given by government personnel to an offeror detailing the reasons its proposal was unsuccessful.

*McVay*

(2) At a minimum, the debriefing information shall include (a) the government's evaluation of the significant weaknesses or deficiencies in the offeror's proposal, if applicable; (b) the overall evaluated cost or price (including unit prices) and technical rating, if applicable, of the successful offeror and the debriefed offeror, and past performance information on the debriefed offeror; (c) the overall ranking of all offerors, when any ranking was developed by the agency during the source selection; (d) a summary of the rationale for award; (e) the acquisitions of commercial items, the make and model of which will be delivered by the successful offeror; and (f) reasonable responses to relevant questions about whether source selection procedures contained in the solicitation, applicable regulations, and other applicable authorities were followed.

*FAR*

(3) The debriefing shall not include point-by-point comparisons of the debriefed offeror's proposal with those of other offerors. Moreover, the debriefing shall not reveal any information prohibited from disclosure by 24.202 or exempt from release under the Freedom of Information Act (FOIA) (5 U.S.C. 552), including (a) trade secrets; (b) privileged or confidential manufacturing processes and techniques; (c) commercial and financial information that is privileged or confidential, including cost breakdowns, profit, indirect cost rates, and similar information; and (d) names of individuals providing reference information about an offeror's past performance.

*FAR*

## DECENTRALIZATION OF PURCHASING

This occurs when personnel from other functional areas—production, engineering, marketing, finance, etc. —decide on sources of supply, negotiate with vendors directly, or perform any of the other major functions of purchasing. Three types of situations justify some decentralization: companies that process single natural raw materials, technically oriented firms that are heavily involved in research, and operation of multisite institutional and manufacturing organizations. Also, the purchase of nontechnical odds and ends often calls for partial decentralization of purchasing.

*DBL*

Compare "Centralization of Purchasing."

## DECISION SUPPORT SYSTEMS

A type of expert system.

*TIPS(2-8)*

See also "Expert Systems."

## DECOUPLING INVENTORY

Inventory retained to make possible the independent control of two operations; sometimes referred to as line-balancing stock.

*Commercial Practices*

## DEDUCTIVE CHANGE

A change resulting in a reduction in contract price because of a net reduction in a contractor's work.

*GUIDE*

## DEFAULT

(1) The actual or anticipated failure of a contractor to fulfill the terms and conditions of the contract, thus giving the contracting officer (CO) the right to terminate the contract.

*NES-89*

(2) The failure to perform a legal obligation or duty.

*FBL*

## DEFAULT TERMINATION

Sanction that the government may impose, under the standard default clause, for a contractor's failure to perform.

*GUIDE*

See also "Cure Notice," "Show Cause Letter," and "Termination."

## DEFECT

The absence of something necessary for completeness or perfection; a deficiency in something essential to the proper use for the purpose for which a thing is to be used. Some structural weakness in part or component that is responsible for damage.

*BLD2*

## DEFECT, LATENT

Defects that existed at the time of acceptance but would not have been discovered by a reasonable inspection.

*NC-A*

## DEFECT, PATENT

Defects that can be discovered without undue effort. If the defects were actually known to the government (buyer) at the time of acceptance they are patent, even if they might otherwise not have been discoverable by a reasonable inspection.

*NC-A*

## DEFECTIVE COST OR PRICING DATA

Certified cost or pricing data subsequently found to have been inaccurate, incomplete, or nonconcurrent as of the effective date of the certificate.

*OPM*

## DEFECTIVE PRICING ACTION

If after contract award, the cost or pricing data relied upon by the procuring contract officer (PCO) are found to be inaccurate, incomplete, or noncurrent as of the date of final agreement on price given on the contractor's or subcontractor's Certificate of Current Cost or Pricing Data, then the government is entitled to a price adjustment, including profit or fee, of any amount by which the price was increased because of the defective data.

*Navy*

## DEFECTIVE SPECIFICATIONS

Mistakes and omissions in the requirements set forth are generally identified in this way. This area is frequently the basis for claims and litigation between contracting parties.

*Cohen*

## DEFENSE ACQUISITION CIRCULAR (DAC)

Circular that is issued to revise or supplement the Department of Defense Supplement to the Federal Acquisition Regulation (Defense Federal Acquisition Regulation Supplement, or DFARS).

*GUIDE*

## DEFENSE ACQUISITION REGULATION (DAR)

The regulation that governed Department of Defense (DOD) procurements directly before the Federal Acquisition Regulation (FAR) became effective in 1984.

*McVay*

## DEFENSE ACQUISITION REGULATORY COUNCIL (DARC)

A council that comprises representatives of the secretaries of Defense, the Army, the Navy, the Air Force, the Defense Logistics Agency (DLA), and the National Aeronautics and Space Administration (NASA). Among other responsibilities, the DARC, along with the Civilian Agency Acquisition Council (CAAC), maintains the Federal Acquisition Regulation (FAR).

*FAI*

## DEFENSE CONTRACT AUDIT AGENCY (DCAA)

Separate and independent entity within the Department of Defense (DOD) that provides contract audit functions and accounting–financial advisory services for all DOD components, as well as for other government agencies.

*GUIDE*

## DEFENSE FEDERAL ACQUISITION REGULATION SUPPLEMENT (DFARS)

Establishes for the Department of Defense (DOD) uniform policies and procedures that implement the Federal Acquisition Regulation (FAR), as well as supplementary material that is unique to DOD. The DFARS is not a stand-alone document and must be read in conjunction with the FAR.

*Navy*

## DEFENSE LOGISTICS AGENCY (DLA)

Component organization within the Department of Defense (DOD) that provides consumable supply items and logistics services common to the military services.

*GUIDE*

## DEFENSE PRIORITIES AND ALLOCATIONS SYSTEM (DPAS)

A set of laws and regulations that establishes priorities for all contracts and subcontracts issued (a) for domestic and imported steel, copper, aluminum, or nickel alloys; and (b) for performance of any of 40 defense-related programs.

*McVay*

See also "Priority Ratings."

## DEFERRED PROCUREMENT

A decision that the initial procurement quantity of high-cost items is to be less than the originally estimated quantity during a specified support period.

*UPM*

## DEFICIENCY REPORT (DR)

Written communication that is issued by the source selection evaluation board through the contracting officer (CO) for the purpose of identifying portions of a proposal that, when compared with the pertinent standard, will fail to meet the government's minimum level of compliance.

*W-HAP*

See also "Clarification Request (CR)."

## DEFICIT

A deficit occurs when more is spent than is received in a fiscal year (FY). It grows as one year's overspending is added to next year's.

*DLA*

## DEFINITE-QUANTITY CONTRACT

A contractual instrument that provides for a definite quantity of supplies or services to be delivered at some later, unspecified date.

*McVay*

## DEFLATED HOURLY RATES

See "Uncompensated Overtime."

## DELAY, EXCUSABLE

(1) A contractual provision designed to protect the contractor from sanctions for late performance. To the extent that the performance has been excusably delayed, the contractor is protected from default termination, liquidated damages, or excess costs of reprocurement or completion. Excusable delays also may lead to recovery of additional compensation if the government constructively accelerates performance.

*NC-A*

(2) Excusable delay protects contractors from penalties for delays that are beyond their control. Examples of excusable delay are acts of God or the public enemy, acts of the government in either its sovereign or contractual capacity, fire, flood, quarantines, strikes, epidemics, unusually severe weather, and freight embargoes.

*FAR*

## DELAY, GOVERNMENT-CAUSED

Acts of the government in either its sovereign or contractual capacity may be found to be excusable causes of delay. For a contractor to be excused by an act of the government in its contractual capacity, the contractor must prove that the government act that caused the delay was wrongful. Sovereign acts that delay the contractor's performance are grounds for excusable delays.

*NC-A*

## DELEGATION

The conferring of authority, from one government agency or representative to another, to accomplish contract administrative tasks. Such authority may be shared or recalled.

*P&L*

## DELINQUENCY

The actual or potential failure by the contractor to meet or maintain the contract delivery or performance schedule.

*AFIT*

## DELIVERY

(1) Transfer of possession. A "Delivery Order" directs an established source to transfer possession of goods from the source to the ordering activity. Applied to shipping, delivery occurs when a bill of lading is surrendered and when title of goods passes to the receiver or consignee.

*SPP*

(2) Constructive or actual delivery; the performance of services for the customer or requisitioner; accessorial

services, when they are normally recorded in the billing and collection cycle immediately following performance.

*MSA*

## DELIVERY ORDER

A written order to a contractor pursuant to an indefinite-delivery type contract, which then becomes the basic obligating document for the transaction. Consummation of an originally partial contractual agreement between the contractor and the government.

*OPM*

See also "Indefinite-Delivery/ Indefinite-Quantity (IDIQ) Contract."

## DEMURRAGE

A fee charged by a carrier against a consignee, consignor, or other responsible party to compensate for the detention of the carrier's equipment (railcar, container, etc.) in excess of allowable free time for loading, unloading, reconsigning, or stopping in transit. The term is also used by suppliers of material delivered in a variety of returnable containers, such as gas cylinders, etc.

*Commercial Practices*

## DEPENDENT DEMAND

Dependent demand is derived or contingent upon the demand for a component or a finished product (i.e., the demand for axles used in the assembly of automobiles is dependent on the demand for the finished automobiles).

*Commercial Practices*

## DEPOSITION

Testimony that is taken under oath and subject to cross-examination in order to discover what the witness is going to say and to ensure the preservation of the witness's testimony should the witness die or disappear or forget before the trial.

*FDL*

## DEPRECIATION

Amount of expense charged against earnings by a company to write off the cost of a plant or machine over its useful life, giving consideration to wear and tear, obsolescence, and salvage value.

*Garrett*

## DESCRIPTIVE LITERATURE

Information, such as cuts, illustrations, drawings, and brochures, that shows the characteristics or construction of a product or explains its operation.

*FAR*

## DESIGN CRITERIA

Either the design constraints, or the preferred or accepted techniques to be used in achieving an acceptable approach to a design requirement.

*AFIT*

## DESIGN SPECIFICATION

(1) A document (including drawings) setting forth the required characteristics of a particular component, part, subsystem, system, or construction item.

*P&L*

(2) A purchase description that establishes precise measurements, tolerances, materials, in-process and finished product tests, quality control, inspection requirements, and other specific details of the deliverable.

*FAI*

## DESIGN-TO-COST (DTC)

(1) A concept that establishes cost elements as management goals to achieve the best balance between life-cycle cost, acceptable performance, and schedule. Under this concept, cost is a design constraint during the design and development phases and a management discipline throughout the acquisition and operation of the system or equipment.

*FAR*

(2) Management concept that historically emphasized cost-effective design (minimizing cost while achieving performance) and targeting an average unit procurement cost (AUPC). DTC concentrated on the contractors' activities associated with tracking or controlling costs and performing cost-performance analyses or trade-offs. Cost as an Independent Variable (CAIV) has refocused DTC to consider cost objectives for the total life cycle of the program and to view CAIV with the understanding that it may be necessary to trade off performance to stay within cost objectives and constraints. DTC is now those actions that are undertaken to meet cost objectives through explicit design activities. Contractual implementation of DTC should go beyond simply incentivizing the contractor to meet cost commitments; it should also incentivize the contractor to seek out additional cost-reduction opportunities.

*DAAT*

## DESK AUDIT

An examination of limited scope made at a point removed from the site of operations by means of reference to documents and other available information.

*AFIT*

See also "Audit."

## DETERMINATION AND FINDINGS

A document that is signed by an authorized government official and that justifies a decision to take a certain action; expressed in terms of meeting the regulatory requirements of the situation.

*OPM*

## DETERMINATION OF RESPONSIBILITY

The process by which a contractor is determined to be a responsible bidder or offeror.

*OPM*

See also "Responsible Contractor."

## DIFFERING SITE CONDITIONS

A provision in construction contracts that provides for adjustment of the contract price should the contractor discover physical conditions of an unusual nature that differ from those ordinarily encountered.

*McVay*

## DIFFERING SITE CONDITIONS— CATEGORY I

A subsurface or latent physical condition differing materially from conditions that are indicated in the contract documents or that may be implied from other language in the contract documents.

*NC-A*

## DIFFERING SITE CONDITIONS— CATEGORY II

Conditions that are unknown and unusual, that differ materially from those ordinarily encountered, and that are not generally recognized as inherent in such work.

*NC-A*

## DIRECT ALLOCATION OF SALARY COSTS

See "Uncompensated Overtime."

## DIRECT COST

(1) Costs specifically identifiable with a contract requirement, including, but not restricted to, costs of material or labor or both that are directly incorporated into an end item.

*L&P*

(2) Costs that are assignable to a specific product, primarily classified as direct labor cost, direct material cost, or purchased cost. Such costs usually are treated as variable and do not include general overhead or common cost allocations.

*Commercial Practices*

## DIRECT COSTING

Type of product costing that charges fixed manufacturing overhead immediately against the revenue of the period in which it was incurred, without assigning it to specific units produced.

*NCMA-CA*

Also known as "Marginal Costing" and "Variable Costing."

## DIRECT LABOR

(1) All labor that is obviously related and specifically and conveniently traceable to specific products.

*NCMA-CA*

(2) Labor specifically identified with a particular final cost objective. Manufacturing direct labor includes fabrication, assembly, inspection, and test for constructing the end product. Engineering direct labor consists of engineering labors, such as reliability, quality assurance (QA), test, design, etc., that are readily identified with the end product.

## DIRECT MATERIAL

Material, including raw material, purchased parts, and subcontracted items, directly incorporated into an end item that is identifiable to a contract requirement.

*L&P*

## DIRECT OFFSET

A general type of industrial or commercial compensation practice required of a contractor by a purchasing government as a condition for the purchase of defense articles or services. The form of compensation, which generally offsets a specific percentage of the cost of the purchase, is directly associated with the items purchased, such as the production of components in the purchasing country for installation in the purchased end item.

*MSA*

## DIRECT PROCUREMENT

The procurement of defense supplies in the United States by a foreign government, contractor, or organization in which the supplies are purchased through commercial channels for use outside the United States.

*AFIT*

## DIRECT PRODUCT PROFITABILITY

Calculation of the net profit contribution attributable to a specific product or product line.

*Commercial Practices*

## DISCHARGE OF A CONTRACT

Results when the obligations incurred by the parties when they entered the agreement are excused, and the parties are no longer bound to perform as promised.

*FAI*

## DISCLOSURE STATEMENT

An official statement in which persons or firms are required to describe their contract cost accounting practices by providing data responsive to the requirements of the government's Cost Accounting Standards (CAS).

*OPM*

## DISCOUNT

See "Prompt Payment Discount," "Quantity Discount," and "Trade Discount."

## DISCOUNTED HOURLY RATES

See "Uncompensated Overtime."

## DISCOVERY

Pretrial or prehearing procedure designed to promote full disclosure of all relevant facts related to a contract dispute.

*GUIDE*

## DISCRIMINATORY PRICE

A selling situation in which a supplier offers similar or identical items for sale, in identical quantities, at different prices to different buyers.

*Commercial Practices*

## DISCUSSION

Any oral or written communication between the government and an offeror, other than communications conducted for the purpose of minor clarification, whether or not initiated by the government, that (a) involves information essential for determining the acceptability of a proposal, or (b) provides the offeror an opportunity to revise or modify its proposal.

*FAR*

## DISPUTES CLAUSE

A contract provision providing for administrative consideration and relief for disputes concerning questions of fact under a government contract that cannot be resolved by agreement between the parties to the contract.

*OPM*

## DISSEMINATION

The government-initiated distribution of information to the public. Not considered dissemination if distribution is limited to government employees or agency contractors or to grantees, intra-agency or interagency use or sharing of government information and responses to requests for agency records under the Freedom of Information Act (FOIA) (5 U.S.C. 552) or Privacy Act.

*OMB A-130*

## DOCUMENTATION

Recorded technical data, or a concept in any form from which information can be derived.

*AFIT*

## DOD VOLUNTARY DISCLOSURE PROGRAM

See "Voluntary Disclosure Program."

## DOMESTIC END PRODUCT

Either (a) an unmanufactured end product mined or produced in the United States, or (b) an end product manufactured in the United States, if the cost of its components mined, produced, or manufactured in the United States exceeds 50 percent of the cost of all its components. (In determining if an end product is domestic, only the end product and its components shall be considered.) The cost of each component includes transportation costs to the place of incorporation into the end product and any applicable duty (whether or not a duty-free entry certificate is issued).

*FAR*

See also "Buy American Act."

## DOMESTIC PREFERENCE

Any one of a number of policies adopted by a nation's government that will maintain discriminatory government procurement rules designed to establish a preference in favor of domestic suppliers.

*TIPS(1-15)*

See also "Buy American Act."

## DOUBLE COUNTING

A cost accounting standards violation that can result from allocating cost items directly to a cost objective without eliminating like cost items from indirect cost pools.

*W-CC*

## DOWN SELECT

To reduce the number of contractors working on a program by eliminating one or more for the next phase.

*DAAT*

## DRAFT REQUEST FOR PROPOSAL (RFP)

Usually sent out to prospective industry bidders authorized by government to receive it in advance of final RFP. Solicits contractors' recommendations to add, delete, or modify requirements, and to give them heads-up on what is anticipated.

*DAAT*

## DRUG-FREE WORKPLACE

A site for the performance of work done in connection with a specific contract at which employees of the contractor are prohibited from engaging in the unlawful manufacture, distribution, dispensing, possession, or use of a controlled substance.

*FAR*

## DUE BILL

A bill levied by a government on the importation, exportation, or use and consumption of goods.

*Commercial Practices*

## DUTY

A tax imposed by the customs authority of the receiving country on imported goods and services.

- Ad valorem—"According to value"
- Specific—determined by product weight or quantity
- Compound—a combination of the above two types.

*NES-94*

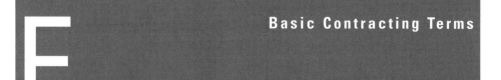
## 8(A) PROGRAM
See "Section 8(a) Subcontract."

## EARLY SUPPLIER INVOLVEMENT (ESI)
A practice that involves one or more selected suppliers with a buyer's product design team early in the specification development process. The objective is to use the supplier's expertise and experience in developing a product specification that is designed for effective and efficient manufacturability.

*Commercial Practices*

See also "Alpha Contracting."

## EARNED VALUE
See "Budgeted Cost of Work Performed (BCWP)."

## EARNED VALUE MANAGEMENT SYSTEM (EVMS)
(1) Industry-developed set of 32 standards adopted for use by Department of Defense (DOD) in 1996 for evaluation of contractor management systems. The EVMS replaced the Cost/Schedule Control Systems Criteria (C/SCSC), which contained 35 standards for evaluation of contractor management systems.

*DAAT*

(2) EVMS is a project management system that combines schedule performance and cost performance to answer the question, "What did we get for the money we spent?" EVMS guidelines incorporate best business practices to provide strong benefits for program or enterprise planning and control. The processes include integration of program scope, schedule, and cost objectives; establishment of a baseline plan for accomplishment of program objectives; and use of earned-value techniques for performance measurement during the execution of a program. The system provides a sound basis for problem identification, corrective actions, and management re-planning as may be required.

*EVM*

(3) EVMS is a project (investment) management tool that effectively integrates the investment scope of work with schedule and cost elements for optimum investment planning and

control. The qualities and operating characteristics of EVMSs are described in American National Standards Institute (ANSI)/Electronic Industries Alliance (EIA) Standard –748–1998, Earned Value Management Systems, approved May 19, 1998. It was reaffirmed on August 28, 2002.

*OMB A-11*

## ECONOMIC ORDER QUANTITY (EOQ)

This concept holds that the appropriate quantity to order may be the one that tends to minimize all costs associated with order-carrying costs, acquisition costs, and cost of the material itself. The EOQ formula states that EOQ occurs when annual carrying cost equals annual acquisition cost (CC = AC).

*DBL*

## ECONOMIC PRICE ADJUSTMENT

An alteration permitted and specified by contract provisions for the upward or downward revision of a stated contract price upon the occurrence of certain specifically defined contingencies.

*OPM*

## ECONOMICS

The study of how people and society choose to use scarce productive resources to produce goods and services and to distribute them among various persons and groups in society.

*ECON*

## ECONOMIES OF SCALE

(1) The reduction in long-term average unit costs as the size (scale) of a firm or operation increases.

*Commercial Practices*

(2) Reductions in unit cost of output resulting from producing additional units. Other factors include: increasing labor specialization as volume of output increases, decreasing unit costs, utilizing management better, buying more efficient equipment, and using more by-products.

*DAAT*

## ECONOMY

A particular system of organization for the production, distribution, and consumption of all things people use to achieve a certain standard of living.

*ECON*

## EDIBANX

Business-to-business payment network that was developed by banks to advance electronic commerce, and that sends and receives payments with attached remittance information.

*NES-00*

## EFFECTIVE COMPETITION

A market condition that exists when two or more responsible offerors acting independently contend for a contract that results in the buyer receiving either (a) the lowest cost or price alternative, or (b) the optimal combination of technical design coupled with a cost-effective price.

*P&L*

## EICHLEAY FORMULA

The best-known and most widely used formula for calculating extended overhead on change proposals. It is used primarily for construction contracts, where it is assumed that almost all overhead is fixed rather than variable. The formula was adopted in Eichleay Corp., ASBCA 5183, 60-2 BCA - 2688, where it computed the daily amount of overhead that the contractor would have charged to the contract had there been no delay, and where it gave the contractor the amount of overhead for each day of delay that occurred.

*NES-87*

See also "Extended Overhead."

## ELASTICITY OF DEMAND

Degree of responsiveness of quantity demanded to a change in price.

*ECON*

## ELECTRONIC DATA INTERCHANGE (EDI)

The computer-to-computer exchange of standard business documentation in machine-processable form.

*EDI*

## ELECTRONIC FUNDS TRANSFER (EFT)

The company-to-company or company-to-bank electronic exchange of value.

*EDI*

EFT means any transfer of funds, other than a transaction originated by cash, check, or similar paper instrument, that is initiated through an electronic terminal, telephone, computer, or magnetic tape, for the purpose of ordering, instructing, or authorizing a financial institution to debit or credit an account. The term includes Automated Clearing House (ACH) transfers, Fedwire transfers, and transfers made at automatic teller machines and point-of-sale terminals.

*FAR*

## ELECTRONIC MAIL (e-Mail)

The transfer of messages over computer networks. Messages are usually in free format.

*EDI*

## ELECTRONIC MAILBOX

A designated holding location for electronic messages. The mailbox can either be on the user's computer, or, as is more common, on a third-party network computer.

*EDI*

## ELECTRONIC PAYMENTS

Any method of making payments electronically. Such payments include wire transfers and Automated Clearing House (ACH) payments. ACH is an organization that acts as a storage and transfer facility for electronic payments.

*EDI*

## ELEMENTS OF A CONTRACT

Elements that must be present in a contract if the contract is to be binding. These elements include the following:

- an offer
- acceptance
- consideration
- execution by competent parties
- legality of purpose
- clear terms and conditions

*FAI*

## ELEMENTS OF COST

Cost categories that directly or indirectly influence the cost of producing material or providing services and that can be apportioned to the contract.

*OPM*

## ENCRYPTION

A method of ensuring data secrecy. The message to be sent is coded using a key available only to the sender and the receiver. The coded message is sent to the receiver and then decoded upon receipt.

*EDI*

## END ITEM

An assembled whole system or equipment ready for its intended use.

*AFIT*

## ENGINEERING CHANGE PROPOSAL (ECP)

(1) A document proposing any design change requiring revision to contract specifications or engineering drawings; ECP may be originated by either party to a contract; it requires detailed documentation and evaluation of technical, cost, and schedule effects.

*OPM*

(2) A proposal to the responsible authority recommending that a change to an original item of equipment be considered, and that the design or engineering change be incorporated into the article to modify, add to, delete, or supersede original parts.

*DAAT*

## ENGINEERING DATA

Engineering documents, such as specifications, drawings, standards, lists, or other information, that are prepared by a design activity relating to the design, performance, manufacture, test, or inspection of items and services.

*AFIT*

## ENHANCED PROLIFERATION CONTROL INITIATIVE (EPCI)

EPCI places greater emphasis on the exporter's responsibility for ensuring that the end use or end user of exporter goods does not violate U.S. export restrictions.

*NES-94*

## ENVIRONMENTAL ASSESSMENT (EA)

(1) A brief document used by the relevant agency to determine whether an environmental impact statement (EIS) is required. The environmental assessment (EA) discusses the proposal, alternatives to the proposal, and a list of the people consulted. The EA affects whether an EIS is required. If the information contained in the EA convincingly evidences that the proposed action will not significantly affect the environment, no EIS is required.

*NES-94*

(2) Contains an estimate of whether or not a proposed system will adversely affect the environment or will be environmentally controversial, in which case an EIS is prepared.

*DAAT*

## EQUAL ACCESS TO JUSTICE ACT (EAJA)

Federal law designed to aid small businesses and individuals in recovering attorney fees if they prevail in certain actions against the government.

*GUIDE*

## EQUAL EMPLOYMENT OPPORTUNITY (EEO)

The right of every individual under the law to be considered for employment without discrimination based on race, color, sex, national origin, age, religion, nondisqualifying mental or physical handicap, or any other nonmerit factor.

*Navy*

## EQUITABLE ADJUSTMENT

(1) The compensation or price adjustment to which a contractor is entitled upon the occurrence of a constructive change or special event.

*OPM*

(2) The courts and boards have recognized four methods for pricing equitable adjustment claims: (a) total cost, (b) modified total cost, (c) jury verdict, and (d) actual costs.

*W-ATCC*

See also "Request for Equitable Adjustment (REA)."

## ESCALATION

A term traditionally used to indicate an upward or downward movement of price.

*OPM*

See also "Economic Price Adjustment."

## ESCALATOR CLAUSE

A contract clause generally permitting an increase in the price of goods or services in the event of certain outcomes, such as an increase in the supplier's raw materials or labor costs. Escalation clauses in a contract typically also provide for de-escalation.

*Commercial Practices*

## ESCALATION

Use of a price index to convert past to present prices or to convert present to future prices; increase resulting from inflation and outlay rates for the appropriation and the branch or the service involved.

*DAAT*

## ESCROW

A legal document or other property delivered into the hands of a third person to be held until the happening of a contingency or performance of a condition.

*BLD2*

## ESTABLISHED CATALOGUE PRICE

A price that is regularly maintained by a manufacturer or vendor, that is published or made available for inspection by customers, and that states prices at which sales either are currently or were last made to a significant number of buyers constituting the general public.

*OPM*

## ESTABLISHED MARKET PRICE

A current price, generated in the usual course of business between buyers and sellers free to bargain, which can be substantiated from sources independent of the seller.

*Commercial Practices*

## ESTABLISHED GOVERNMENT SOURCES

Government and nongovernment sources of supplies, equipment, and services that are designated by law or regulation as mandatory sources, in a set order of priority, for particular items and services.

*SPP*

## ESTABLISHED MARKET PRICE

A current price, established in the usual and ordinary course of trade between buyers and sellers free to bargain, which can be substantiated from sources independent of the manufacturer or vendor.

*OPM*

## ESTIMATE AT COMPLETION (EAC)

(1) Actual direct costs, plus indirect costs or costs allocable to the contract, plus the estimate of costs (direct and indirect) for authorized work remaining.

*DAAT*

(2) This is a re-estimate of the total project budget. The original budget is multiplied by the actual cost and is divided by the earned value. It is a way of saying that if the current cost performance trends continue, the final cost can be predicted (EAC = BAC x CPI).

*Verzuh*

(3) The current estimated total cost for program-authorized work. It equals actual cost to a point in time plus the estimated costs to completion (Estimate to Complete).

*OTB*

## ESTIMATE TO COMPLETE (ETC)

The budget amount that is needed to finish the project and that is based on the current Cost Performance Index. Estimate to complete equals current cost performance index times (estimate at completion minus actual costs) ETC=CPI(EAC-AC).

*Verzuh*

## ESTOPPEL

A rule of law that bars, prevents, and precludes a party from alleging or denying certain facts because of a previous allegation or denial or because of his or her previous conduct or admission.

*FBL*

## ETHICS

Of or relating to moral action, conduct, motive, or character as in an ethical emotion; also, treating of moral feelings, duties, or conduct; containing precepts of morality; moral; professionally right or befitting; or conforming to professional standards of conduct

*BLD*

## EVALUATION BOARD

See "Source Selection Evaluation Board (SSEB)."

## EVALUATION FACTORS

Factors that will be considered in evaluating proposals tailored to each acquisition that have an effect on the source-selection decision. Price or cost to the government shall be included as an evaluation factor in every source selection. Quality shall also be addressed in every source selection. Quality may be expressed in terms of technical excellence, management capability, personnel qualifications, prior experience, past performance, and schedule compliance. Any other relevant factors such as cost realism may also be included.

*FAR*

## EVOLUTIONARY ACQUISITION (EA)

The preferred Department of Defense (DOD) strategy for rapid acquisition of mature technology for the user according to Department of Defense Instruction (DODI) 5000.2. An evolutionary approach delivers capability in increments, recognizing up front the need for future capability improvements. There are two approaches to achieving an EA: Spiral Development and Incremental Development, as noted below.

(1) Spiral Development: In this process, a desired capability is identified, but the end-state requirements are not known at program initiation. Requirements are refined through demonstration, risk management, and continuous user feedback. Each increment provides the best possible capability, but the requirements for future increments depend on user feedback and tech-nology maturation. According to DOD 5000.1, spiral development is the preferred process for executing an EA strategy.

(2) Incremental Development: In this process, a desired capability is identified, an end-state requirement is known, and that requirement is met over time by developing several increments, each of which depends on available mature technology.

*DAAT*

## EXCESS PERSONAL PROPERTY

Property under control of an agency or activity that the agency or activity has declared is excess to its needs.

*SPP*

## EXCESS REPROCUREMENT COSTS

The contractor is liable to the government for any excess costs incurred by the government to repurchase supplies or services similar to those terminated for default.

*FAR*

## EXCLUSIVE (NONEXCLUSIVE) LICENSE

A license covering a patent (or patents), technical or proprietary data, technical assistance, know-how, or any combination of these, which is granted by a U.S. firm to a foreign firm or government to produce, co-produce, or sell a defense article or service within a given sales territory without competition from any other licensees or from the licensor. A "Nonexclusive License" is a license as described above, except that competition may be permitted with other licensees or the licensor.

*MSA*

## EXCULPATORY CLAUSES

Contract language designed to shift responsibility to the other party. A "no damages for delay" clause would be an example of one used by customers.

*Cohen*

## EXCUSABLE DELAY
See "Delay, Excusable."

## EXECUTED CONTRACT
A written document, signed by both parties and mailed or otherwise furnished to each party, which expresses the requirements, terms, and conditions to be met by both parties in the performance of the contract.

*OPM*

## EXEMPT COMMODITIES
Goods that are not subject to import duties, or specific goods that can be transported exempt of regulation by the Interstate Commerce Commission (ICC).

*Commercial Practices*

## EXEMPT EMPLOYEE
An employee who is "exempt" from the provisions of the Service Contract Act (SCA). Professional services and the like are deemed exempt.

*W-ESCA*

See also "Uncompensated Overtime."

## EXEMPTION
An exemption is a determination made that a commercial activity may be converted to or from in-house, contract, or Interservice Support Agreement (ISSA) performance, without cost comparison, and that may be justified by reasons other than cost.

*OMB A-76*

## EXPANSION
An expansion is the modernization, replacement, upgrading, or enlargement of an in-house commercial activity or capability. If the expansion involves a 30 percent increase in the operating cost of the activity, a 30 percent increase in the total capital investment to perform the activity, or an increase of 65 full-time equivalents (FTE) or more, a cost comparison is required prior to authorizing in-house performance. A consolidation of two or more existing commercial activities is not an expansion, unless the total operating cost is 30 percent greater than the total of the individual components or it requires an increase of 65 FTE or more.

*OMB A-76*

(The above definition notwithstanding, all aircraft purchase decisions should be justified through formal cost comparison.)

## EXPEDITED PROCEDURE
Procedure under the Contract Disputes Act (CDA), whereby an appellant before an agency board of contract appeals can elect, for claims of $100,000 or less, to have a decision issued on a claim within four months after making the election.

*GUIDE*

See also "Accelerated Procedure."

## EXPERT SYSTEMS
Computerized knowledge base of basic facts and heuristic (problem-solving) knowledge that assists humans in eliminating infeasible decision options up front.

*TIPS(2-8)*

## EXPIRED APPROPRIATION
An appropriation that is no longer available for new obligations because the time available for incurring such obligations has expired. Expired appropriations are maintained by fiscal year (FY) identity for five years. During this five-year period, obligations may be adjusted and outlays are made from these accounts. Unobligated balances may not be withdrawn from expired accounts. After the five-year period has elapsed, all obligated and unobligated balances are cancelled and the expired account is closed.

*DAAT*

## EXPIRED COST
A cost that should be released to the current period as an expense or loss.

*NCMA-CA*

## EXPORT ADMINISTRATION REGULATIONS (EAR)
Export of commodities not regulated by the State Department through the International Traffic in Arms Regulation (ITAR) is administered by the Commerce Department through the Export Administration Regulations (EAR). Under the EAR, most commodities can be exported under the authority of a general license. Authority to export commodities that are dual-use items (those that can be used both for defense or spacecraft and for commercial purposes) is sought under a validated license. A validated license is necessary to protect national security or foreign policy interests, or because the commodity is in short supply in the United States.

*TIPS(2-10)*
See also "International Traffic in Arms Regulation (ITAR)."

## EXPORT CONTROL ACT (1965)
The Act governs all U.S. exporting activities and mandates the Commerce Control List (previously referred to as the "Commodity Control List) for private and government (nonmunitions) sales and transactions. The Commerce Control List includes all commodities subject to Department of Commerce export controls and then identifies those products subject to licensing control.

*NES-94*

## EXPORTING
The act of sending or carrying merchandise abroad, especially for trade or sale.

*NES-94/AHD*

## EXPORT–IMPORT BANK ("EXIMBANK")

An independent U.S. government agency that provides loans, loan guarantees, and credit risk insurance coverage to U.S. exporters and foreign importers.

*NES-94*

## EXPRESS

Direct, explicit, exact, precise, and specific language that manifests these characteristics and is not left to interpretation or inference.

*L&P*

## EXPRESS AUTHORITY

See "Agent Authority."

## EXTENDED OVERHEAD

This concept was devised as a means of recovering management and other fixed costs during a period of delay where the overhead during the period will not be fully recovered by the formula of overhead as a "markup" on direct costs. Equity requires that the government pay for the additional management attention given to the project during delays. In such cases, contractors need to recover their fixed overhead costs using a different formula than overhead as a markup on direct costs.

*NES-87*

See also "Eichleay Formula."

## EXTENDED WORK WEEK

See "Uncompensated Overtime."

## EXTRAORDINARY CONTRACTUAL RELIEF

Form of relief for contractors under federal law giving the president the power to authorize federal agencies to enter into contracts, amendments, or modifications of contracts, without regard to other provisions of law relating to the making, performance, amendment, or modification of contracts, when the president believes the action will facilitate national defense.

*GUIDE*

## FACILITIES
A property category that refers to property used in production, maintenance, research, development, or testing. It includes plant equipment (such as machine tools, test equipment, and furniture) and real property (i.e., land, buildings, and other structures).

*W-GPB*

## FACILITIES CAPITAL
The net book value of tangible capital assets and of those intangible capital assets that are subject to amortization.

*FAR*

## FACILITIES CAPITAL COST OF MONEY (FCCM)
An imputed cost of capital committed to facilities determined by applying a cost-of-money rate determined by the Secretary of the Treasury to facilities capital used in contract performance.

*FAR*

## FACT-FINDING
The process of identifying and obtaining information necessary to complete the evaluation of proposals. This process may include fact-finding sessions with offerors.

*FAI*

## FACTORY BURDEN
See "Factory Overhead."

## FACTORY OVERHEAD
All factory costs other than direct labor and direct material.

*NCMA-CA*

Also known as "Factory Burden," "Indirect Manufacturing Costs," and "Manufacturing Overhead."

## FAIR AND REASONABLE
A subjective evaluation of what each party deems as equitable consideration in areas such as terms and conditions, cost or price, assured quality, and timeliness of contract performance, or any other areas subject to negotiation.

*P&L*

## FAIR AND REASONABLE PRICE
A price that is fair to both parties, considering the agreed-upon conditions, promised quality, and timeliness of contract performance. Although generally a fair and reasonable price is a function of the law of supply and demand, there are statutory, regulatory, and judgmental limits on the concept.

*ASPM*

## FAIR LABOR STANDARDS ACT

Federal Act (1938) that set a minimum standard wage (periodically increased by later statutes) and a maximum work week of 40 hours in industries engaged in interstate commerce. The Act also prohibited the labor of children under 16 years of age in most employments, and under 18 years of age in dangerous occupations. The Act created the Wage and Hour Division in the Department of Labor.

*BLD*

See also "Professional Services."

## FAIR MARKET VALUE

The value of an item as determined by negotiation between purchasers and suppliers, which would be acceptable as a basis for a purchase and sale.

*Commercial Practices*

## FAST PAYMENT PROCEDURE

A procedure used with small purchases that provides payment to the contractor immediately upon receipt of its invoice (and before inspection and acceptance has taken place), provided the contractor certifies that the supplies have been delivered to a "Point of First Receipt" (such as a common carrier) and are as ordered.

*McVay*

See also "Point of First Receipt."

## FAST TRACK PROGRAM

An acquisition program in which time constraints require the design, development, production, testing, and support acquisition processes to be compressed or overlapped.

*DSMC*

## FEDBIZOPPS (FBO)

FedBizOpps.gov is the single government point-of-entry (GPE) for federal government procurement opportunities over $25,000. Government buyers are able to publicize their business opportunities by posting information directly to FBO over the Internet. Through one portal—FedBizOpps—commercial vendors seeking federal markets for their products and services can search, monitor, and retrieve opportunities solicited by the entire federal contracting community.

*FBO*

## FEDERAL ACQUISITION CIRCULAR (FAC)

Document issued by the Defense Acquisition Regulatory Council (DARC) and the Civilian Agency Acquisition Council (CAAC) to amend the Federal Acquisition Regulation (FAR).

*GUIDE*

## FEDERAL ACQUISITION INSTITUTE (FAI)

Since 1976, FAI has been working to promote the development of a professional acquisition workforce. In addition to providing information, management tools, and training opportunities, FAI collects and analyzes acquisition workforce data, coordinates governmentwide research and studies to improve the procurement process, and assists agencies with recruitment of qualified candidates for acquisition fields. In conjunction with its partners, FAI seeks to ensure availability of exceptional training, to provide compelling research, to promote professionalism, and to improve acquisition workforce management. (Note: definition revised in sixth edition.)

*FAI-web*

## FEDERAL ACQUISITION REGULATION (FAR)

The governmentwide procurement regulation mandated by Congress and issued by the Department of Defense (DOD), the General Services Administration (GSA), and the National Aeronautics and Space Administration (NASA). Effective April 1, 1984, the FAR supersedes both the Defense Acquisition Regulation (DAR) and the Federal Procurement Regulation (FPR). All federal agencies are authorized to issue regulations implementing the FAR.

*NCMA-SB*

## FEDERAL ACQUISITION REGULATORY COUNCIL

A council that comprises the Administrator for the Office of Federal Procurement Policy (OFPP), the Secretary of Defense, the Administrator of National Aeronautics and Space Administration (NASA), and the Administrator of the General Services Administration (GSA). Under the Office of Federal Procurement Policy Act, the Council assists in the direction and coordination of governmentwide procurement and policy procurement regulatory activities.

*FAI*

## FEDERAL ACQUISITION REFORM ACT (1996) (FARA)

Also referred to as the "Clinger-Cohen Act," FARA provides suppliers of commercial items under federal contracts and subcontracts an exception from the requirement to submit certified cost or pricing data, and it removes the contracting officer's (CO's) discretion to request certified cost and pricing data when the exception applies. It also exempts commercial item contracts and subcontracts from cost accounting standards (CAS). Further, FARA establishes a new definition of commercial-off-the-shelf (COTS) items and provides that procurements for such items be exempt from certain provisions of law that are to be incorporated in the FAR. Finally, FARA requires agencies to establish special simplified procedures for purchases of value greater than the simplified acquisition threshold (SAT), but not greater than $5 million, when the contracting officer reasonably expects, based on market research, that only offers of commercial items will be received. In addition to the above, the General Service

Administration's (GSA's) central authority over computer procurements is eliminated, and a chief information officer (CIO) in each agency will coordinate information technology (IT) purchases.

*NES-97*

## FEDERAL ASSISTANCE (GRANTS AND COOPERATIVE AGREEMENTS)

(1) The furnishing of assistance (anything of value) by the federal government by grant or cooperative agreement to a recipient to accomplish a public purpose. It is different from procurement in that it is not an acquisition of products or services for the direct benefit or use of the federal government.

*OPM*

(2) Refers to federal financing for public purposes through transfer of funds to state or local governments or to other recipients. The principal distinction between an assistance arrangement and procurement is found in the purpose of the funding. If the purpose is to sponsor property or to support services not for the government's express use or benefit, assistance arrangements are used. Within the category of assistance, there are two principal types of instruments: the grant and the cooperative agreement. The distinction between the grant and the cooperative agreement relates to management. Grants have little or no federal involvement in management,

whereas cooperative agreements involve collaborative management from the sponsoring agency.

*Sherman3*

See also "Cooperative Agreement" and "Grants."

## FEDERAL COURTS ADMINISTRATION ACT

P.L. 102-572 that, in 1992, changed the name of the U.S. Claims Court to the U.S. Court of Federal Claims.

## FEDERAL COURTS IMPROVEMENT ACT

Federal law that, in 1982, replaced the U.S. Court of Claims as the primary federal court involved in government contract litigation with two new courts—the U.S. Claims Court and the U.S. Court of Appeals for the Federal Circuit.

*GUIDE*

See also "United States Claims Court," "United States Court of Appeals for the Federal Circuit," and "United States Court of Claims."

## FEDERAL FINANCIAL MANAGE-MENT IMPROVEMENT ACT (1996)

The Act is designed to improve federal financial management, and it aims to uniformly implement accounting standards in federal financial management systems. Under the Act, each agency head is required to determine whether the agency's financial systems substantially comply with federal financial management system requirements, applicable federal accounting standards, and the U.S. government standard general ledger at the transaction level.

*CM-1/99*

## FEDERAL PRISON INDUSTRIES (FPI)

A wholly owned government corporation administered by a presidentially appointed board of directors. The chief function of this self-supporting corporation is to provide training and employment for inmates confined in federal penal and correctional institutions. Functioning under the trade name of UNICOR, FPI provides a wide range of supplies and services available for federal purchase. FPI is a required source of supply.

*W-PSP*

See also "Required Sources of Supplies and Service."

## FEDERAL PROCUREMENT DATA CENTER (FPDC)

The FPDC is charged with developing and implementing a governmentwide procurement data system capable of generating consistent and accurate statistical reports of governmentwide procurement activity.

*Sherman2*

See also "Federal Acquisition Institute (FAI)."

## FEDERAL PROCUREMENT INSTITUTE (FPI)

See "Federal Acquisition Institute (FAI)."

## FEDERAL PROCUREMENT REGULATIONS (FPR)

(1) The rules that governed the purchases made by civilian agencies before the Federal Acquisition Regulation (FAR) became effective.

*McVay*

(2) The FPR were issued in 1959 to provide detailed procurement guidance and requirements for nonmilitary agencies. The lead agency for the FPR was the General Services Administration (GSA). The FPR was authorized by the Federal Property and Administrative Services Act of 1949.

*Culver*

## FEDERAL PROPERTY AND ADMINISTRATIVE SERVICES ACT

General federal statute that governs contracting by the civilian agencies of the government.

*GUIDE*

## FEDERAL REGISTER

A daily government publication that informs the public of proposed rules, final rules, and other legal notices issued by federal agencies.

*FAI*

## FEDERAL SENTENCING GUIDELINES

Guidelines published by the U.S. Sentencing Commission that establish the parameters and set policies for judges in sentencing convicted companies. Under the Guidelines, there are three possible penalties: restitution, monetary fine, and probation. The company may experience more severe punishment if it does not have "an effective [compliance] program to prevent and detect violations of law."

*TIPS(4-5)*

See also "Compliance Program."

## FEDERAL SPECIFICATION OR STANDARD

A specification or standard issued or controlled by the General Services Administration (GSA) and listed in the GSA Index of Federal Specifications, Standards, and Commercial Item Descriptions.

*FAR*

## FEDERAL SUPPLY SCHEDULE (FSS) PROGRAM

Directed and managed by the General Services Administration (GSA), FSS provides federal agencies with a simplified process for obtaining commonly used supplies and services at prices associated with volume buying. There are four types of Federal Supply Schedules: single-award, multiple-award, new item introductory, and international. Schedules are designated as manda-tory- or optional-use for specific government agencies.

*FAR*

See also "International Federal Supply Schedule," "Multiple Award Schedule (MAS)," "New Item Introductory Schedule," and "Single Award Schedule (SAS)."

## FEDWIRE

An online transfer system operated by the Federal Reserve Banking System that is used primarily for large dollar volume and small volume payments that need immediate confirmation.

*NES-98*

## FEE

(1) An agreed-to amount of reimbursement beyond the initial estimate of costs.

*OPM*

(2) The term "Fee" is used when discussing cost-reimbursement contracts, whereas "Profit" is used in relation to fixed-price contracts.

## FIDUCIARY

A person who handles another person's money or property in a capacity that involves a confidence or trust. Examples of fiduciaries are executors or guardians of the estates of minors or deceased persons.

*FBL*

## FIELD CONTRACTING ACTIVITY

A level of government contracting activity that supports the operational requirements of a post, camp, station, national park, hospital, institute, or field installation, and that involves a highly diversified range of assignments.

*OPM*

## FIELD PRICING SUPPORT

The analysis of contractor pricing proposals by any or all field technical and other specialists.

*OPM*

## FILL RATE

The proportion of all stock requisitions that are filled from stock that is present on the shelf. The inverse of this is stock-out rate, which is the percentage of orders for which there is no stock on the shelves and, therefore, the order cannot be filled (resulting in a back order). These measurements can be calculated for any time period; in some retail or distribution firms, the rate might be computed daily or weekly.

*Commercial Practices*

## FINAL COST OBJECTIVE

A cost objective that has allocated to it both direct and indirect costs and that, in the contractor's accumulation system, is one of the final accumulation points.

*FAR*

## FINAL DECISION

For purposes of the Contract Disputes Act (CDA), a contracting officer's (CO's) unilateral adjudication of a contract claim that is a prerequisite to jurisdiction over the claim by a board of contract appeals or federal court.

*GUIDE*

## FINAL VOUCHER

See "Invoice."

## FINANCIAL ACCOUNTING

Involves the measuring and recording of financial data of an enterprise for purposes of providing relevant financial information to interested users, both internal and external to the entity.

*NCMA-CA*

## FINANCIAL ACCOUNTING DATA SHEET

Commits the government to availability of funds for specific amounts as displayed on the data sheet. It is the final proof that the contracting officer (CO) needs to show that funds are available to obligate the government. The data sheet becomes the last page of any contract or modification involving money. The data sheet is part of the contract, as opposed to the financial data addendum sheet (FAD sheet), which is attached to the procurement request (PR) and which indicates funding availability.

*Navy*

Also known as "Data Sheet."

## FINANCIAL ACCOUNTING STANDARDS BOARD (FASB)

A professional board created by the American Institute of Certified Public Accountants. Previously named the Accounting Principles Board (APB), the APB was replaced in 1973 by the FASB. The FASB was considered an improvement over the APB, because the FAS Board was more autonomous and carried a broader representation of accountants than the APB. FASB publishes its pronouncements in its "Statement of Financial Accounting Standards." FASB also publishes "Statements of Financial Accounting Concepts," which set forth fundamental objectives and concepts on which further FASB pronouncements will be based.

*NCMA-CA*

## FINANCIAL DATA ADDENDUM (FAD) SHEET

A document that indicates funds are available for a particular procurement. It indicates the appropriate funding citation and dollar limitation that is established for procuring the designated item. It is attached to the procurement request (PR) or is forwarded by separate funding procurement request to initiate the funding action. The FAD sheet is distinguished from the data sheet, which becomes part of the executed contract.

*Navy*

Also known as "FAD Sheet."

## FINANCING

See "Contractor Financing."

## FINISHED GOODS INVENTORY

The cost of a manufacturer's completed product that is being held for sale.

*NCMA-CA*

## FIRM BID RULE

A rule that prohibits the bidder from withdrawing its bid for the period specified in the Invitation for Bids (IFBs), usually 60 days after bid opening.

*McVay*

## FIRM-FIXED-PRICE (FFP) CONTRACT

A contract that provides for a price that is not subject to any adjustment by reason of costs experienced by the contractor in the performance of the contract.

*OPM*

## FIRST ARTICLE

(1) Preproduction models, initial production samples, test samples, first lots, or pilot samples submitted for testing and evaluation for conformance with specified contract requirements before or in the initial stages of production.

*AFIT*

(2) First article testing and approval is used by the federal government to

ensure the vendor can furnish a product that conforms to all contract requirements for acceptance. This procedure, although costly, can be a significant contributor to risk reduction. Assuming that more than one product is to be built, the risk to the remaining products is minimized when based on the lessons learned during the first article inspection.

*W-GSD*

## FIRST-IN, FIRST-OUT (FIFO)
An inventory costing method where the stock of merchandise or material that is acquired earliest is assumed to be used first; the stock acquired latest is assumed to be still on hand.

*MGMT*

Compare "Last-In, First-Out (LIFO)."

## FISCAL YEAR (FY)
The federal budget cycle, which runs from October 1 to September 30, is known as the government's fiscal year.

*DLA*

## FISHBONE DIAGRAM
Another name for the cause-and-effect diagram. (The finished product resembles a fish skeleton.) Also known as "Ishikawa Diagram" after the Japanese engineer who developed it.

*DGCQI*

See also "Cause and Effect Diagram."

## FITNESS FOR USE
The condition of goods and services that meet the needs of the people who use them.

*DGCQI*

## FIXED COST
(1) A cost that, for a given period of time and range of activity that is called the "relevant range," does not change in total but becomes progressively smaller on a per-unit basis as volume increases.

*NCMA-CA*

(2) Operating expenses that are incurred to provide facilities and organization that are kept in readiness to do business without regard to actual volumes of production and sales. Examples of fixed costs consist of rent, property tax, and interest expense.

*Garrett*

## FIXED PRICE
A form of pricing that includes a ceiling beyond which the government (buyer) bears no responsibility for payment.

*OPM*

## FIXED-PRICE-INCENTIVE (FPI) CONTRACT
A type of contract that provides for adjusting profit and establishing the final contract price by application of a

formula that is based on the relationship of total final negotiated cost to total target cost. The final price is subject to a price ceiling, which is negotiated at the outset. There are two types of FPI contracts: firm target and successive targets.

*Navy*

## FIXED-PRICE REDETERMINABLE (FPR) CONTRACT

A fixed-price type of contract that contains provisions for subsequently negotiated adjustment, in whole or in part, of the initially negotiated base price.

*OPM*

## FIXED-PRICE WITH ECONOMIC PRICE ADJUSTMENT CONTRACT

A fixed-price contract that permits an element of cost to fluctuate to reflect current market prices.

*McVay*

## FLEXIBLE BUDGET

A budget, usually referring to overhead costs only, that is prepared for a range, rather than a single level, of activity; one that can be automatically geared to changes in the level of volume.

*NCMA-CA*

Also known as a "Variable Budget."

## FLOWCHART

A chart that symbolically shows the input from suppliers, the sequential work activities, and the output to the customer.

*DGCQI*

## FLOW DOWN

The transfer and translation of prime contract requirements to subcontracts.

*NES-89*

See also "Mandatory Flow Down Clauses."

## FOB POINT

See "Free on Board (FOB)."

## FORCE MAJEURE CLAUSE

(1) Excusable conditions for non-performance (e.g., strikes and acts of God) are contained in this clause.

*Cohen*

(2) A French term that refers to an unexpected or uncontrollable event that upsets the plan or releases one from obligation; literally, means "superior force."

*TIPS(2-10)*

## FOREIGN CORRUPT PRACTICES ACT

In 1977, Congress passed legislation making certain payments to foreign government officials illegal, even if such payments are legal or a common practice in the foreign country.

*TIPS(2-10)*

## FOREIGN MILITARY SALES (FMS)

(1) Actions on the part of the Department of Defense (DOD) on behalf of another government to make procurements using that government's funds.

*OPM*

(2) That portion of U.S. security assistance authorized by the Arms Export Control Act, as amended, and conducted on the basis of formal contracts or agreements between the U.S. government and an authorized recipient government or international organization. FMS includes government-to-government sales of defense articles or defense services, from DOD stocks or through new procurement under DOD-managed contracts, regardless of the source of financing.

*MSA*

See also "Conventional Arms Transfer."

## FOREIGN TRADE ZONE

A site sanctioned by the Customs Service in which imported goods are exempted from customs duties until withdrawn for domestic sale or use. These zones are ideal for commercial warehouses or foreign production plants.

*Commercial Practices*

## FORM, FIT, and FUNCTION DATA

A type of data that provides a basic technical description of an item's characteristics and capabilities. Its primary purpose is to describe an item to such a degree as to allow the government to procure comparable items. The government generally requires unlimited rights to all form, fit, and function data.

*TIPS(2-5)*

See also "Rights in Technical Data."

## FORWARD BUYING

The practice of buying materials in a quantity exceeding specified current requirements, but not beyond the actual foreseeable requirements. Even though not known with precision, it is reasonably certain that a longer-term production need for the material does exist. Any purchases beyond this point fall into the speculative buying category. Forward buying can be used in stable markets or in unstable markets where prices appear to be rising. One potential hazard in forward buying, however, is the possible price risk involved, depending on the volatility of the market in which the purchase is made. The buyer must also consider the additional inventory carrying costs and the attendant tie-up of working capital that accompany forward buys.

*DBL*

## FORWARD PRICING

Action involving negotiations and a resultant agreement between a contractor and the buyer to use certain rates or indices for a specified future period of time in pricing contracts or contract modifications.

*P&L*

## FOUR CORNERS DOCTRINE

A theory of contract interpretation that the contract itself should include all of the terms and conditions that the parties wish to be part of the agreement; the notion that the agreement should be contained within the four corners of the document.

*W-GCLB*

See also "Contract Interpretation."

## FRAUD

An intentional perversion of truth for the purpose of inducing another in reliance upon it to part with something of value belonging to him or her or to surrender a legal right. A false representation of a matter of fact, whether by words or conduct, by false or misleading allegations, or by concealment of that which should have been disclosed, and which deceives and is intended to deceive another so that he or she shall act upon it to his or her legal injury. Anything calculated to deceive.

*BLD2*

## FREE ON BOARD (FOB)

This term is used in conjunction with a physical point to determine (a) the responsibility and basis for payment of freight charges, and (b) unless otherwise agreed, the point at which title for goods passes to the buyer or consignee. FOB origin—The seller places the goods on the conveyance by which they are to be transported. Cost of shipping and risk of loss are borne by the buyer. FOB destination—The seller delivers the goods on the seller's conveyance at destination. Cost of shipping and risk of loss are borne by the seller.

*FAR*

## FREEDOM OF INFORMATION ACT (FOIA)

(1) Provides that information is to be made available to the public either by (a) publishing it in the Federal Register; (b) providing an opportunity to read and copy records at convenient locations; or (c) upon request, providing a copy of a reasonably described record.

*FAR*

(2) The Freedom of Information Act, 5 U.S.C. - 552, enacted in 1966, requires disclosure of government records to any person except as stated in specific exceptions.

*TIPS(1-12)*

## FRINGE BENEFITS

Allowances and services provided to employees in addition to their salaries and wages. Fringe benefits may include, but are not limited to, vacation, sick leave, holidays, military leave, insurance, and supplemental unemployment benefits.

*BP(90-11)*

## FULL AND OPEN COMPETITION

All responsible sources are permitted to compete.

*FAR*

## FULL COSTS

When applied to the expenses incurred in the operation of an information processing service organization (IPSO), comprises all direct, indirect, general, and administrative costs incurred in the operation of an IPSO. These costs include, but are not limited to, personnel, equipment, software, supplies, contracted services from private sector providers, space occupancy, intra-agency services from within the agency, inter-agency services from other federal agencies, other services that are provided by state and local governments, and judicial and legislative branch organizations.

*OMB A-130*

## FULL DISCLOSURE

An accounting principle that states the accountant should adequately disclose all relevant information to facilitate a clear understanding of the preparation of financial statements and to avoid erroneous implications.

*NCMA-CA*

## FULL-SCALE DEVELOPMENT (FSD) PHASE

The period when the system or equipment and the principal items necessary for its support are designed, fabricated, tested, and evaluated. The intended output is, as a minimum, a preproduction system that closely approximates the final product, which is the documentation necessary to enter the production phase, and the test results that demonstrate that the production product will meet stated requirements.

*DOD-MMH*

## FULL-TIME ACCOUNTING

See "Uncompensated Overtime."

## FUNCTIONAL SPECIFICATION

A purchase description that describes the deliverable in terms of performance characteristics and intended use, including those characteristics that at minimum are necessary to satisfy the intended use.

*FAI*

## FUTURES CONTRACTS

Contracts for the purchase or sale and delivery of commodities at a future date, primarily used as a hedging device against market price fluctuations or unforeseen supply shortages.

*Commercial Practices*

## GENERAL ACCOUNTING OFFICE (GAO)

Government agency, headed by the Comptroller General of the United States, that is charged by law to settle and adjust claims by and against the government and that, in the government contract area, renders advance opinions for government disbursement officers, audits their accounts, and decides the merits of protests regarding contract awards.

*GUIDE*

## GENERAL AGREEMENT ON TARIFFS AND TRADE (GATT) (1947)

A multilateral agreement that was implemented in 1979 and that became effective in 1981 when Congress affirmed the negotiated treaty. GATT has played a critical role in reducing escalated tariffs and promoting free trade.

*NES-94*

## GENERAL AND ADMINISTRATIVE (G&A)

(1) Indirect expenses related to the overall business. Expenses for a company's general and executive offices, executive compensation, staff services, and other miscellaneous support purposes.

*OPM*

(2) Any indirect management, financial, or other expense that

- is not assignable to a program's direct overhead charges for engineering manufacturing, material, etc., but is routinely incurred by or allotted to a business unit
- is for the general management and administration of the business as a whole

*L&P*

## GENERAL PROVISIONS

A collection of contract clauses that are not specific to a given procurement, but are part of a common contract language.

*OPM*

## GENERALLY ACCEPTED ACCOUNTING PRINCIPLES (GAAP)

A technical term encompassing conventions, rules, and procedures of accounting that are "generally accepted" and that have "substantial authoritative support." The GAAP have been developed by agreement on the basis of experience, reason, custom, usage, and, to a certain extent, practical necessity rather than being derived from a formal set of theories.

*NCMA-CA*

## GENERAL LEDGER
The book of all accounts.

*NES-02*

## GLOBAL SOURCING
The procurement of goods or services outside the continental limits of the United States. In many firms, the term global implies the development of a longer term, planned continuing relationship with international suppliers.

*Commercial Practices*

## GOALS OF THE ACQUISITION PROCESS
Among the goals of the acquisition process are quality, cost, timeliness, risk, competition, integrity, and socioeconomic objectives.

*FAI*

## "GOING CONCERN" CONCEPT
An accounting concept that assumes the economic entity will last indefinitely (without evidence to the contrary). This concept is critical in order to support and justify important accounting concepts, such as depreciation of property, amortization of assets, and other considerations.

*NCMA-CA*

## GOODWILL
One of the intangible values beyond its net worth that a business acquires from suppliers and customers. It is promoted by granting more business as a reward for good service, by sharing plans and forecasts, and by working together to solve problems, to achieve mutual research and development (R&D), etc.

*Commercial Practices*

## GOVERNMENT ACCOUNTABILITY OFFICE (GAO)
Formerly the General Accounting Office. An agency of the Legislative Branch, responsible solely to Congress, which functions to audit all negotiated government office contracts and to investigate all matters relating to the receipt, disbursement, and application of public funds. The GAO determines whether public funds are expended in accordance with appropriations.

*DAAT*

## GOVERNMENT-CAUSED DELAY
See "Delay, Government-Caused."

## GOVERNMENT CONTRACTOR DEFENSE
(1) Allows a government contractor to escape liability from state law claims brought by injured persons when those claims arise from a contractor's compliance with federal government specifications.

*BP(89-13)*

(2) The U.S. Supreme Court explained the government contractor defense in Boyle v. United Technologies Corp. Thus, the government contractor defense is also known as the "Boyle Rule." The following steps must be used to apply the Boyle Rule: (a) there must be a uniquely federal interest that conflicts with state law, (b) the government must approve precise contract specifications, (c) the contractor must conform to specifications, and (d) the contractor must warn the government of potential dangers.

*TIPS(1-9)*

## GOVERNMENT-FURNISHED PROPERTY (GFP)
Property in the possession of or acquired by the government and subsequently delivered or otherwise made available to the contractor.

*AFIT*

See also "Property."

## GOVERNMENT INFORMATION
Information created, collected, processed, disseminated, or disposed of by or for the federal government.

*OMB A-130*

## GOVERNMENT INFORMATION LOCATOR SYSTEM (GILS)
GILS is intended to make federal information available and easily accessible to companies over the Internet. Each agency will be responsible for managing its own information.

*NES-96*

## GOVERNMENT MANAGEMENT REFORM ACT (1994)
The Act is intended to provide a more effective, efficient, and responsive government, primarily through reform in the areas of human resources and financial management. First, the Act requires that the executive branch begin making all federal wage, salary, and retirement payments to recipients by electronic funds transfer (EFT) unless another means of payment has been determined to be appropriate by the Secretary of Treasury. Second, the Act establishes a pilot program in each of six executive agencies to test the use of a franchise fund. Third, and perhaps most important, beginning in fiscal year (FY) 1996, the Act required all major federal departments and agencies to prepare and submit to the director of the Office of Management and Budget (OMB) annual audited financial statements covering all accounts and associated activities of each office, bureau, and activity of the agency. Finally, the Act requires annual governmentwide financial statements reflecting the consolidated financial position and results of operation of the entire federal government, beginning with FY1997.

*CM-1/99*

## GOVERNMENT-OWNED, CONTRACTOR-OPERATED (GOCO)

A facility owned by the government but provided to a contractor for operation to produce goods for the government's use.

*OPM*

## GOVERNMENT PERFORMANCE AND RESULTS ACT (1993)

The Act proposes (a) to improve the American people's confidence in the federal government by systematically holding federal agencies accountable for achieving program results; (b) to initiate program reform by measuring program performance against program goals and publicly reporting the results; and (c) to improve the operational effectiveness, efficiency, and public accountability of the federal government by focusing on results, service quality, and customer satisfaction. Starting in fiscal year (FY) 1994, the Act required agencies to prepare and publish a strategic plan, a performance plan, and a performance report.

*CM-1/99*

## GOVERNMENT PUBLICATION

Information that is published as an individual document at government expense or as required by law. (44 U.S.C. 1901)

*OMB 1-130*

## GOVERNMENT PURPOSE LICENSE RIGHTS (GPLR)

A type of data rights that are unique to the Defense Federal Acquisition Regulation Supplement (DFARS) and that are designed as a compromise between the polar rights offered by the "unlimited rights" and "limited rights" categories. GPLR allow the government to use the data for "governmental purposes," including re-procurement purposes, while the contractor retains exclusive commercial rights. The DFARS provides that GPLR generally revert to unlimited rights after no more than five years; however, time limits may be negotiated or extended.

*TIPS(2-5)*

See also "Rights in Technical Data."

## GOVERNMENTAL ACCOUNTING

Similar to financial accounting, which involves the measuring and recording of financial data of governmental units to interested users; however, govern-mental accounting uses accounting conventions that are different from those applied to financial accounting.

*NCMA-CA*

## GOVERNMENTWIDE ACQUISITION CONTRACT

Governmentwide acquisition contract (GWAC) means a task-order or deliv-ery-order contract that is for informa-tion technology and is established by one agency for governmentwide use. The GWAC is operated by an executive agent designated by the Office of Management and Budget (OMB) pursuant to 40 U.S.C. 11302(e).

*FAR*

## GOVWORKS

GovWorks is a Federal Acquisition Center under the National Business Center of the Department of the Interior. The organization is a federal service-for-fee acquisition center operating under the authority of the U.S. Department of the Interior Franchise Fund. GovWorks helps federal contracting agents and program managers acquire products and services.
See **www.govworks.gov.**

*GW*

## GRACE COMMISSION

A commission of volunteer business-people and labor leaders appointed by the president in 1982 with a mission to investigate the entire federal bureaucracy and to seek out every possible savings opportunity. In its final report on January 16, 1985, the Commission made 2,478 specific recommendations that it estimated would save $424 billion over the next three years. Many recommendations dealt with government acquisition of services and supplies, including major systems and spare parts.

*Culver*

## GRAMM-RUDMAN-HOLLINGS BALANCED BUDGET AND EMERGENCY DEFICIT CONTROL ACT

A 1985 law that provided that the federal budget should be balanced by fiscal year (FY) 1991. Per the Act, if Congress does not meet the prescribed deficit target in any year, the law requires automatic, across-the-board spending cuts divided evenly between defense and domestic spending.

*TIPS(1-5)*

## GRANDFATHER CLAUSE

A contractual or legal provision that protects the existing interests of affected parties.

*Commercial Practices*

## GRANTS

(1) Contribution, gift, or subsidy made by the government for specified purposes. Grants are frequently made conditional upon an action specified by the grantee, such as the maintenance of certain standards or a proportional contribution of funds.

*AFIT*

(2) Under a grant arrangement, there is little or no federal involvement in the management of the work being funded. Substantial funding of non-federal, governmental undertakings is provided by the grant process. In addition, research grants are awarded in substantial number by some

government agencies.

*Sherman3*

See also "Cooperative Agreement" and "Federal Assistance (Grants and Cooperative Agreements)."

## GRATUITY

Something of monetary value, freely given to someone else with no explicit expectation of return or reward. In actual practice, the motive behind dispensing a gratuity is often suspect, as if the giver were bribing or buying special consideration.

*SPP*

## GREEN TIME

See "Uncompensated Overtime."

## GROSS DOMESTIC PRODUCT (GDP)

A measure of a nation's domestic output, which is the total value of all finished goods and services produced within the country during a specified time period, typically one calendar year.

*Commercial Practices*

## GROSS NATIONAL PRODUCT (GNP)

The total dollar value of all the final goods (as distinguished from goods still in the process of production) produced by all the firms in the economy.

*ECON*

## GUARANTEED LOANS

(1) An extraordinary method of contract financing in which the government guarantees payment to the lending institution should the contractor be unable to pay.

*McVay*

(2) Guarantees made by federal reserve banks, on behalf of designated guaranteeing agencies, to enable a contractor to obtain financing from private sources under contracts for the acquisition of supplies or services for the national defense.

*FAI*

See also "Contractor Financing."

# H,I,J

## HAND-TO-MOUTH BUYING

Purchasing over a short period of time to meet only immediate short-term requirements.

*Commercial Practices*

## HARD SAVINGS

Cost reductions that are reasonable, measurable, and reduce the established level of approved expenditures.

*AFIT*

## HEDGING

A futures purchase or sale entered into for the purpose of balancing a sale or purchase already made, or under contract, in order to offset the effectiveness of potential market price fluctuations.

*Commercial Practices*

## HERZBERG'S THEORY

A behavioral science theory that addresses those situations in which people feel good about their jobs and those in which they feel bad about their jobs. The factors linked with good times are called "satisfiers" or "motivators" because they are associated with wanting to achieve better job performance. Motivators include achievement, recognition, work itself, responsibility, advancement, and growth. The factors associated with bad times are called "dissatisfiers" and include policy and administration, supervision, relationship with supervisor, work conditions, salary, and relationship with subordinates. If one is to improve motivation, "motivators" must be present. Under Herzberg's Theory, participation in the contract negotiation process may provide the needed recognition and growth to motivate some people.

*W-AN*

See also "Motivation Theories."

## HISTORICAL COSTS

An accounting convention that is the foundation for the valuation of assets and the initial recording of economic transactions. Various other costing methods have evolved over time (e.g., present value of future cash flow, etc.), but the historical costs method has been generally accepted by accountants to be the most useful and reliable basis for accounting because (a) historical costs are definite and determinable, and (b) historical costs are objective and verifiable.

*NCMA-CA*

Also known as "Sunk Costs."

## HISTORICAL PRICES

A type of secondary comparison used in performing price analysis. The current quotation can be compared with historical prices from past acquisitions to determine the reasonableness of a currently offered price. Some adjustment to a historical price is probably necessary, however, to account for changes such as increased costs, improved technology, different specifications, size or quantity of the purchase, delivery terms, government-furnished property (GFE), and packaging requirements.

*W-ICPA*

See also "Secondary Comparison."

## IDLE TIME

A time interval during which either the workman, the equipment, or both do not perform useful work.

*DOD-MMH*

## IMMATERIALITY

See "Materiality and Immateriality."

## IMPLIED AUTHORITY

See "Agent Authority."

## IMPLIED WARRANTY OF SPECIFICATIONS

See "Spearin Doctrine."

## IMPLY

To indirectly convey meaning or intent; to leave the determination of meaning up to the receiver of the communication according to circumstances, general language used, or conduct of those involved.

*L&P*

## IMPORTING

The purchase of commodities by one country from a source in a foreign country for trade or resale by the purchaser.

*NES-94/AHD*

## IMPREST FUND

A cash fund of a fixed amount established by advance of funds, without charge to an appropriation, from an agency finance or disbursing officer to a duly appointed cashier, for disbursement as needed from time to time in making payment in cash for relatively small purchases.

*FAR*

## IMPROVEMENT CURVE

See "Learning Curve."

## IN-HOUSE SAVINGS

Net life-cycle cost savings achieved by in-house agency staff using value engineering (VE) techniques.

*OMB A-131*

## IN SCOPE

Phrase used to denote that an action performed or requested to be performed by a contractor for the buyer could reasonably be considered to be within the requirements of the contract.

*P&L*

## INCENTIVE
Motivating the contractor in calculable monetary terms to turn out a product that meets significantly advanced performance goals, to improve on the contract schedule up to and including final delivery, to substantially reduce costs of the work, or to complete the project under a weighted combination of some or all of these objectives.

*DAAT*

## INCENTIVE ARRANGEMENT
A negotiated pricing arrangement that structures a series of relationships designed to motivate and reward the contractor for performance in accordance with the contract specifications; it involves target costs, fees, or profits. In the case of award fee arrangements, it involves the payment of a fee tied to negotiated incentive criteria.

*OPM*

## INCIDENTALS
Small items and expenses. In small purchases procurement, incidentals are usually taken care of from the imprest fund.

*SPP*

## INCIDENTAL DAMAGES
Any commercially reasonable charges,

expenses, or commissions incurred in stopping delivery, in the transportation, care, and custody of goods after the buyer's breach, or in connection with the return or resale of the goods or otherwise resulting from the breach.

*Garrett*

## INCOTERMS
When referenced in contract documents, Incoterms enable parties contracting for the purchase and sale of goods internationally to simply and concisely allocate their responsibilities for transportation costs, customs fees and documentation requirements, risks of loss or damage, and insurance and other responsibilities.

*NES-94*

## INCREMENTAL BUDGET
The budget is based on the previous period's budget and actual results. The budget amount is then changed in accordance with expectations for the next period.

*MGMT*

## INCREMENTAL COST
Defined narrowly, "incremental cost" is the additional cost associated with increases in a given set of costs. For example, the incremental cost of increasing production for 1,000 units to 1,200 per week would be the additional cost of the extra 200 units. Defined broadly, "incremental" is a

synonym for "differential;" that is, an incremental may be a positive or negative amount.

*MGMT*

## INCREMENTAL DEVELOPMENT
See "Evolutionary Acquisition (EA)."

## INCREMENTAL FUNDING
(1) The obligation of funds to a contract (which contains a total price or estimated cost) in periodic installments as the work progresses, rather than in a lump sum.

*Commercial Practices*

(2) The provision (or recording) of budgetary resources for a program or project that is based on obligations estimated to be incurred within a fiscal year (FY) when such budgetary resources will cover only a portion of the obligations to be incurred in completing the program or project as planned. This provision differs from full funding, where budgetary resources are provided or recorded for the total estimated obligations for a program or project in the initial year of funding. It is most commonly used for research and development (R&D), as opposed to production, which must be fully funded.

*DAAT*

## INDEFINITE-DELIVERY/INDEFINITE-QUANTITY (IDIQ) CONTRACT
A type of contract in which the exact date of delivery or the exact quantity, or a combination of both, is not specified at the time the contract is executed; provisions are placed in the contract to later stipulate these elements of the contract.

*OPM*

See also "Delivery Order."

## INDEMNIFICATION CLAUSE
(1) This clause describes protections provided by the parties to each other.

*Cohen*

(2) A contract clause by which one party engages to secure another against an anticipated loss resulting from an act or forbearance on the part of one of the parties or of some third person.

*Garrett*

## INDEMNIFY
To make good; to compensate; to reimburse a person in case of an anticipated loss.

*Garrett*

## INDEPENDENT CONTRACTOR
The following elements are essential to establish the relationship of an independent contractor to its client, as contrasted with the relationship of an agent to its principal. An independent contractor must (a) exercise independent judgment as to the means used to accomplish the result, (b) be free from control orders from any other person,

and (c) be responsible only under the contract with the client for the result obtained.

*Commercial Practices*

## INDEPENDENT RESEARCH AND DEVELOPMENT (IR&D)
The cost of effort that is neither sponsored by a grant nor required in performing a contract; it falls within any of the following four areas: (a) basic research, (b) applied research, (c) development, and (d) systems and other concept formulation studies.

*FAR*

## INDEPENDENT REVIEW OFFICER (IRO)
The agency official who certifies, prior to a bid opening, that the government's performance and cost comparison estimates have been prepared in accordance with Circular A-76 and its Supplement.

*OMB A-76*

## INDEX NUMBERS
The Department of Labor's Bureau of Labor Statistics (BLS) offers publications that provide statistical samples that assist the cost estimator. The Wholesale Prices and Price Indexes is a monthly report on price movements at the primary market level, including statistical summary tables and indexes for groups of products and commodities. An annual supplement contains changes in the relative importance of components of the index, revisions in coverage, and annual averages. The Consumer Price Index Detailed Report is a monthly report that contains detailed data that are used to measure retail price changes, purchasing power of the consumer's dollar, and inflation.

*CE*

## INDEX OF FEDERAL SPECIFICATIONS, STANDARDS, AND COMMERCIAL ITEM DESCRIPTIONS
See "Federal Specification or Standard."

## INDICTMENT
A formal accusation of a crime by a grand jury.

*FBL*

## INDIRECT COST
Any cost not directly identifiable with a specific cost objective, but subject to two or more cost objectives.

*OPM*

## INDIRECT LABOR
All labor that is not specifically associated with or cannot be practically traced to specific units of output.

*NCMA-CA*

## INDIRECT MANUFACTURING COSTS
See "Factory Overhead."

## INDUSTRIAL BASE

A nation's resources that represent its capacity and capability to produce goods at an appropriate rate in terms of national defense and commercial competitiveness. The defense industrial base is only one portion of the whole industrial base (i.e., those industries that at any particular time support the nation's security through the provision of defense material and supporting goods and services).

*TIPS(3-2)*

## INDUSTRIAL MODERNIZATION INCENTIVES PROGRAM (IMIP)

IMIP provides government incentives to contractors to motivate investment of their own funds in facility improvements, which should result in reduced acquisition costs and improved productivity.

*DSMC*

## INDUSTRY SPECIFICATION

Type of specification that is prepared by technical or industry associations and that is approved for use by federal agencies.

*GUIDE*

## INFLATION

An ongoing general rise in prices. The steeper the rise, the faster the decline of a dollar's purchasing power.

*ECON*

## INFORMATION

Any communication or representation of knowledge such as facts, data, or opinions in any medium or form, including textual, numerical, graphic, cartographic, narrative, or audiovisual forms.

*OMB A-130*

## INFORMATION DISSEMINATION PRODUCT

Any book, paper, map, machine-readable material, audiovisual production, or other documentary material, regardless of its physical form or characteristic, that is disseminated by an agency to the public.

*OMB A-130*

## INFORMATION LIFE CYCLE

The stages through which information passes, typically characterized as creation or collection, processing, dissemination, use, storage, and disposition.

*OMB A-130*

## INFORMATION MANAGEMENT

The planning, budgeting, manipulating, and controlling of information throughout its life cycle.

*OMB A-130*

## INFORMATION PROCESSING SERVICES ORGANIZATION (IPSO)

A discrete set of personnel, information technology, and support equipment with the primary function of providing services to more than one agency on a reimbursable basis.

*OMB A-130*

## INFORMATION RESOURCES

Includes both government information and information technology (IT).

*OMB A-130*

## INFORMATION RESOURCES MANAGEMENT

The process of managing information resources to accomplish agency missions. The term encompasses both information itself and related resources, such as personnel, equipment, funds, and information technology (IT).

*OMB A-130*

## INFORMATION SYSTEM

A discrete set of information resources organized for the collection, processing, maintenance, transmission, and dissemination of information in accordance with defined procedures, whether automated or manual.

*OMB A-130*

## INFORMATION SYSTEMS LIFE CYCLE

The phases through which an information system passes, typically characterized as initiation, development, operation, and termination.

*OMB A-130*

## INFORMATION TECHNOLOGY (IT)

(1) The hardware and software operated by a federal agency or by a contractor of a federal agency or other organization that processes information on behalf of the federal government to accomplish a federal function, regardless of the technology involved, whether computers, telecommunications, or others. IT includes automatic data processing (ADP) equipment as that term is defined in Section 111(a)(2) of the Federal Property and Administrative Services Act of 1949.

*OMB A-130*

(2) Any equipment or interconnected system or subsystem of equipment that is used in the automatic acquisition, storage, manipulation, management, movement, control, display, switching, interchange, transmission, or reception of data or information by the executive agency. IT includes computers, ancillary equipment, software, firmware and similar procedures, services (including support services), and related resources, including National Security Systems (NSSs). It does not include any equipment that is acquired by a federal contractor incidental to a federal contract.

*DAAT*

## INHERENTLY GOVERNMENTAL ACTIVITY

An inherently governmental activity is one that is so intimately related to the public interest as to mandate performance by federal employees. Activities that meet these criteria are not in competition with commercial sources, are not generally available from commercial sources and, therefore, are not subject to Circular A-76 or its supplement. Guidance to avoid an unacceptable transfer of official responsibility to contract performance may be found in the OFPP Policy Letter 92-1.

*OMB A-76*

Also called "inherently federal functions."

## INITIAL PRODUCT INSPECTION
The product verification inspection performed during early stages of production on selected characteristics of an item to obtain confidence that the contractor can produce the item in accordance with contract requirements.

*AFIT*

## INJUNCTION
An order of a court of equity that tells a person to do or refrain from doing some act or acts.

*FBL*

## INSIDER TRADING
Trading in securities, or buying or selling property or assets on the basis of nonpublic information that has been acquired during a consultancy contract.

*UNI*

## INSPECTION
The examination (including testing) of supplies and services (including, when appropriate, raw materials, components, and intermediate assemblies) to determine whether the supplies and services conform to the contract requirements.

*GSA*

## INSPECTION REQUIREMENTS
Instructions issued by the purchasing officer or technical representative regarding the type and extent of government inspections required for specific contracts.

*AFIT*

## INTEGRATED ACQUISITION ENVIRONMENT (IAE)
A single point where federal buyers and sellers can access information and support services. IAE is under the auspices of the Office of Management and Budget's (OMB's) Office of Federal Procurement Policy and the Chief Acquisition Officers Council, formerly ACQNET. See **http://acquisition.gov**.

*IAE*

## INTEGRATED LOGISTICS SUPPORT (ILS)
The composite of actions necessary to ensure the effective and economical performance of the systems and equipment that, functioning together,

compose a total system and, in turn, an operating force.

*Navy*

## INTEGRATED SUPPLY
A special type of partnering arrangement, usually developed between a purchaser and a distributor on an intermediate to long-term basis. The objective of an integrated supply relationship is to minimize, for both buyer and supplier, the labor and expense involved in the acquisition and possession of maintenance, repair, and operating (MRO) supplies, which are items that are repetitive, generic, high transaction and that have a low unit cost.

*Commercial Practices*

## INTEGRATION, HORIZONTAL
A firm that owns several plants, each of which does the same thing, is said to have "horizontal integration." An example is a retail store.

*ECON*

## INTEGRATION, VERTICAL
Firms that own several plants, each of which handles a different stage in the production process, are said to have "vertical integration." An example is an automobile company that owns iron mines, an ore-carrying freighter, steel mills, stamping plants, and assembly plants.

*ECON*

## INTELLECTUAL PROPERTY
Includes inventions, trademarks, patents, industrial designs, copyrights, and technical information such as software, data designs, technical know-how, manufacturing information and know-how, techniques, Technical Data Packages (TDPs), manufacturing data packages, and trade secrets.

*DAAT*

## INTERDIVISION WORK AUTHORIZATION (IDWA)/INTERDIVISION WORK ORDER (IDWO, IWO)
See "Interorganizational Transfer (IOT)."

## INTERESTED PARTY
A protest may be filed only by an interested party. An interested party is an actual or prospective bidder or offeror whose direct economic interest would be affected by the award of the contract or by failure to award the contract.

*W-HAP*

See also "Protest."

## INTERIM VOUCHER
See "Invoice."

## INTERNAL CONTROL
The coordinated methods and measures in an organization designed to (a) promote efficiency, (b) encourage adherence to prescribed manage-

ment plans and policies, (c) check the accuracy and validity of organization data, and (d) safeguard assets.

*NCMA-CA*

## INTERNATIONAL COMMERCIAL TERMS (INCOTERMS)

The terms clarify destination, risk and liability, point of title transfer, and cost inclusions.

*NES-94*

See also INCOTERMS.

## INTERNATIONAL FEDERAL SUPPLY SCHEDULE

Provides sources of supplies to U.S. government activities overseas.

*W-PSP*

See also "Federal Supply Schedule (FSS) Program."

## INTERNATIONAL TARIFF IN ARMS REGULATIONS (ITAR)

Implements the Munitions Control Act. The Department of State governs the exportation of weapons through the U.S. Munitions Control List.

*NES-94*

## INTERNATIONAL TRADE COMMISSION (ITC)

The ITC is responsible for monitoring trade and determining when "dumped" goods cause, or threaten to cause, material injury to any U.S. industrial product.

*NES-94*

## INTERNATIONAL TRAFFIC IN ARMS REGULATION (ITAR)

A document prepared by the Office of Munitions Control, Department of State, providing licensing and regulatory provisions for the export of defense articles, technical data, and services. The ITAR also provides the U.S. Munitions List.

*MSA*

See also "Export Administration Regulation (EAR)."

## INTERORGANIZATIONAL TRANSFER (IOT)

The assignment of work under a contract to one or more separate divisions or subunits of the prime contractor.

*NES-89*

Also known as "Interdivision Work Authorization (IDWA)" and "Interdivision Work Order (IDWO, IWO)."

## INVENTORIABLE COST

A cost associated with units produced; it may be looked upon as "attaching" or "clinging" to units produced.

*NCMA-CA*

## INVENTORY

(1) Inventories include raw materials, goods in process, and finished goods.

*NES-02*

(2) The amount of property on hand at any given time.

*SPP*

## INVENTORY CONTROL

The effective management of inventories, including decisions about which items to stock at each location, how much to stock at each location, how much stock to keep on hand at various levels of operation, when to buy, how much to buy, how to control pilferage and damage, and how to manage shortages and backorders.

*Commercial Practices*

## INVENTORY HOLDING (CARRYING) COST

The cost of keeping inventory on hand, including the opportunity cost of invested funds; storage and handling costs; and taxes, insurance, shrinkage, and obsolescence–risk costs. Firms usually state an item's holding cost per time period as a percentage of the item's value, typically between 20 and 40 percent per year.

*Commercial Practices*

## INVENTORY POSITION

A measure of an inventory item's ability to satisfy future demand, considering scheduled receipts and on-hand inventory.

*Commercial Practices*

## INVENTORY RECOVERY

A systematic, centralized organizational effort to manage the surplus equipment or material and the scrap recovery or marketing or disposition activities in a manner that recovers as much of the original capital investment as possible.

*Commercial Practices*

## INVENTORY TURNOVER

A measure of the velocity of total inventory movement through the firm. The turnover rate is found by dividing annual sales (at cost) by the average aggregate inventory value maintained during the year. Many firms calculate production inventory turnover rate as the annual inventory purchase value divided by the average production inventory value.

*Commercial Practices*

## INVESTMENT GOODS

See "Capital."

## INVITATION FOR BIDS (IFB)

The solicitation is called an "Invitation for Bids" when using the sealed-bid method of procurement.

*NCMA-SB*

See also "Request for Proposal (RFP)."

## INVOICE

A contractor may submit an invoice (a bill) to the government for payment for contract performance. Such invoice payments are not made for the purpose of financing work in process. Invoice payments are made to honor a contractual obligation to pay for work accepted. Under cost-reimbursement contracts, contractors may submit two types of invoices: interim vouchers and final vouchers. Interim vouchers are submitted before completion of the contract. Final vouchers are submitted when the contract is completed.

*W-MFPP*

## ISHIKAWA DIAGRAM
See "Fishbone Diagram."

## ISO 9000
A comprehensive set of process and procedure quality management standards developed by the International Organization for Standardization (ISO). Suppliers selling to firms that have adopted the ISO 9000 standards must produce their products using processes and methodologies that use the quality management standards specified by ISO 9000.

*Commercial Practices*

## INTERSERVICE SUPPORT AGREEMENT (ISSA)
The provision of a commercial activity, in accordance with an ISSA, on a reimbursable basis. The ISSA includes franchise funds, revolving funds, and working capital funds.

*OMB A-76*

## JACKET
Term used to describe the folder in which a procurement request and all associated papers flow through the system. A label is applied to the front of each jacket to identify the Purchase Request (PR) number. The original PR and copies are forwarded in the jacket to the contract specialist.

*Navy*

## JAVITS-WAGNER-O'DAY (JWOD) ACT
Another name for P.L. 92-28, which requires the government to buy some of its supplies and services from non-profit agencies that employ Americans who are blind or have other severe limitations, such as the Committee for Purchase from People Who Are Blind or Severely Disabled.

*W-PSP*

See also "Committee for Purchase from People Who Are Blind or Severely Disabled."

## JOB ANALYSIS
A detailed examination of a job to determine the duties, responsibilities, and specialized requirements that are necessary for its performance.

*DAAT*

## JOB ORDER COST SYSTEM
One in which a contractor accounts for output and costs incurred by specifically identifiable physical units. A job order may cover the production of one unit or may represent a composite number of identical units.

*Cohen*

## JOB SHOP
A company specializing in the supply of personnel on a temporary basis.

*Cohen*

## JOINT CONTRACT
A contract in which the parties bind themselves both individually and as a unit.

*Garrett*

## JOINT COST
A cost that is common to all the segments in question and that is not clearly or practically allocable except by some questionable allocation base.

*NCMA-CA*

Also known as "Common Cost."

## JOINT PRODUCTS COSTS
Costs of two or more manufactured goods, of significant sales values, that are produced by a single process and that are not identifiable as individual products up to a certain state of pro-duction known as the split-off point.

*NCMA-CA*

## JOINT VENTURE
In a joint venture, the parties jointly own and manage either a partnership or a corporation established for the express purpose of entering into a contract with the customer. Neither party alone enjoys direct privity of contract with the customer; only the joint venture itself has direct privity.

## AI
See also "Team Arrangement."

## JURISDICTION
The authority (of a board of contract appeals, federal court, or arbitrator) to hold a hearing, to grant relief, and to make determinations that are binding on the parties.

*GUIDE*

## JURY VERDICT BASIS
A means of pricing equitable adjustments used when the two parties rely on different costing approaches. This technique is not limited to use in court; it can also be used during negotiations. It requires compromise. The evidence is presented by both parties, the information is evaluated, and the "jury verdict" method is used to determine a reasonable claim amount.

*W-ATCC*

See also "Actual Cost Basis," "Modified Total Cost Basis," and "Total Cost Basis."

## JUST-IN-TIME (JIT) INVENTORY
(1) A manufacturing and inventory philosophy in which inventory is scheduled for delivery only as needed on the production line.

*EDI*

(2) The minimum inventory required to meet production schedules.

*DGCQI*

## JUST-IN-TIME (JIT) SYSTEM

The basic JIT concept is an operations management philosophy whose dual objectives are to reduce waste and to increase productivity. Operationally, JIT minimizes inventory at all levels; materials are purchased, transported, and processed just in time for their use in a subsequent stage of the manufacturing process.

*Commercial Practices*

## JUSTIFICATION AND APPROVAL (J&A)

A document to justify procurement using other than full and open competition. This document is required prior to commencing negotiation for a contract resulting from an unsolicited proposal or any other contract award that does not provide for full and open competition.

*Navy*

# K, L

## KANBAN SYSTEM

A system of production flow control that uses kanban cards to pull in-process inventories through a manufacturing process in which items are called for only as they are needed in the next step of the production process.

*Commercial Practices*

## KEY FUNCTIONAL CHARACTERISTICS

The functional qualities or characteristics that critically affect a configuration item's ability to fulfill operational requirements.

*AFIT*

## KEY PERSONNEL CLAUSE

A solicitation provision that requires offerors to identify which personnel will be working on the contract. The government states its personnel qualification requirements, and the contractor responds with documentation (e.g., resumes) detailing how its key personnel meet the government's requirements. Some key personnel clauses may require the contractor to price its effort on the basis of each key person's actual rate rather than on the average bid rate used on the majority of proposals. The contractor must bid the key personnel in good faith, but generally has a right of substitution, with the contracting officer's (CO's) approval. The government has certain recourse, such as renegotiation and right of refusal, if the promised key personnel are not provided.

*TIPS(4-1)*

## KICKBACKS

Payment back of a portion of the purchase price to a buyer or public official by the seller to induce purchase or to influence improper future purchases or leases. A federal statute makes kickbacks a criminal offense in connection with a contract for construction or repair of a public building or a building financed by loans from the government.

*BLD*

## LABOR HOUR CONTRACT

(1) A contract that provides for reimbursement of the contractor's labor costs at a fixed hourly rate.

*McVay*

(2) A variation of the time-and-materials contract, differing only in

that materials are not supplied by the contractor.

*FAI*

## LABOR PRODUCTIVITY
The rate of output of a worker or group of workers per unit of time, usually compared to an established standard or expected rate of output.

*DAAT*

## LABOR SURPLUS AREA
A geographic area identified by the Department of Labor in accordance with 20 C.F.R. 654, Subpart A, as an area of concentrated unemployment or underemployment or an area of labor surplus.

*FAR*

## LAST-IN, FIRST-OUT (LIFO)
A cost-flow assumption that the stock acquired earliest is still on hand; the stock of merchandise or material acquired latest is used first.

*MGMT*

Compare "First-In, First-Out (FIFO)."

## LAW OF AGENCY
See "Agency."

## LEAD TIME
The period of time from the date of a purchase order (PO) to the date of delivery of the order.

*Commercial Practices*

## LEADER–FOLLOWER CONCEPT
A government contractual relationship for the delivery of an end item through a prime or subcontract relationship or to provide assistance to another company. Variants include (a) a prime contract awarded to established source (leader) that is obligated to subcontract to and assist another source (follower), (b) a contract awarded requiring the leader to assist the follower that has the prime contract for production, or (c) a prime contract awarded to the follower for production. The follower is obligated to subcontract with a designated leader for assistance. (The leader may be producing under another contract.)

*DAAT*

## LEARNING CURVE
A tool of calculation used primarily to project resource requirements in terms of the direct manufacturing labor hours or the quantity of material (for this purpose, usually referred to as an improvement curve) required for a production run. Used interchangeably with the term "improvement curve," the concept of a learning curve was adopted from the observation that individuals who perform repetitive tasks exhibit a rate of improvement resulting from increased manual dexterity.

*ASPM*

## LEASE

(1) When used with reference to tangible personal property, "lease" means a contract by which the owner of such property grants another the right to possess, use, and enjoy it for a specified period of time in exchange for periodic payment of a stipulated price.

*BLD2*

(2) A lease is a legal contract between two parties: the lessor, who owns the asset, and the lessee, who uses the asset.

*NES–02*

## LEASE-TO-OWNERSHIP PROGRAM (LTOP)

A contract for the lease of property that provides for the automatic transfer of property title to the government (buyer) upon the expiration of the lease.

*F&F*

## LEASE-WITH-OPTION PURCHASE (LWOP)

A contract for the lease of property that provides the government (buyer) with the option of purchasing the property at one or more points during the lease, or upon its expiration.

*F&F*

## LEASE OR BUY DECISION

The decision concerning whether to contract for the possession and use of an asset owned by another party for a period of time in return for lease payments, as opposed to purchasing the asset.

*Commercial Practices*

## LESSONS LEARNED

Capitalizing on past errors in judgment, materiel failures, wrong timing, or other mistakes to ultimately improve a situation or system.

*DAAT*

## LETTER CONTRACT

A written preliminary contractual instrument that authorizes the immediate commencement of activity under its terms and conditions, pending definitization of a fixed-price or cost-reimbursement pricing arrangement for the work to be done. It includes specifications of the government's (buyer's) maximum liability and must be superseded by a definite contract within a specified time.

*OPM*

## LETTER OF CREDIT

(1) An international business document that assures the seller that payment will be made by the bank issuing the letter of credit upon fulfillment of the sales agreement.

*Commercial Practices*

(2) A letter of credit is a contract between the banks representing the

exporter and the importer; it includes all the terms and conditions of the sale.

*NES-02*

## LETTER OF INTENT (LOI)

An obligation instrument that can be used to protect price and availability of long-lead-time items and for other purposes.

*AFIT*

## LEVEL OF EFFORT (LOE)

The devotion of talent or capability to a predetermined level of activity, over a stated period of time, on the basis of a fixed-price or cost-reimbursement pricing arrangement. Payment is usually based on effort expended rather than on results achieved.

*OPM*

## LEVEL UNIT PRICING

The requirement in most multi-year contracts to price each year's deliveries at the same unit price.

*McVay*

## LIABILITIES

Liabilities are the various claims against a firm; they include accounts payable, notes payable, obligations under capital leases, and long-term debts.

*NES-02*

## LICENSE

See "Exclusive (Nonexclusive) License."

## LIEN

A legal claim on property for the purpose of satisfying a debt.

*Commercial Practices*

## LIFE-CYCLE COST

The total cost of a system, building, or other product computed over its useful life. It includes all relevant costs involved in acquiring, owning, operating, maintaining, and disposing of the system or product over a specified period of time, including environmental and energy costs.

*OMB A-131*

## LIMITATION OF COSTS CLAUSE

Applicable only to fully funded cost-reimbursement contracts. Under this clause, the contracting officer (CO) should be given 60 days of notice in writing when costs incurred will exceed 75 percent of the estimated cost. The government is not obligated to reimburse the contractor for costs incurred in excess of the estimated costs, and the contractors are not obligated to continue performance under a contract causing them to incur costs in excess of the estimated costs.

*TIPS(1-5)*

See also "Notification Clause."

## LIMITATION OF FUNDS CLAUSE

Used for incrementally funded cost-reimbursement contracts. Similar to the Limitation of Costs clause, this clause requires the contractor to give the contracting officer (CO) 60 days of written notice when costs incurred will exceed 75 percent of the funds allotted to the contract.

*TIPS(1-5)*
See also "Notification Clause."

## LIMITED PRODUCTION

See "Low Rate Initial Production."

## LIMITED RIGHTS

In technical data, refers to the rights to use, duplicate, or disclose technical data in whole or in part, by or for the government, with the express written permission of the party furnishing the technical data. Such data may be released or disclosed outside the government; used by the government for manufacture (or if software documentation, for preparing the same or similar software); or used by a party other than the government except under certain restricted circumstances.

*DSMC*
See also "Rights in Technical Data."

## LIQUIDATED DAMAGES

A contract provision providing for the assessment of damages on the contractor for its failure to comply with certain performance or delivery requirements of the contract; used when the time of delivery or performance is of such importance that the government (buyer) may reasonably expect to suffer damages if the delivery or performance is delinquent.

*OPM*

## LIQUIDATION

Term used when the contractor pays back or reimburses the government for contractor financing or loan given in the form of progress payments. (A progress payment is a financing method to support the future delivery of a product.) When the product is delivered and accepted by the government, the progress payments are liquidated or offset against the delivery price. At delivery, instead of paying the full line-item price, the government will subtract from the line-item price a percentage (the liquidation rate) as payback for the financing. Generally, the liquidation rate is the same percentage as the progress payment rate.

*NES-93*
See also "Contractor Financing" and "Progress Payment."

## LOAN GUARANTEES

See "Guaranteed Loans."

## LOCAL BUYING

Patronizing local suppliers can have the following benefits: improved community relations, smaller quantities of materials provided at lower prices, local inventories adapted for continuing local users, minimal transportation costs, and shorter lead times.

*DBL*

## LOCAL SUPPLIER
A business located within the purchasing activity's recognized metropolitan area.

*SPP*

## LOGISTICS
(1) The process of planning, implementing, and controlling the efficient, cost-effective flow and storage of raw materials, in-process inventory, finished goods, and related information from point of origin to point of consumption for the purpose of conforming to customer requirements.

*Commercial Practices*

(2) The science of planning and carrying out the movement and maintenance of forces. In its most comprehensive sense, logistics involves those aspects of military operations that deal with (a) design and development, acquisition storage, movement, distribution, maintenance, evacuation, and disposition of materials; (b) movement, evacuation, and hospitalization of personnel; (c) acquisition or construction, maintenance, operation, and disposition of facilities; and (d) acquisitioning or furnishing of services.

*MSA*

## LONG-LEAD ITEMS/ LONG-LEAD-TIME MATERIALS
Components of a system or piece of equipment for which the times to design and fabricate are the longest and, therefore, to which an early commitment of funds may be desirable in order to meet the earliest possible date of system completion. Might be ordered during "Full Scale Development" (FSD) to arrive for production start.

*DSMC*

## LOT SIZE
The quantity of goods purchased or produced in anticipation of demand.

*Commercial Practices*

## LOW-RATE INITIAL PRODUCTION
A low rate of output at the end of full-scale development (FSD) or beginning of production. Reduces the government's (buyer's) exposure to large retrofit problems and costs while still providing adequate numbers of hard-tooled production items for final development and operational tests before a full production decision. Part of an acquisition strategy, it is a risk-reduction method that is also known as "Limited Production" and "Pilot Production."

*DSMC*

## LUMP SUM
A lot price or a fixed-total price paid in one sum.

*Commercial Practices*

## "M" ACCOUNT

Another term for the Treasury Memorandum Account, which was established in 1956 (a) to help lighten the burden of General Accountability Office (GAO) audits and Congress's lengthy appropriations process every year, and (b) to facilitate congressional appropriations without established ceilings. Individual agency M accounts were abolished in 1991.

*TIPS(2-6)*

## MAINTENANCE, REPAIR, AND OPERATING (MRO)

MRO supplies are consumed in the operations process, but do not become part of the product of the operation (e.g., soap, lubricating oil, machine repair parts, office supplies, etc.).

*Commercial Practices*

## MRP II (Manufacturing Resource Planning)

An expansion of a basic MRP system that includes the following additional capabilities: (a) a capacity planning capability, (b) a financial interface that permits planning to be done in financial terms as well as operations planning terms, and (c) a simulation

capability that can be used in doing alternative planning work.

*Commercial Practices*

## MAASTRICT TREATY (1991)

Drafted in 1991 by "The 12" countries included in the European Community and ratified in 1993. It established a single currency and central banking system by the year 1999, as well as a political union and framework for coordinating defense and foreign policies.

*NES-94*

## MAILBOX RULE

The idea that the acceptance of an offer is effective when deposited in the mail if the envelope is properly addressed.

*Garrett*

## MAINTAINABILITY

The ability of an item to be retained in or restored to a specified condition when maintenance is performed by personnel having specified skill levels, using prescribed procedures and resources, at each prescribed level of maintenance and repair.

*DOD-MMH*

## MAJOR INFORMATION SYSTEM

An information system that requires special management attention because of its importance to an agency mission; its high development, operating, or maintenance costs; or its significant role in the administration of agency programs, finances, property, or other resources.

*OMB A-130*

## MAJOR SYSTEMS ACQUISITION

See "OMB Circular A-109, Major Systems Acquisition."

## MAKE-OR-BUY PROGRAM

The part of a contractor's written plan for the development or production of an end item outlining the subsystems, major components, assemblies, subassemblies, and parts intended to be manufactured, test-treated, or assembled by the contractor (make); and those the contractor intends to procure from another source (buy).

*DSMC*

## MANAGEMENT CONTROL SYSTEM

The process by which managers ensure that resources are obtained and used effectively and efficiently in the accomplishment of an organization's objectives. A management control system is an explicit set of activities, policies, procedures, and reports intended to institutionalize the formal aspects of the management control process.

*MCS*

## MANAGEMENT PLAN

The document that outlines the changes that will result in the government's Most Efficient Organization (MEO) to perform a commercial activity in-house. It provides the staffing patterns and operating procedures that serve as a baseline for in-house cost estimates

*OMB A-76*

## MANAGEMENT RESERVE (MR)

(1) Management reserve is held for growth within the currently authorized work scope, rate changes, and other program unknowns. MR is held for current and future needs, and it must not be used to offset accumulated overruns or underruns. The use of MR provides the project manager with a capability to adjust for these uncertainties. MR is not a contingency that can be eliminated from contract price during subsequent negotiations or used to absorb the cost of contract changes. The contractor should not be required to use existing MR to provide budgets for authorized, but undefinitized, work or other modifications to authorized contractual efforts or as a source of funding for added work scope.

*EVMIG*

(2) MR is budget to cover unexpected work that is deemed in scope to the contract but cannot be identified in advance. Because MR is budget that is not as yet tied to work, it does not form

part of the performance measurement baseline. The MR budget should be commensurate with the level of risk identified by the project or withheld for management control purposes.

*NDIA*

## MANAGER, KEY FUNCTIONS OF
The broad skills or functions of a manager are planning, organizing, staffing, directing, and controlling.

*NCMA-CP2*

## MANAGERIAL ACCOUNTING
See "Cost Accounting."

## MANDATORY FLOW-DOWN CLAUSES
Federal Acquisition Regulation (FAR) clauses that are cited in the prime contract and that specifically require the inclusion of the text of the clause, either verbatim or substantially verbatim, in all subcontracts entered into in support of the prime contract.

*OPM*

See also "Flow Down."

## MANDATORY SOURCE
See "Established Government Sources."

## MANDATORY USE SCHEDULE
See "Federal Supply Schedule (FSS) Program."

## MANUFACTURING OVERHEAD
See "Factory Overhead."

## MANUFACTURING RESOURCE PLANNING
A production planning and control system used to schedule production jobs, purchase materials, check capacity requirements, forecast product demands, and redirect material supplies in the face of changing schedules.

*P&L*

## MANUFACTURING TECHNOLOGY (MANTECH)
Any action having the objective of the timely establishment or improvement of the manufacturing process, techniques, or equipment required to support current and projected programs. MANTECH includes assurance of the availability to produce, reduce lead time, ensure economic availability of end items, reduce costs, increase efficiency, improve reliability, or enhance safety and antipollution measures.

*DSMC*

## MARCH-IN RIGHTS
With respect to any invention of a contractor conceived or first actually reduced to practice in the performance of work under a government contract in which a contractor has acquired title, the agency shall have the right to require the contractor to grant a nonexclusive, partially exclusive, or exclusive license in any field of use to a responsible applicant or applicants. If the contractor refuses

such a request, the agency is granted a license if the agency determines that such action is necessary.

*FAR*

## MARGINAL COSTING

See "Direct Costing."

## MARKET DATA

A type of secondary comparison used in performing price analysis. Market data are used to evaluate trends and technology in a particular market. Newspapers and trade journals can be used to validate assumptions.

*W-ICPA*

See also "Secondary Comparison."

## MARKET DIVISION

Agreements or understandings by which competitors divide a market in which they compete; exclusive allocation of customers, territories, or products within a market.

*BCG*

## MARKET GRADE

A product that is of fair, average quality, meaning the item meets the standards of the trade and its quality is appropriate for ordinary use; it is used in applying the implied warranty of merchantability.

*Commercial Practices*

## MARKET INTELLIGENCE

Information on competitors or competitive teams operating in the marketplace or industry.

*Garrett*

## MARKET RESEARCH

The process used for collecting and analyzing information about the entire market that is available to satisfy the minimum agency needs. The research will arrive at the most suitable approach to acquiring, distributing, and supporting supplies and services.

*FAR*

## MARKET SURVEILLANCE

Includes all the activities that acquisition personnel perform continuously to keep themselves abreast of technology and product developments in their areas of expertise.

*DAAT*

## MARKET SURVEY

Attempts to ascertain whether other qualified sources exist that are capable of satisfying the government's requirement.

*FAR*

## MASLOW'S HIERARCHY OF NEEDS

A behavioral science theory that sets forth a hierarchy of human needs in order of importance: (a) physiological (satisfying basic biological needs), (b) safety (avoiding risks or threats), (c) social (belonging through group membership), (d) self-esteem (perceiving status), and (e) self-actualization (growing personally). Each level must be met before other levels demand attention. Maslow's hierarchy of needs implies that since unmet needs can motivate behavior, managers should try to fulfill unmet needs. Participation in a contract negotiation process may or may not motivate someone, depending on where the person is in Maslow's hierarchy at the time.

*W-AN*

See also "Motivation Theories."

## MASTER SOLICITATION

A document containing special clauses and provisions that have been identified as essential for the acquisition of a specific type of supply or service that is acquired repetitively.

*FAR*

## MATCHING PRINCIPLE

An important accounting principle that provides the basis for accrual accounting. The matching principle is concerned with matching expenses to the related revenue as a means of providing an accurate presentation of an entity's performance.

*NCMA-CA*

See also "Accrual Accounting."

## MATERIAL

A property category that includes property that may be incorporated into or attached to a deliverable end item (i.e., steel used to make bolts) or that may be consumed or expended in performing a contract (i.e., solvents, cleansers, paint). It also includes assemblies, components, parts, raw and processed materials, and small tools and supplies that may be consumed while performing a contract.

*W-GPB*

## MATERIAL INSPECTION AND RECEIVING REPORT

A validated report of contractor-furnished supplies or services inspected, accepted, or both by the government.

*AFIT*

## MATERIAL MANAGEMENT

The process of procuring and moving materials, parts, or finished inventory from the point of purchase to assembly plants, warehouses, or the final customer.

*F&F*

## MATERIAL MANAGEMENT AND ACCOUNTING SYSTEM (MMAS)

The contractor's system for planning, controlling, and accounting for the acquisition, use, and disposition of material. Such a system may be manual or automated and may be integrated with planning, engineering, estimating, purchasing, inventory, or accounting systems, etc., or it may be essentially a stand-alone system.

*P&L*

## MATERIAL REQUIREMENTS PLANNING (MRP)

A technique used to determine the quantity and timing requirements of "dependent demand" materials used in the manufacturing operation (those materials whose use is directly dependent on the scheduled production of a larger component or finished product). In practice, the actual number-crunching and paperwork generation usually is accomplished by computer, which takes the master production schedule output for a given product and calculates precisely the specific part and component requirements for that product during the given period of operation.

*DBL*

## MATERIALITY AND IMMATERIALITY

An accounting principle that holds that financial reporting is not concerned with insignificant items or minor amounts that would not affect the decisions of interested users. Decisions have to be made regarding the relative importance and size (i.e., materiality) of the expense items in order to determine the most cost-effective and meaningful expression of a company's operating costs.

*NCMA-CA*

## MATERIALS MANAGEMENT

An integrated systems approach to the coordination of materials activities and the control of total materials costs. It advocates assigning to a single operating department all major activities that contribute to the cost of materials. In the classic materials management organization, the following activities report to the materials manager: purchasing, inbound traffic, production scheduling, inventory control, and stores and receiving.

*DBL*

## McCLELLAND'S THEORY

A behavioral science theory that sets forth human needs in no particular order of importance: achievement, affiliation, and power. These motives affect the performance of people at their jobs. McClelland's achievement, affiliation, and power motives can be used to evaluate whether someone is appropriate for a lead contract negotiator position or a contract negotiation team member position.

*W-AN*

See also "Motivation Theories."

## MEAN TIME BETWEEN FAILURE (MTBF)

For a particular interval, the total functional life of a population of an item divided by the total number of failures (requiring corrective maintenance actions) within the population. The definition holds for time, rounds, miles, events, or other measures of life unit. A basic technical measure of reliability recommended for use in the research and development (R&D) contractual specification environment, where "time" and "failure" must be carefully defined for contractual compliance purposes.

*DAAT*

## MEAN TIME BETWEEN MAINTENANCE (MTBM)
A measure of reliability that represents the average time between all maintenance actions, both corrective and preventive.

*DAAT*

## MEASURING UNIT
In accounting, a standard unit of measure is necessary to provide a "yardstick" for measuring and comparing performance on financial statements. The U.S. dollar is the unit of measure used by virtually all companies in the United States for financial reporting purposes. However, the accounting process assumes that the U.S. dollar remains stable. There are inherent flaws with this assumption (i.e., inflation and deflation of the dollar).

*NCMA-CA*

## MEMORANDUM OF AGREEMENT (MOA)/ MEMORANDUM OF UNDERSTANDING (MOU)
(1) The documentation of a mutually agreed to statement of facts, intentions, procedures, and parameters for future actions and matters of coordination.

*AFIT*

(2) An MOU may express mutual understanding of an issue without implying commitments by parties to the understanding.

*DSMC*

(3) MOUs are bilateral agreements that are between two parties and that include policy statements regarding a specific commodity, service, or area of trade.

*NES-94*

## MENTOR–PROTÉGE PROGRAM
The U.S. Small Business Administration's (SBA's) Mentor–Protégé program enhances the capability of 8(a) participants to compete more successfully for federal government contracts. The program encourages private-sector relationships and expands SBA's efforts to identify and respond to the developmental needs of 8(a) clients. Mentors provide technical and management assistance, financial assistance in the form of equity investments or loans, subcontract support, and assistance in performing prime contracts through joint venture arrangements with 8(a) firms.

*SBA*

## METHOD OF PROCUREMENT
The process used for soliciting offers, evaluating offers, and awarding a contract. In federal contracting, contracting officers (COs) use one of

the following methods for any given acquisition:

- small purchase
- sealed bidding
- negotiation
- two-step sealed bidding

*FAI*

## MILESTONES

Key event points upon which activities are measured for progress.

*Cohen*

## MILITARY ASSISTANCE PROGRAM (MAP)

See "Conventional Arms Transfer."

## MILITARY SPECIFICATIONS (MILSPEC)

Specifications and standards maintained by Department of Defense (DOD) and published in the DOD Index of Specifications and Standards.

*FAI*

## MILITARY STANDARD REQUISITIONING AND ISSUE PROCEDURES (MILSTRIP)

A uniform procedure established by the Department of Defense (DOD) to govern requisition and issue of material within standardized priorities.

*AFIT*

## MILLER ACT

The Miller Act (40 U.S.C 270a–270f)

requires performance and payment bonds for any construction contract exceeding $100,000, except that this requirement may be waived (a) by the contracting officer (CO) for as much of the work as is to be performed in a foreign country upon finding that it is impracticable for the contractor to furnish such bond, or (b) as otherwise authorized by the Miller Act or other law. (Threshold revised in the sixth edition)

*FAR*

## MINIMUM REORDER POINT

A predetermined inventory level that triggers a need to place an order. This minimum level (considering safety stock) provides inventory to meet anticipated demand during the time it takes to receive the order.

*Commercial Practices*

## MINORITY BUSINESS ENTERPRISE (MBE)

Any legal entity that is organized to engage in commercial transaction and that is at least 51 percent owned and controlled by one or more minority persons.

*Commercial Practices*

## MISTAKE IN BID

A procedure that enables a bidder to correct or withdraw its bid when a mistake has been made in preparing the bid.

*McVay*

## MODEM
Modulator–demodulator. A device that converts information from a computer into an audio tone that can be passed over telephone wires.

*EDI*

## MODIFICATION
See "Contract Modification."

## MODIFIED TOTAL COST BASIS
A means of pricing equitable adjustments. Under this approach, information on specific costs incurred is included in addition to a total cost portion of the claim. This basis is probably the most frequently used of all costing approaches in claims preparation.

*W-ATCC*

See also "Actual Cost Basis," "Jury Verdict Basis," and "Total Cost Basis."

## MODULAR CONTRACTING
A contracting approach under which the need for a system is satisfied in successive acquisitions of interoperable increments. Each increment complies with common or commercially acceptable standards applicable to information technology (IT) so that the increments are compatible with the other increments of IT that compose the system.

*DAAT*

## MONOPOLIZATION
Maintaining or expanding a large market share through illegal or threatening tactics intended to impair the commercial viability of competitors.

*BCG*

## MONOPOLY
Form of market structure in which the entire market for a good or service is supplied by a single seller or firm.

*ECON*

## MONOPSONY
Market structure in which a single buyer purchases a good or service.

*ECON*

## MOST EFFICIENT ORGANIZATION (MEO)
The MEO refers to the government's in-house organization to perform a commercial activity. It may include a mix of federal employees and contract support. It is the basis for all government costs entered on the Cost Comparison Form (CCF). The MEO is the product of the management plan and is based on the performance work statement (PWS).

*OMB A-76*

## MOST FAVORED CUSTOMER
It is a General Services Administration (GSA) policy that GSA requires most favored customer pricing from vendors; that is, GSA will not award a contract to a firm that does not offer

the government a discount equal to or better than that offered to any other customer.

*W-CC*

## MOTIVATION THEORIES

The study of behavioral science offers several theories about an individual's motivations. An individual's motivations become important in negotiations. If one is to ensure that negotiation objectives are met, it is important to understand why people behave the way they do.

*W-AN*

See also "Herzberg's Theory," "Maslow's Hierarchy of Needs," and "McClelland's Theory"

## MULTIPLE AWARD SCHEDULE (MAS)

Contracts made with multiple suppliers, pursuant to the Federal Supply Schedule (FSS) Program, for relatively the same items at varying prices for delivery within the same geographic area.

*W-PSP*

See also "Federal Supply Schedule (FSS) Program."

## MULTI-YEAR CONTRACT

(1) A method of procuring known requirements for supplies or services for more than one year, even though the total funds obligated are not available

at the time of entering into the contract.

*OPM*

(2) A fixed-price contract, lasting up to five years, that is funded on a yearly basis, with cancellation costs being paid the contractor if the contract is canceled before completion.

*McVay*

(3) A procurement of more units of products than can be funded by the government (buyer) in a single year. The total purchase is divided into annual segments that are negotiated at one time. Under multi-year considerations, the government (buyer) pays lower unit prices because of larger buys; however, the contractor is protected from annual cancellations through clauses in the contract.

*DOD-MMH*

## MUNITIONS LIST

The U.S. Munitions List is an enumeration of defense articles and defense services published in the International Traffic in Arms Regulation (ITAR).

*MSA*

## MUTUAL ASSENT

Consists of an offer made by one party and the unconditional acceptance of that offer by another party.

*Commercial Practices*

## MUTUAL MISTAKE

A mistake is a belief that is not in accord with the facts. If the government participated in the mistake, relief is sought by contractors under the theory of mutual mistake.

*NC-A*

## NATIONAL DEFENSE ACTIVITY

A national defense activity is a commercial activity that is approved by the Secretary of Defense, or designee, as being subject to deployment in a direct military combat support role.

*OMB A 76*

## NATIONAL INDUSTRIES FOR THE BLIND (NIB)

See "Committee for Purchase from People Who Are Blind or Severely Disabled."

## NATIONAL INDUSTRIES FOR THE SEVERELY HANDICAPPED (NISH)

See "Committee for Purchase from People Who Are Blind or Severely Disabled."

## NATIONAL PERFORMANCE REVIEW (NPR)

A study requested by President Bill Clinton. Its purpose was to look at federal practices in a variety of disciplines, to judge how well the programs worked, and to recommend changes for improvement. Vice President Al Gore's report, titled From Red Tape to Results: Creating a Government that Works Better and Costs Less, was issued in September 1993. It includes some recommendations that specifically concern procurement, many of which are the same or similar to suggestions in the Section 800 Panel report.

*TIPS(5-2)*

See also "Section 800 Panel."

## NATIONAL SECURITY

A national security activity is a commercial activity that is approved by the Director of Central Intelligence, or designee, as being necessary to meet the national security.

*OMB A-76*

## NATIONAL STOCK NUMBER

A 13-digit stock number consisting of a four-digit Federal Supply Classification and a nine-digit National Item Iden-tification Number.

*MSA*

## NEGOTIATED CEILING

Maximum negotiated value for which the government (buyer) is liable for payment to the contractor.

*AFIT*

See also "Adjusted Ceiling."

## NEGOTIATED CONTRACT COST

The estimated cost negotiated in a cost-plus-fixed-fee (CPFF) contract, or the negotiated contract target cost in either a fixed-price-incentive or a cost-plus-incentive-fee (CPIF) contract.

*AFIT*

## NEGOTIATION

(1) A process between buyers and sellers seeking to reach mutual agreement on a matter of common concern through fact-finding, bargaining, and persuasion.

*L&P*

(2) Government acquisition of supplies or services, including construction, by other-than-sealed bidding procedures.

*L&P*

## NEGOTIATION TECHNIQUES

Specific methods used during negotiations to reach agreement. Example techniques include blaming a third party, appealing to emotions, conceding straw issues (give-aways), playing good guy–bad guy roles, making the other side appear unreasonable, and pressuring the other side (prolonging negotiation, approaching the other party's superiors, walking out of negotiations).

*W-AN*

## NATIONAL ENVIRONMENTAL POLICY ACT (NEPA) (1969)

Dictates the national environmental policy, which affects the administration of all other federal environmental laws. The Act imposes environmental responsibilities on all federal government agencies, which include consideration of environmental factors when making significant decisions, such as proposals for legislation or other major federal actions that will significantly affect the quality of the environment.

*NES-94*

## NEW ITEM INTRODUCTORY SCHEDULE

Introduces new or improved products into the federal supply system.

*W-PSP*

## NEW REQUIREMENTS

A new requirement is a newly established need for a commercial product or service.

*OMB A-76*

See also "Federal Supply Schedule Program."

## NONDEVELOPMENTAL ITEM (NDI)

(1) A generic term describing either a commercial product or an item developed and used prior to a planned acquisition. Use of an NDI reduces R&D costs and speeds up the acquisition process.

*DSMC*

(2) Any previously developed item of supply used exclusively for governmental purposes by a federal agency, a state or local government, or a foreign government with which the United States has a mutual defense cooperation agreement; any item described in the paragraph above that requires only minor modification or modifications of a type customarily available in the commercial marketplace in order to meet the requirements of the procuring department or agency; or any item of supply being produced that does not meet the requirements of the paragraphs above solely because the item is not yet in use.

*NES-97/FAR*

Also known as an "Off-the-Shelf" item. See also "Commercial Item."

## NONEXCLUSIVE LICENSE
See "Exclusive (Nonexclusive) License."

## NONPROBABILITY SAMPLING
See "Sampling."

## NONRECURRING COSTS
Costs that are generally incurred on a one-time basis. For example, nonrecurring production costs could include costs such as plant or equipment relocation, plant rearrangement, special tooling and special test equipment, preproduction engineering, initial spoilage and rework, and specialized workforce training.

*FAR*

## NORMAL COSTING
A type of product costing that applies to units produced (as costs of production), the actual direct materials consumed, the actual direct labor used, and an estimated or predetermined portion of overhead calculated on the basis of a normal or average schedule of production.

*NCMA-CA*

## NORMAL WORKWEEK
A normal workweek has 40 hours.

*IAN*

## NORTH AMERICAN FREE TRADE AGREEMENT (NAFTA)
The Agreement expands the intent of the Canadian Free Trade Agreement (CFTA), which was to reduce trade restrictions between the U.S. and Canadian borders. This expansion includes all of the countries in North America in one regional agreement. The passage of NAFTA will eliminate existing tariffs by the year 2008.

*NES-94*

## NOTICE OF AWARD
A notification to the lowest, responsive construction contractor that it must obtain a performance bond and a payment bond before it can be awarded a contract.

*McVay*

## NOTIFICATION CLAUSE

For certain types of cost reimbursable contracts, buyers will include provisions that they be notified when invoiced costs reach a percentage of the total contract. This clause allows for proper planning, particularly when it appears that costs identified for the job will not be sufficient to complete the work.

*Cohen*

See also "Limitation of Costs Clause" and "Limitation of Funds Clause."

## NOT OTHERWISE SPECIFIED

A classification indicating commodities not completely identified.

*Commercial Practices*

## NOT-TO-EXCEED (NTE) PRICE

A maximum price that the contractor may not exceed while negotiations are under way to establish the final price. NTE permits the contractor to perform the contract while negotiations are being conducted and protects the government (buyer) from excessive expenditures; it also is a ceiling for a particular cost element in a cost reimbursable contract.

*NCMA-SB*

## NOVATION AGREEMENT

A legal instrument executed by (a) the contractor (transferor), (b) the successor in interest (transferee), and (c) the government (buyer) by which, among other things, the transferor guarantees

performance of the contract, the transferee assumes all obligations under the contract, and the government (buyer) recognizes the transfer of the contract and related assets.

*FAR*

## NO-YEAR FUNDING

Congressional funding that does not require obligation in any specific year or years.

*FAR*

## OBJECTIVITY
An accounting principle that holds that financial accounting information should be verifiable and substantially capable of reproduction for reviews made by independent and qualified preparers using the same set of facts and assumptions. This principle is critical to the audit process.

*NCMA-CA*

## OBLIGATION
(1) A legal requirement for the disbursement of funds according to orders placed, contracts awarded, services received, or other contractual documents.

*AFIT*

(2) A duty to make a future payment of money. The duty is incurred as soon as an order is placed or a contract is awarded for the delivery of goods and the performance of services. The placement of an order is sufficient. An obligation "legally" encumbers a specified sum of money, which will require outlay(s) or expenditures in the future.

*DAAT*

## OBLIGATION AUTHORITY
(1) Congressional or administrative authority to incur obligations; it is independent from the authority to make expenditures in payment thereof.

*AFIT*

(2) A congressional authorization to procure goods and services within a specified amount by appropriation or other authorization.

*DAAT*

(3) The administrative extension of such authority by apportionment or funding.

*DAAT*

(4) The amount of authority so granted.

*DAAT*

## OBLIGATION OF FUNDS
Legally binding commitments, such as contract awards, that are made by federal agencies during a given period and that will require outlays during the same or some future period.

*FAI*

## OFFER

(1) A legally binding promise, made by one party to another, to enter into a contractual agreement if the offer is accepted. In sealed bidding, offers made in response to Invitations for Bids (IFBs) are called "bids." In negotiated acquisitions, offers made in response to Requests for Proposals (RFPs) are called "proposals."

*FAI*

(2) A proposal to make a contract. It is made orally, in writing, or by other conduct, and it must contain the terms legally necessary to create a contract. Acceptance of the proposal creates the contract.

*FBL*

(3) A response to a solicitation that, if accepted, would bind the offeror to perform the resultant contract.

*DAAT*

(4) The manifestation of willingness to enter into a bargain, so made as to justify another person in understanding that his or her assent to that bargain is invited and will conclude it.

*Garrett*

(5) An unequivocal and intentionally communicated statement of proposed terms made to another party. An offer is presumed revocable unless it specifically states that it is irrevocable. An offer once made will be open for a reasonable period of time and is binding on the offeror unless revoked by the offeror before the other party's acceptance.

*Garrett*

See also "Proposal."

## OFFICE OF FEDERAL PROCUREMENT POLICY (OFPP)

An organization within the Office of Management and Budget (OMB) that provides leadership and direction to federal procurement programs.

*FAI*

## OFFICE OF MANAGEMENT AND BUDGET (OMB)

A federal office that recommends and monitors federal programs and funding levels, that develops and issues governmentwide policy guidance on management concerns, and that reviews proposed regulations.

*FAI*

## OFFSET AGREEMENTS

One of various industrial and commercial compensation practices required of defense contractors by foreign governments as a condition for the purchase of defense articles or services in either government-to-government or direct commercial sales. The responsibility for negotiating offset arrangements resides with the U.S. firm involved.

*DAAT*

## OFFSETS
(1) A cost balancing action whereby a claim may be canceled or lessened by a counterclaim.

*P&L*

(2) In foreign military sales, an "offset" is additional "compensation" obtained by a foreign buyer from the seller.

*W-CC*

## OFF-THE-SHELF
Procurement of existing systems or equipment without a research, devel opment, test, and evaluation program or with minor development to make the system suitable for government needs. It may be a commercial system or equipment or a system or equipment already in the government's inventory.

*DSMC*

Also known as "Commercial-Off-the-Shelf." See also "Nondevelopmental Item (NDI)."

## OLIGOPOLY
A market dominated by a few sellers.

*ECON*

## OMB CIRCULAR A-76, PERFORMANCE OF COMMERCIAL ACTIVITIES
A directive of the Office of Management and Budget (OMB) that requires government-operated activities be contracted out whenever it is cost-effective.

*FAR*

## OMB CIRCULAR A-109, MAJOR SYSTEMS ACQUISITION
A directive of the Office of Management and Budget (OMB) created as a result of the Commission on Government Procurement's recommendations that establishes policies to be followed by executive branch agencies in the acquisition of major systems. A "major system" is defined as a combination of elements that will function together to produce the capabilities required to fulfill a mission need. The circular states management objectives, management structure, and key decision points.

*OMB A-109*

See also "Progressive Down-Selection."

## OMB CIRCULAR A-120, GUIDE-LINES FOR THE USE OF ADVISORY AND ASSISTANCE SERVICES
A directive of the Office of Management and Budget (OMB) that specifically prohibits the government's use of advisory and assistance services obtained for professional or technical advice that is readily available within the government agency (except when the contract has been entered into and reviewed under the provisions of OMB Circular A-76, "Performance of Commercial Activities").

*TIPS(1-6)*

## OMB CIRCULAR A-130, MANAGEMENT OF FEDERAL INFORMATION RESOURCES

This circular provides uniform governmentwide information resources management policies as required by the Paperwork Reduction Act of 1980 and amended by the Paperwork Reduction Act 1995, 44 U.S. Chapter 35. To assist agencies in an integrated approach to information resources management, the Act requires that the Director of the Office of Management and Budget (OMB) develop and implement uniform and consistent information resources management policies; oversee the development and promote the use of information management principles, standards, and guidelines; and evaluate agency information resources management practices with the policies, principles, standards, and guidelines promulgated by the director.

*OMB A-130*

## ON-LINE INSPECTION

Any inspection or test that can be performed on an item without impeding the flow of the item through the receiving (or manufacturing) process.

*AFIT*

## ONE-YEAR APPROPRIATIONS

Appropriations generally used for current administrative, maintenance, and operational programs, including the procurement of items classified as "expense." These appropriations are available for obligation for a single fiscal year (FY).

*DAAT*

## OPEN-END CONTRACT

An agreement for the supply of goods or services that contains varying limits, or no limit, on time and quantity, and which usually involves recurring orders and changes of various types.

*AFIT*

## OPEN MARKET

The collective name for private, commercial business sources of supplies and services. For example, in government small purchasing, open market sources can be used under two conditions: (a) no mandatory sources can meet the need, or (b) the open market can provide the same supplies or services at substantial savings.

*SPP*

## OPEN SYSTEM

A system that implements specifications maintained by an open, public consensus process for interfaces, services, and support formats, to enable properly engineered components to be used across a wide range of systems with minimal change, to interoperate with other components on local and remote systems, and to interact with users in a manner that facilitates portability.

*DAAT*

## OPERATING PROFIT

The amount of gross profit earned from the normal operations of the company; the amount of sales in excess of total operating expenses.

*NES-02*

## OPERATION & MAINTENANCE (O&M) COSTS

Costs associated with equipment, supplies, and services required to train, operate, and maintain forces in a recipient country. O&M costs include (a) spare parts other than concurrent spares and initial stockages, (b) ammunition and missiles used in training or replacements for such items expended in training or operations, (c) rebuild and overhaul costs (excluding modernization) of equipment subsequent to initial issue, (d) training and other services that do not constitute investment costs, and (e) administrative costs associated with overall program management and administration.

*MSA*

## OPPORTUNITY COST

The maximum alternative earning that might have been obtained if the productive good, service, or capacity had been applied to some alternative use.

*NCMA-CA*

## OPPORTUNITY PROFILE

A stage of the capture management life cycle, during which a seller evaluates and describes the opportunity in terms of what it means to your customer, what it means to your company, and what will be required to succeed.

*Garrett*

## OPTION

A unilateral right in a contract by which, for a specified time, the government (buyer) may elect to purchase additional quantities of the supplies or services called for in the contract, or may elect to extend the period of performance of the contract.

*AFIT*

## OPTIONAL USE SCHEDULE

See "Federal Supply Schedule (FSS) Program."

## ORDER OF PRECEDENCE

A solicitation provision that establishes priorities so that contradictions within the solicitation can be resolved.

*McVay*

## THE ORGANIZATIONAL BREAKDOWN STRUCTURE (OBS)

The OBS reflects the way the project is organized. When one is to assign work responsibility to appropriate organizational elements, any work breakdown structure (WBS) and organizational structure must be interrelated with each other; that is, organizational responsibility must be established for identified units of work.

*EVMIG*

## ORGANIZATIONAL CONFLICT OF INTEREST (OCI)

An OCI exists when the nature of the work to be performed under a proposed contract may, without some restriction on future activities, (a) result in an unfair competitive advantage to the contractor, or (b) impair the contractor's objectivity in performing the contract work.

*FAR*

See also "Conflict of Interest."

## OTHER DIRECT COSTS (ODC)

Labor hours, materials and subcontracts, and travel costs are considered "direct costs;" that is, they are costs directly incurred in designing, manufacturing, testing, or producing the product itself. Added to these direct costs is the category "other direct costs," which includes such elements as computer services, reproduction services, and training.

*CE*

## OTHER TRANSACTIONS

Anything other than grants, cooperative agreements, or contracts.

*NES-99*

## OUTLAYS

(1) Actual expenditures. Checks issued, interest occurred on the public debt, or other payments. Total budget outlays consist of the sum of the outlays from appropriations and other funds in the budget, less receipts (i.e., refunds and reimbursements).

*MSA*

(2) Payments (e.g., checks issued, cash disbursed, and electronic fund transfers, or EFTs) by a federal department or agency.

*FAI*

## OUTSOURCING

(1) A version of the make-or-buy decision in which a firm elects to purchase an item that previously was made in-house; it is commonly used for services.

*Commercial Practices*

(2) A contractual process of obtaining another party to provide goods, services, or both that were previously done internal to an organization.

*Garrett*

## OUT-YEARS

The four fiscal years following the target years.

*AFIT*

## OVERHEAD

An accounting cost pool that generally includes general indirect expenses that are necessary to operate a business but are not directly account-able to a specific good or service produced. Some examples are building rent, utilities, salaries of corporate officers, janitorial services, office supplies and furniture, etc.

*Navy*

See also "Extended Overhead."

## OVERSEAS PRIVATE INVESTMENT CORPORATION (OPIC)

Offers finance and insurance for overseas investments, along with investment and foreign country information.

*NES-94*

## OVER TARGET BASELINE (OTB)

When the total budget allocated to work exceeds the Contract Budget Base (CBB). Sometimes, available budgets for the remaining work are insufficient to ensure valid perfor-mance measurement. The need for an OTB could result from a major event or program review.

*EVMIG*

## OVERTIME

Time worked by a contractor's employee in excess of the employee's normal workweek.

*FAR*

## OVERTIME PREMIUM

The difference between the contractor's regular rate of pay to an employee for the shift involved and the higher rate paid for overtime. It does not include shift premium.

*FAR*

P

## PACKARD COMMISSION
Established by the president in 1985 as the President's Blue Ribbon Commission on Defense Management, it is commonly called the "Packard Commission" in reference to its chairperson. The Commission was tasked to examine defense issues, cite problems, and recommend solutions. In June 1986, the Commission's final report, titled A Quest for Excellence, was issued citing 37 broadly worded recommendations.

*TIPS(3-2)*

## PAPERWORK REDUCTION ACT
A 1980 act that, among other objectives, seeks to ensure that automatic data processing (ADP) and telecommunications technologies are acquired and used by the federal government in a manner that improves service delivery and program management (44 U.S.C. 3501 et seq.).

*NS*

(Amended 1995 - 44 U.S.C. 35)

*OMB A-130*

## PARAMETRIC COST ESTIMATING
(1) Statistical and parametric estimating involves collecting and organizing historical information through mathematical techniques and relating this information to the work output being estimated. The format most commonly used for statistical and parametric estimating is the estimating relationship, which relates some physical characteristic of the work output (weight, power requirements, size, or volume) with the cost or labor hours required to produce it. Estimating relationships have the advantage of providing a quick estimate even though very little is known about the work output except its physical characteristics. Conversely, because of their dependence on past (historical) data, they may erroneously indicate cost trends.

*CE*

(2) A cost-estimating methodology using statistical relationships between historical costs and other program variables, such as system physical or performance characteristics, contractor output measures, or workforce loading.

*DAAT*

## PAROL EVIDENCE
Oral or verbal evidence; in contract law, the evidence is drawn from sources exterior to the written instrument.

*Garrett*

## PAROL EVIDENCE RULE

A rule that seeks to preserve the integrity of written agreements by refusing to permit contracting parties to attempt to alter a written contract with evidence of any contradictory prior or contemporaneous oral agreement (parole to the contract).

*Garrett*

## PARTIAL PAYMENT

A payment authorized under a contract, to be made upon completion of the delivery of one or more complete units called for, delivered, and accepted by the government (buyer) under the contract; also, a payment made against a termination claim upon prior approval before final settlement of the total termination claim.

*OPM*

## PARTIAL SET-ASIDE

When small business sources cannot satisfy the government's entire requirement at a reasonable price (i.e., a total set-aside is not appropriate), the contracting officer may elect to set aside only a portion of the acquisition for small businesses.

*W-SBC*

See also "Set-Aside."

## PATENTS

A property right granted by the government of the United States of America to an inventor "to exclude others from making, using, offering for sale, or selling the invention throughout the United States or importing the invention into the United States" for a limited time in exchange for public disclosure of the invention when the patent is granted.

*Patent Office*

## PAYMENT

The amount payable under the contract supporting data required to be submitted with invoices, and other payment terms such as time for payment and retention.

*Garrett*

See also "Compensation Clause."

## PAYMENT BOND

A bond that ensures payments as required by law to all persons supplying labor or material in the prosecution of the work provided for in the contract. A payment bond is required only when a performance bond is required, and if the use of a payment bond is in the government's (buyer's) interest.

*FAR*

## PECUNIARY LIABILITY

The statutory obligation of an individual to reimburse the government for loss or improper application of funds or property.

*AFIT*

## PENALTY

Includes the imposition by an agency or court of a fine or other punishment; a judgment for monetary damages or equitable relief; or the revocation suspension, reduction, or denial of a license, privilege, right, grant, or benefit.

*USC-44-35*

## PER DIEM

Although this term literally means per day, it is used in various ways to take on more specific meanings. For example, from a transportation perspective, a per diem charge is the daily rate for use of rail cars of one railroad by another railroad.

*Commercial Practices*

## PERFORMANCE

The execution of the terms of a contract. If a buyer offers to purchase from a supplier, the supplier performs by furnishing the buyer's requirements.

*FAI*

## PERFORMANCE-BASED CONTRACT (PBC)

A documented business arrangement in which the buyer and seller agree to use a performance work statement, performance-based metrics, and a quality assurance plan to ensure contract requirements are met or exceeded.

*Garrett*

## PERFORMANCE BOND

A bond that secures the performance and fulfillment of all the undertakings, covenants, terms, conditions, and agreements contained in the contract.

*AFIT*

## PERFORMANCE MEASUREMENT BASELINE (PMB)

The assignment of budgets to scheduled segments of work produces a plan against which actual performance can be compared. The PMB represents the time-phased scope, schedule, and associated budget through the end of the contract.

*NDIA*

See also "Budgeted Cost of Work Scheduled (BCWS)."

## PERFORMANCE REQUIREMENTS SUMMARY (PRS)

A synopsis of the scope of work and output performance measurements that may be used in conjunction with aviation cost comparisons that rely on the data system of the General Services Administration's (GSA's) Facilities Asset Management Information System (FAMIS) for identifying contract costs.

*OMB A-76*

## PERFORMANCE RISK ASSESSMENT GROUP (PRAG)

(1) A group of experienced government personnel who are appointed by the source selection advisory council chairperson to permit performance risk to be used, if appropriate. Performance risk may be separately assessed for each evaluation factor or as a whole with the assessment provided directly to the source selection advisory council or authority for final decision, or indirectly through the Source Selection Evaluation Board (SSEB).

*ACC*

(2) PRAG was originally developed by the U.S. Army Communications, Electronics Command, but similar initiatives have been developed throughout the government. The PRAG requires the government to maintain a historical database of contract actions across multiple agencies. Any contract between any government agency and any contractor is a candidate for the database.

*NES-96*

## PERFORMANCE SPECIFICATION

A purchase description that explains the deliverable in terms of desired operational characteristics. Performance specifications tend to be more restrictive than functional specifications, in that they limit alternatives that the buyer will consider and define separate performance standards for each such alternative.

*Garrett*

## PERFORMANCE STANDARD

A performance standard reflects the minimum, sector-specific, federal requirement for the performance of a commercial activity. It incorporates both quality measures and cost measures.

*OMB A-76*

## PERFORMANCE WORK STATEMENT (PWS)

(1) A statement of the technical, functional, and performance characteristics of the work to be performed; PWS determines performance factors, including the location of the work, the units of work, the quantity of work units, and the quality and timeliness of the work units. It serves as the scope of work and is the basis for all costs entered on the Cost Comparison Form (CCF).

*OMB A-76*

(2) A statement of work (SOW) expressed in terms of desired performance results, often including specific measurable objectives.

*Garrett*

## PERIODIC INVENTORY METHOD

An inventory accounting system that requires a physical count of inventory to determine the ending amounts of raw material, work in process, and finished goods, and, hence, also the costs of goods sold.

*NCMA-CA*

## PERIODIC REVIEW SYSTEM

A fixed-order interval inventory control system in which an item's inventory position is reviewed on a scheduled periodic basis, rather than continuously. An order is placed at the end of each review, and the order quantity usually varies. This system is different from a fixed-order quantity system in which the order quantity typically is fixed and the time between orders varies.

*Commercial Practices*

## PERPETUAL INVENTORY METHOD

An inventory accounting system whereby a continuous record is kept that tracks raw materials, work in process, finished goods, and cost of goods sold on a day-to-day basis.

*NCMA-CA*

## PERSONAL SERVICES CONTRACT

A contract that, by its express terms or as administered, makes the contractor personnel appear, in effect, as government employees.

*FAI*

## PHYSICAL CONFIGURATION AUDIT (PCA)

A technical examination of a designated configuration item to verify that the item "as built" conforms to the technical documentation that defines the item.

*DOD-MMH*

## PILOT PRODUCTION

A limited production run of a new system used to demonstrate the capability to mass produce an item.

*AFII*

Also known as "Low Rate Initial Production."

## PLANNED ORDER RELEASE (POR)

A planned authorization for a supplier to release (ship) material against an existing contract. As used in material requirements planning (MRP) system operation, the POR indicates when a release for a specified quantity of an item is to be issued; the release date is the planned receipt date minus the lead time.

*Commercial Practices*

## PLANNED VALUE

See "Budgeted Cost of Work Scheduled (BCWS), and "Budget at Completion."

## PLANNING ESTIMATE

The estimates of operational or technical characteristics, schedule, and the program acquisition cost developed at the time of approval for program initiation.

*AFIT*

## PLANNING FACTOR

An estimating relationship used to compute the amount and type of effort or resources that will be necessary to develop, produce, acquire, or operate a given system.

*AFIT*

## PLANNING PACKAGE

A planning package is the logical aggregation of work within a control account, normally the far-term effort, that can be identified and budgeted in early baseline planning, but that cannot yet be defined into discrete, apportioned, or level of effort (LOE) work packages. Planning package plans must reflect the manner in which the work is to be performed.

*NDIA*

## POINT OF FIRST RECEIPT

Often referred to in discussions of "Fast Payment Procedure." The point of first receipt is designated by the government. It is the point where goods or services leave the supplier's hands, and from which they are forwarded to the eventual user. Post offices or common carriers are examples of such points.

*SPP*

## POINT OF ORIGIN

The location where a transportation company receives a shipment from the shipper.

*Commercial Practices*

## POST-AWARD ORIENTATION

A meeting of government (buyer) and contractor (supplier) personnel held soon after contract award to ensure that everyone understands the contract requirements.

*McVay*

## POST-MEO PERFORMANCE REVIEW

When services are preformed in-house, as a result of a cost comparison, including those involving an interservice support agreement (ISSA), a formal review and inspection of the most efficient organization (MEO) should be conducted. Typically, this review should be conducted following the end of the first full year of performance. Post-MEO performance reviews confirm that the MEO has been implemented in accordance with the transition plan, established the MEO's ability to perform the services of the performance work statement (PWS) and to confirm that actual costs are within the estimates contained in the in-house cost estimate. Adjustments may be for formal mission or scope of work changes.

*OMB A-76*

## PRE-AWARD INQUIRY

Questions and comments from prospective offerors about specifications, terms, and conditions in a solicitation received before the opening date of the IFB or closing date of the RFP.

*FAI*

## PRE-AWARD SURVEY

An evaluation of a prospective contractor's ability to perform a specific contract, performed by the contract administration office or the purchasing office, with assistance from an audit organization at the request of either office. The evaluation addresses the physical, technical, managerial, and financial capability of the prospective contractor. Also addressed are the adequacy of the contractor's systems and procedures, and past performance record.

*P&L*

## PRE-BID CONFERENCE

A conference held with prospective bidders in sealed-bid procurements before the submission of a bid to clarify any ambiguous situations, to answer bidder questions, and to ensure that all bidders have a common basis of understanding regarding the supplies or services required. Also known as a "Pre-proposal Conference" in a negotiated procurement.

*OPM*

## PREFERENTIAL PROCUREMENT PROGRAMS

These are special "commercial" source programs, such as Federal Prison Industries (FPI) and the workshops administered by the Committee for Purchase from the Blind and Other Severely Handicapped (CPBOSH) under the Javits-Wagner-O'Day Act (JWOD).

*OMB A-76*

## PREPRODUCTION INSPECTION

Examination and testing performed, witnessed, or participated in by the government on one or more items submitted by a contractor to prove, before the initiation of production, that its production methods are capable of yielding items that comply with the technical requirements of the contract.

*AFIT*

## PRE-PROPOSAL CONFERENCE

A meeting held with contractors after the request for proposals (RFPs) in negotiated procurements have been sent out. The goal is to promote uniform interpretation of work statements and specifications by all prospective contractors.

*NCMA-SS*

See also "Pre-bid Conference."

## PRESENT VALUE OF FUTURE CASH FLOWS

A dollar today is worth more because of the interest cost. Thus, dollar benefits that accrue in the future cannot be compared directly with investments made in the present. Discounting is a technique for converting various cash flows occurring over time to equivalent amounts at a common point in time considering the time value of money to facilitate a valid comparison.

*AFIT*

Also known as "Time Value of Future Cash Flows."

## PRESIDENT'S BLUE RIBBON COMMISSION ON DEFENSE MANAGEMENT

See "Packard Commission."

## PRE-SOLICITATION CONFERENCE

A meeting held with potential contractors or subcontractors before a formal solicitation to discuss technical and other problems connected with a proposed procurement. The conference is also used to elicit the interest of prospective contractors in pursuing the task, such as a research and development (R&D) effort.

*DSMC*

## PRICE

(1) A monetary unit given, received, or asked for in exchange for supplies or services.

*ASPM*

(2) The amount of money or equivalent paid or charged for supplies or services, including cost and profit or fee.

*L&P*

## PRICE ANALYSIS

(1) The process of examining and evaluating a prospective price without evaluation of the separate cost elements and proposed profit of the individual offeror.

*OPM*

(2) Price analysis evaluates an offer by comparing it with indicators of reasonableness. Primary comparisons include competitive analysis and published prices. Secondary comparisons include comparative analysis (previous contracts, prior quotations), market data, price index, cost estimating relationships, government price lists, government estimates, and discounts. Auxiliary techniques include value analysis and visual analysis.

*W-ICPA*

## PRICE ANALYSIS, METHODS OF

See "Auxiliary Techniques," "Primary Comparison," and "Secondary Comparison."

## PRICE-ANDERSON ACT

The Act was intended by Congress to encourage private participation in the field of nuclear energy by requiring the then-named Atomic Energy Commission (AEC) to ensure protection of AEC licensees from liability arising from accidents and to compensate the public if such an accident did occur.

*NES-94*

## PRICE FIXING

Any agreement, understanding, or arrangement among competitors to raise, lower, fix, or stabilize prices, as well as any agreement between a supplier and customer as to the price at which the customer may resell goods purchased.

*BCG*

## PRICE INDEX

A number, usually a percentage, expressing the relation of the actual price of a commodity at a given point in time to its price during a specified base period. The information can be used to chart price level changes.

*Commercial Practices*

## PRICE NEGOTIATION MEMORANDUM (PNM)

The document that relates the story of the negotiation. A sales document establishing the reasonableness of the agreement reached with the successful offeror, as well as a permanent record of the decisions made by the negotiator in establishing that the price was fair and reasonable.

*OPM*

## PRICE REDUCTION

(1) A contract clause that entitles the government to obtain a price reduction

of any significant amount, including profit or fee, by which the contract price was increased as a result of defective cost or pricing data. An audit investigation by an outside party (often the Defense Contract Audit Agency or DCAA) must precede this administrative action. On the basis of the audit results, a unilateral modification to the contract, thereby reducing the price, is issued by the contracting officer (CO).

*TIPS(2-2)*

(2) A clause in a multiple award schedule (MAS) that dictates the MAS price schedule will be adjusted to retain the price relationship between the parties, in the event that a general decrease in price is offered to all of the vendors' customers in the same category as the government.

*W-CC*

## PRICE VARIANCE

The difference between the actual price and the standard price, multiplied by the total number of items acquired. The term "price variance" is usually linked with direct materials; the term "rate variance," which is conceptually similar to the price variance, is usually linked with direct labor.

*NCMA-CA*

See also "Rate Variance."

## PRICING ARRANGEMENT

An agreed-to basis between contractual parties for the payment of amounts for specified performance; it is usually expressed in terms of a specific cost-reimbursement or fixed-price type arrangement.

*OPM*

## PRICING PROPOSAL
See "Contract Pricing Proposal."

## PRIMARY COMPARISON
A means of accomplishing price analysis. An example of a primary comparison is competitive evaluation, whereby independent, current, responsible, responsive offers are compared against each other. Another example of a primary comparison is published catalog prices.

*W-ICPA*

Compare "Auxiliary Techniques" and "Secondary Comparison."

## PRIME COST
The sum of direct material and direct labor.

*NCMA-CA*

## PRIME, OR PRIME CONTRACTOR
Revised sixth edition. The entity with whom an agent of the United States enters into a prime contract for the purpose of obtaining supplies, materials, equipment, or services of any kind.

*DAAT*

## PRIOR COURSE OF DEALING
An important type of extrinsic evidence used in the interpretive process to establish the meaning of ambiguous language. Also used to demonstrate that an explicit requirement of the contract is not binding because that requirement was not enforced in the past.

*NC-A*

## PRIORITY RATINGS
"DO" and "DX" are the two types of priority ratings contained in the Defense Priorities and Allocations System (DPAS) Regulation that specify rules relating to the status, placement, acceptance, and treatment of priority-rated contracts and orders. "DO" ratings have equal preferential status and take priority over all unrated orders. "DX" ratings have equal preferential status and take priority over DO-rated and unrated orders.

*Sherman*

See also "Defense Priorities and Allocations System (DPAS)."

## PRIVATIZATION
Privatization is the process of changing a public entity or enterprise to private control and ownership. It does not include determinations as to whether a support service should be obtained through public or private resources. The government retains full responsibility and control over the delivery of those services.

*OMB A-76*

## PRIVITY OF CONTRACT

(1) The direct legal (contractual) relationship that exists between parties that allows either party to (a) enforce contractual rights against the other party and (b) seek remedy directly from the other party with whom this relationship exists.

*P&L*

(2) The legal relationship between two parties to the same contract. The government has "privity of contract" with the prime contractor. Therefore, the government's relationship with subcontractors is indirect in nature. Government involvement with sub-contractors is channeled through the prime contractor's directed activities; only the prime contractor is authorized to direct the subcontractor.

*DSMC*

## PROBABILITY SAMPLING

See "Sampling."

## PROCEDURAL SUPPORT DATA

Recorded procedures that are used by the contractor during the development program for assembly, operation, or maintenance tasks connected with production, testing, or inspection.

*AFIT*

## PROCESS

A group of sequential, logically related tasks that use organizational resources to provide a product or a service to internal or external customers.

*DGCQI*

## PROCESS CAPABILITY ANALYSIS

A statistical technique used during development and production cycles to analyze the variability of a process relative to product specifications.

*DGCQI*

## PROCESS COSTING

A method of costing products with average costs computed on the basis of total costs divided by equivalent units of work performed. Usually used in high-volume, similar-product situations.

*NCMA-CA*

## PROCUREMENT

The complete action or process of acquiring or obtaining goods or services using any of several authorized means.

*AFIT*

## PROCUREMENT AUTHORIZATION

A document that establishes the approved material procurement program, and that authorizes and directs the action to be taken to place the approved material program under procurement.

*AFIT*

## PROCUREMENT AUTOMATED SOURCE SYSTEM (PASS)

(1) A centralized inventory and referral system containing the names and capabilities of small businesses interested in obtaining government contracts or subcontracts.

*McVay*

(2) A database maintained by the Small Business Administration (SBA) that lists the capabilities of contractors certified under the SBA's 8(a) program for the benefit of government agencies and larger contractors who wish to utilize such 8(a) firms.

*F&F*

## PROCUREMENT, CATEGORIES OF

The major categories of procurement are supplies, construction, services, and research and development (R&D). Within each of these major categories are numerous specialized types of procurement. The classification of the procurement is extremely important for purposes of funding, types of contracts to be used, applicability of contract clauses, and coverage of socioeconomic provisions.

*NC-F*

## PROCUREMENT INTEGRITY

A set of rules of conduct, contained in the 1989 amendments to the Office of Federal Procurement Policy Act, 41 U.S.C. 423, that were formalized for the purpose of upholding the integrity of

the government procurement process. The rules are implemented by Federal Acquisition Regulation (FAR) 3.104.

*NS*

## PROCUREMENT LEAD TIME

The time interval between the initiation of procurement and the receipt into the supply system of material purchased as a result of such action.

*AFIT*

See also "Administrative Lead Time."

## PROCUREMENT PACKAGE

All information required to obtain bids or proposals; the technical information necessary to accurately describe the item to be procured.

*AFIT*

## PROCURING CONTRACTING OFFICER (PCO)

The government agent designated by a warrant having the authority to obligate the government. The PCO negotiates and signs the actual contractual document. Administration of the contract after award may be delegated to an Administrating Contracting Officer (ACO).

*DSMC*

## PROCUREMENT REQUEST (PR)

Document that describes the required supplies or services so that procurement can be initiated. Some procuring activities actually refer to the document by this title; others use a different title such as Procurement Directive. Combined with specifications, the statement of work (SOW), and Contract Data Requirements List (CDRL), it is called the PR Package, or a basis for solicitation.

*DAAT*

## PRODUCT VERIFICATION INSPECTION

Physical inspection or test of a product by the government after inspection and acceptance by the contractor's quality organization.

*AFIT*

## PRODUCTION READINESS REVIEW (PRR)

A formal examination of a program to determine whether (a) the design is ready for production, (b) the production engineering problems have been resolved, and (c) the producer has accomplished adequate planning for the production phase.

*DOD-MMH*

## PROFESSIONAL SERVICES

The Fair Labor Standards Act defines a "professional" employee as one who exercises discretion and independent judgment and who performs work that is predominantly intellectual and varied in character, as opposed to skilled or technical. The categories of executive, administrative, and professional employees are exempt from the Service Contract Act (SCA) and

provisions for minimum wage rates, fringe benefits requirements, and rules governing overtime compensation.

*W-ESCA*

See also "Fair Labor Standards Act," "Service Contract Act," and "Uncompensated Overtime."

## PROFIT

The net proceeds from selling a product or service when costs are subtracted from revenues. The net may be positive (profit) or negative (loss).

*L&P*

See also "Anticipatory Profit" and "Fee."

## PROFIT CENTER

The smallest organizationally independent segment of a company charged by management with profit and loss responsibilities.

*FAR*

## PROFIT OBJECTIVE

The part of the estimated contract price objective that the contracting officer (CO) concludes is appropriate for the procurement at hand. It is developed after a thorough review of proposed contract work and after all available knowledge regarding an offeror, as well as an analysis of the offeror's cost estimate and a comparison of it with the government's estimate or projection of cost.

*OPM*

## PROFITABILITY ACCOUNTING
See "Responsibility Accounting."

## PRO FORMA INVOICE
A document prepared in advance of a sale to provide evidence of the final form and amount of invoice.

*Commercial Practices*

## PROGRAM EVALUATION AND REVIEW TECHNIQUE (PERT)
One of the best known (along with the Critical Path Method, or CPM) techniques derived from the basic critical path scheduling concept. PERT emerged in 1958 through the joint efforts of the U.S. Navy; the Booz, Allen & Hamilton consulting firm; and the Lockheed Missile and Space Division in connection with the Polaris weapons program. With the passage of time, PERT and CPM have become very similar in concept. Currently, they differ only with respect to various details of application. In practice, the application of CPM and PERT generally is accomplished with a computer program. It uses network diagrams to show time and dependency relationships between the activities that make up the total project. The purpose of the technique is to keep all the "parts" arriving on schedule so that the total project can be completed as planned.

*DBL*

## PROGRAM MANAGEMENT
The process whereby a single leader exercises centralized authority and responsibility for planning, organizing, staffing, controlling, and leading the combined efforts of participating or assigned civilian and military personnel and organizations. The leader manages a specific acquisition program or programs throughout the system life cycle.

*DAAT*

## PROGRAM MANAGER (PM)
(1) An individual charged with the responsibility for design, development, and acquisition of the system or equipment, plus the design, development, and acquisition of the integrated logistic support (ILS).

*AFIT*

(2) A designated individual with responsibility for and authority to accomplish program objectives for development, production, and sustainment to meet the user's operational needs.

*DAAT*

## PROGRAM WORK BREAKDOWN STRUCTURE (PWBS)
The WBS structure that encompasses an entire program. It consists of at least three levels of the program with associated definitions and is used by the government's Program Manager (PM) and contractor to develop and extend a Contract Work Breakdown Structure (CWBS).

*DAAT*

## PROGRESS PAYMENT

(1) A payment made as work progresses under a contract on the basis of percentage of completion accomplished, or for work performed at a particular stage of completion.

*OPM*

(2) An interim payment for delivered work in accordance with contract terms; it is generally tied to meeting specified performance milestones.

*Garrett*

See also "Contractor Financing" and "Liquidation."

## PROGRESSIVE DOWN-SELECTION

A method used with major systems acquisitions, whereby a planned series of competitions is held in sequential phases. Each phase has successively fewer awards among a group of competitively selected participating contractors, finally resulting in a single award for the development or production of the system. This method can eliminate the gaps between the major systems' five separate phases:

(a) concept exploration,
(b) definition,
(c) demonstration and validation,
(d) design and development, and
(e) production and operations.

*TIPS(3-12)*

See also "OMB Circular A-109 Major Systems Acquisition."

## PROMISORY NOTE

A written promise from one party to another to pay a specific sum of money at a specific time to the bearer or other designated party.

*Commercial Practices*

## PROMPT PAYMENT DISCOUNT

A discount offered by a bidder for payment by the government (buyer) within a designated time period.

*GUIDE*

## PROPERTY

The Federal Acquisition Regulation classifies property into five categories: (a) facilities, (b) material, (c) special tooling, (d) special test equipment, and (e) agency-peculiar property.

*W-GPB*

See also "Government-Furnished Property (GFP)."

## PROPERTY ADMINISTRATION

Upon receipt of government property, the contractor is responsible and accountable for the property as prescribed by the terms of the contract. This accountability includes any government property in the possession or control of a subcontractor. Accordingly, the contractor is required to establish and maintain a system to control, protect, and maintain all government property.

*W-GPB*

See also "Property Control System."

## PROPERTY CONTROL SYSTEM

Contractors must have control systems that adequately meet the requirements of the government property clauses.

*W-GPB*

See also "Property Administration."

## PROPOSAL

Normally, a written offer by a seller describing its offering terms. Proposals may be issued in response to a specific request or may be made unilaterally when a seller feels there may be an interest in its offer (which is also known as an "Unsolicited Proposal").

*Cohen*

See also "Contract Pricing Proposal," "Offer," and "Unsolicited Proposal."

## PROPOSAL EVALUATION

An assessment of both the proposal and the offeror's ability (as conveyed by the proposal) to successfully accomplish the prospective contract. An agency shall evaluate competitive proposals solely on the factors specified in the solicitation.

*FAR*

See also "Evaluation Factors."

## PROPRIETARY INFORMATION

Data that are owned by a contractor, that are not publicly available, and that may be used only with the permission of the owner.

*NCMA-SB*

## PROPRIETARY RIGHT

A broad contractor term used to describe data belonging to the contractor. These data could be intellectual property, financial data, etc. This term is generally used in the submission of a proposal to protect the contractor's sensitive information from disclosure and is not a category of rights applicable to technical data (TD) under all contracts.

*DAAT*

## PROSPECTIVE PRICING

A pricing decision that is made in advance of performance and that is based on analysis of comparative prices, cost estimates, past costs, or combinations of such considerations.

*OPM*

## PROTEST

A written objection by an interested party to a solicitation by an agency for offers covering a proposed contract for the acquisition of supplies or services, or a written objection by an interested party to a proposed award or the award of such a contract.

*FAR*

See also "Interested Party."

## PROVISIONED ITEM

A line item in the contract for which firm requirements (quantity or type) are not known at the time of contract preparation. A line item is, therefore, established for generic types of supplies or services (i.e., spare and repair parts, support equipment, engineering support, government property repair, and data). Requirements for these line items are initiated by a requisition.

*Navy*

## PROVISIONING
The process of determining or meeting the range and quantity of items required to support and maintain or function for a set period of time.

*OPM*

## PRUDENT BUSINESSPERSON CONCEPT
Phrase used as a measure of reasonableness in assessing an offer or counteroffer, or other action taken under a contract. Related to making a procurement decision that is based on sound fiduciary or business principles.

*P&L*

## PUBLIC INFORMATION
Any information, regardless of form or format, that an agency discloses, disseminates, or makes available to the public.

*USC-44-3502*

## PURCHASE DESCRIPTION
(1) A description of the essential physical characteristics and functions required to meet the government's (buyer's) minimum needs.

*FAR*

(2) A simplified specification that is used when an item is purchased infrequently.

*McVay*

See also "Purchase Order (PO)" and "Purchase Request (PR)."

## PURCHASE ORDER (PO)
A document, signed by a contracting officer (CO) and addressed to a contractor. A PO requests the future delivery of supplies, equipment, or material, or the future performance of nonpersonal services in accordance with certain terms in exchange for a promise by the government to pay the stated price. A PO is considered an offer to contract rather than an acceptance of contract.

*OPM*

## PURCHASE REQUEST (PR)
An exact description of a product or service. A PR is used in invitations for bids, requests for proposals (RFPs), and contracts to tell prospective suppliers precisely what is required.

*OPM*

Also known as a "Purchase Description."

## PURCHASE REQUISITION
A written or computerized request to the purchasing department for a procurement of goods or services from suppliers.

*Commercial Practices*

## PURCHASING

(1) The process of buying supplies and services using a variety of contractual arrangements.

*L&P*

(2) In government, the process of buying readily available supplies and services using procedures such as purchase orders, blanket purchase agreements (BPAs), and prenegotiated schedules.

*L&P*

## QUALIFIED BIDDERS LIST (QBL)

A list of bidders who have had their products examined and tested and who have satisfied all applicable qualification requirements for that product or have otherwise satisfied all applicable qualification requirements.

*FAR*

## QUALIFIED MANUFACTURERS LIST (QML)

A list of manufacturers who have had their products examined and tested and who have satisfied all applicable qualification requirements for that product.

*FAR*

## QUALIFIED PRODUCT

An item that has been examined and tested for compliance with specification requirements and that is qualified for inclusion in a qualified products list.

*GUIDE*

## QUALIFIED PRODUCTS LIST (QPL)

A list of products that have been examined and tested and that have satisfied all applicable qualification requirements.

*FAR*

## QUALITY

The composite of all attributes or characteristics, including per-for-mance, that satisfy a user's needs.

*GAO*

## QUALITY ASSURANCE (QA)

(1) A planned and systematic pattern of actions necessary (a) to provide adequate confidence that material, data, supplies, and services conform to established technical require-ments, and (b) to achieve satisfactory performance.

*AFIT*

(2) All those tasks performed by persons outside an organization to improve and monitor the quality of its output. This QA would include inspec-tions done by authorized government representatives to make sure that the quality of a contractor's delivered products and services complies with the terms of the government contract.

*USCG*

## QUALITY ASSURANCE SURVEILLANCE

The method by which federal employees will supervise in-house or contract performance to ensure that the standards of the performance work statement (PWS) are met within the costs bid.

*OMB A-76*

## QUALITY CONTROL (QC)

(1) The process of measuring quality performance, comparing it with the standard, and acting on the difference.

*DGCQI*

(2) All those tasks done within an organization to improve the quality of its output. This QC would include inspection systems set up by a contractor to monitor its own output at key intervals in the contracting process.

*USCG*

## QUANTITY DISCOUNT

A price reduction given to a buyer for purchasing increasingly larger quantities of materials. A quantity discount is normally offered (a) for purchasing a specific quantity of items at one time, (b) for purchasing a specified dollar total at one time, or (c) for purchasing a specified dollar total over an agreed-upon time period (also known as a "Cumulative Discount").

*DBL*

See also "Trade Discount."

## QUANTITY VARIANCE

The standard price that is for a given resource and that is multiplied by the difference between the actual quantity used and the total standard quantity allowed for the number of good units produced.

*NCMA-CA*

## QUI TAM ACTION

An action brought by an informer (sometimes known as a "whistleblower"). Part of the penalty goes to any person who brings such action and the remainder to the state or some other suit (e.g., the government). Called a "Qui Tam Action" because the plaintiff states that he or she sues for the state as well as for himself or herself.

*BLD*

## QUICK CLOSEOUT

Basically, a faster method of completing the closeout process for a cost-reimbursement contract. Final indirect rates are negotiated on a contract basis, rather than by fiscal year (FY) as in regular closeout methods. Quick closeout can be done only in limited circumstances: if the contract is physically complete, the amount of unsettled indirect costs to be allocated to the contract is relatively insignificant, and an agreement can be reached on a reasonable estimate for allocable dollars.

*W-CCC*

See also "Closeout."

## QUOTATION

A statement of price, either written or verbal, that may include, among other things, a description of the product or service; the terms of sale, delivery, or period of performance; and payment. Such statements are usually issued by sellers at the request of potential buyers. In federal government procurement, quotations do not constitute an offer that can be accepted to form the basis of a binding contract. Rather, quotations are solicited to obtain market information for planning purposes.

*P&L*

## RATE VARIANCE
The difference between actual wages paid and the standard wage rate, multiplied by the total actual hours of direct labor used.

*NCMA-CA*

See also "Price Variance."

## RATIFICATION
In a broad sense, the confirmation of a previous act done either by the party itself or by another, as confirmation of a voidable act. The affirmance by a person of a prior act that did not bind him or her, but which was done or professedly was done on his or her account, whereby the act, as to some or all persons, is given the effect as if originally authorized by him or her.

*BLD*

## RATING SYSTEM
The source selection plan establishes the factors against which all proposals will be evaluated, the weights to be assigned to each factor, and the applicable rating system. A rating system may be based on colors, points, or adjectives. An example of a color-based rating system follows: blue = exceptional; green = acceptable; yellow = marginal; and red = unacceptable.

An example of an adjective-based rating system is excellent, very good, good, fair, and poor.

*W-HAP*

## REAL GROWTH
The growth (decline) of a budget after considering inflation. For example, a $10,000 budget that goes to $11,000 is only five percent real growth if inflation for the covered period is five percent; with no inflation, it would be 10 percent growth.

*DLA*

Also known as "Decline."

## REASONABLE COST
(1) A cost is reasonable if, in its nature and amount, it does not exceed that which would be incurred by a prudent person in the conduct of competitive business.

*FAR*

(2) A business decision reached jointly by a buyer and seller, a product of judgment influenced by bargaining strength and economic realities dictated by the marketplace.

*DAAT*

## REASONABLE OR COMPETITIVE PRICES

The expected range of prices resulting from experience obtained through the competitive free enterprise system for like or similar activities. Determinations are to be made by the contracting officer (CO).

*OMB A-76*

## REBATE

A legitimate refund to a purchasing organization in consideration for the purchase of a stipulated quantity or dollar volume within a specified time frame.

*Commercial Practices*

## RECIPROCITY

An agreement or understanding that one company will buy goods or services from a supplier in exchange for the supplier's purchase of equipment, programs, or services from that company.

*BCG*

## RECORDS

All books, papers, maps, photographs, machine-readable materials, or other documentary materials, regardless of physical form or characteristics, made or received by an agency of the U.S. government under federal law or in connection with the transaction of public business. The records may be preserved or appropriate for preservation by that agency or its legitimate successor as evidence of the organization, functions, policies, decisions, procedures, operations, or other activities of the government or because of the informational value of the data in them. Not included are (a) library and museum material made or acquired and preserved solely for reference or exhibition purposes, (b) extra copies of documents preserved for only convenience of reference, and (c) stocks of publications and processed documents. (44 U.S. C. 3301)

*OMB A-130*

## RECORDS MANAGEMENT

The planning, controlling, directing, organizing, training, promoting, and other managerial activities involved with respect to records creation, records maintenance and use, and records disposition in order to achieve adequate and proper documentation of the policies and transactions of the federal government and of the effective and economical management of agency operations. (44 U.S.C. 2901 (2))

*OMB A-130*

## RECORD RETENTION

After contract closeout is completed, Federal Acquisition Regulation (FAR) 4.805 establishes retention periods for contract files. The record retention requirements apply both to prime contracts and subcontracts. Contractors must make books, records, documents, and other supporting evidence available to the comptroller general and contracting agencies for a certain period after final payment. The calculation of a retention period starts at the end of the contractor's fiscal year (FY) in which an entry is made that charges a cost to a government contract.

*W-CCC*

See also "Closeout."

## RECURRING COMMERCIAL ACTIVITY

A recurring commercial activity is one that is required by the government on a consistent and long-term basis. This definition does not imply an hourly, daily, monthly, or annual requirement, but must, in a general sense, be repetitive in nature, wherein the expected workload can be reasonably estimated.

*OMB A-76*

## RECURRING COSTS

Costs that are required to operate and maintain an operation and that (a) vary or occur with the quantity being produced, and (b) occur repeatedly during the life cycle of a program, system, product, or service.

*P&L*

## REGULAR DEALER

A person who owns, operates, or maintains a store, warehouse, or other establishment in which the materials, supplies, articles, or equipment of the general character described by the specifications and required under the contract are bought, kept in stock, and sold to the public in the usual course of business.

*FAR*

See also "Walsh-Healey Public Contracts Act."

## RELIABILITY

(1) The duration or probability of failure-free performance under stated conditions.

*DOD-MMH*

(2) The ability of a system and its parts to perform its mission without failure, degradation, or demand on the support system.

*DAAT*

See "Mean Time Between Failure (MTBF)" and "Mean Time Between Maintenance (MTBM)."

## RENEGOTIATION BOARD

Created as an independent establishment in the executive branch by the Renegotiation Act of 1951 (65 Stat. 7; 50 U.S.C.A. App 1211), and organized on October 8, 1951. The Board seeks the elimination of excessive profits on defense and space contracts and related subcontracts. This elimination is accomplished through informal and nonadversary proceedings before the Board and its regional boards. Contractors not agreeing with Board determinations may petition the Court of Claims for redetermination.

*BLD*

## REPLEVIN

A legal action whereby the owner of goods can legally recover them from someone who is holding them unlawfully.

*FBL*

## REQUEST FOR DEVIATION

When a product or service must deviate in only a minor fashion from the original requirement.

*NES-96*

## REQUEST FOR EQUITABLE ADJUSTMENT (REA)

A letter or proposal from a contractor requesting a change to the contract price or schedule.

*Navy*

See also "Equitable Adjustment."

## REQUEST FOR INFORMATION (RFI)

A formal invitation to submit general or specific information concerning the potential future purchase of goods, services, or both.

*Garrett*

## REQUEST FOR PROPOSAL (RFP)

(1) Solicitation document used in negotiated procurement when the buyer reserves the right to award without further oral or written negotiation. Only the acceptance of the buyer is required in order to create a binding contract. Of course, the buyer can choose to negotiate further at its option.

*DSMC*

(2) A formal invitation that contains a scope of work and that seeks a formal response (proposal), thereby describing both methodology and compensation, to form the basis of a contract.

*Garrett*

## REQUEST FOR QUOTATION (RFQ)

(1) The solicitation form used in negotiated procurement when award will be made after negotiation with the offeror. Because the prospective subcontractor's quotation is not a formal offer, the prime contractor and subcontractor must reach a bilateral negotiated agreement before a binding contract exists.

*DSMC*

(2) A formal invitation to submit a price for goods, services, or both, as specified.

*Garrett*

## REQUEST FOR TECHNICAL PROPOSALS

Solicitation document used in two-step sealed bidding. Normally in letter form, it asks only for technical information; price and cost breakdowns are forbidden.

*DSMC*

## REQUEST FOR WAIVER

A contractor uses this request to ask that a particular requirement for a product or service be overlooked or waived. The waiver request would ask for permission to ignore a specific requirement.

*NES-96*

## REQUIRED SOURCES OF SUPPLIES AND SERVICES

The U.S. government buyer must first examine sources offered from or through the government before fulfilling the requirement with an outside source. The Federal Acquisition Regulation (FAR), Part 8, details the required sources of supplies and services and their order of priority.

*W-PSP*

See also "Committee for Purchase from People Who Are Blind or Severely Disabled," "Federal Prison Industries (FPI)," and "Wholesale Supply Sources."

## REQUIREMENTS

(1) Technical requirements specify what the product should do and how the seller will support it.

(2) Administrative requirements specify how the customer/buyer relationship will work.

*NES-97*

## REQUIREMENTS CONTRACT

A type of contract that provides for the filling of all actual purchase requirements for supplies or services for a designated activity during a specified contract period.

*OPM*

## REQUIREMENTS CREEP

The tendency of the user (or developer) to add to the original mission responsibilities or performance requirements for a system while it is still in development.

*DAAT*

## REQUISITION

A request for supplies or services originating from the party actually requiring them.

*SPP*

See also "Purchase Request (PR)."

## RESCISSION

The unmaking of a contract, or an undoing of it from the beginning, not merely a termination. It may be effected by mutual agreement of parties or by one of the parties declaring rescission of contract without consent of the other if a legally sufficient ground does, therefore, exist. An action of equitable nature in which a party seeks to be relieved of its obligations under a contract on the grounds of mutual mistake, fraud, impossibility, etc.

*BLD*

## RESEARCH AND DEVELOPMENT (R&D) CONTRACT

A contract for basic research (directed toward increasing knowledge); applied research (directed toward improving or expanding new scientific discoveries, technologies, materials, processes, or techniques); or development (directed production of, or improvements in, useful products to meet specific performance requirements through the systematic application of scientific knowledge).

*OPM*

## RESPONSIBILITY ACCOUNTING

A system of accounting that recognizes various responsibilities throughout the organization and that reflects the plans and actions of each of these centers by allocating particular revenues and costs to the one having the pertinent responsibility.

*NCMA-CA*

Also known as "Activity Accounting" and "Profitability Accounting."

## RESPONSIBLE CONTRACTOR

A capable party that has the financial resources, personnel, facilities, integrity, and overall capability to fulfill specific contractual requirements satisfactorily.

*NCMA-SB*

## RESPONSIVE

(1) Describes a bid that meets, without any material deviation, the expressed requirements of a solicitation.

*NCMA-SB*

(2) When a bidder fully complies with and does not materially deviate from the terms, conditions, and specifications set forth in an invitation for bids (IFB) (sealed-bid method), it is deemed "responsive."

*L&P*

(3) When an offeror materially complies with a solicitation and is capable of being made compliant through discussions, it is deemed "responsive."

*L&P*

## RESTRICTED COMPUTER SOFTWARE

Computer software that is developed at private expense and is a trade secret; that is commercial or financial and is confidential or privileged; or that is published, copyrighted computer software, including minor modifications of such computer software.

*FAR*

## RESTRICTED RIGHTS

A form of limited rights that applies only to computer software. Data that are protected under restricted rights are referred to as "restricted computer software."

*TIPS(2-5)*

See "Rights in Technical Data."

## RETROACTIVE PRICING

A pricing decision made after some or all of the work specified under contract has been completed. The pricing is based on a review of performance and recorded cost data.

*Commercial Practices*

## RETURN ON INVESTMENT (ROI)

A measure of income or profit divided by the investment required to help obtain the income or profit. That is, given the same risks for any given amount of resources required, the investor wants the maximum income.

*MGMT*

## REVENUE RECOGNITION AND REALIZATION

Generally accepted accounting principles (GAAP) state that revenue should be recognized (realized) when the earning process is virtually complete and when an exchange has taken place. There are exceptions to this rule, particularly in the case of percentage-of-completion construction contracts where revenue is recognized over the life of the construction project. The purpose of the revenue realization principle is to provide an accurate representation of the economic substance of revenue-related transactions.

*NCMA-CA*

## REVERSE AUCTION

A single buyer of a single item (or lot of items) receives decreasing offers from prospective sellers. The auction ends at a predetermined time, and the item is purchased from the lowest offeror for the lowest offer price.

*Linster*

## REVERSE ENGINEERING

Process whereby a product is analyzed to determine the composition of its various design elements for the purpose of producing a like product or performance capability.

*P&L*

## REVERSE MARKETING

An aggressive approach to developing a relationship with a supplier. The buyer takes the initiative in making the proposal for the relationship and the specific business transaction a reversal of the usual buyer and supplier marketing practice.

*Commercial Practices*

## REVOLVING DOOR

The process of government employees leaving government service to join private industry. Restrictions on such employment are contained in 18 U.S.C. 207 (civilian employees) and 37 U.S.C. 801 (military employees). These provisions are amplified and interpreted by regulations issued by the Office of Government Ethics at 5 C.F.R. 2637 and 2641. Additional restrictions are contained in the procurement integrity rules. Special statutory provisions

governing post-government employment with defense contractors are
contained in 10 U.S.C. 2397 et seq.

*NS*

## RIGHTS IN TECHNICAL DATA

The right for the government to acquire
technical data. If the government has
funded or will fund a part of or the entire
development of the item, component,
or process, then the government is
entitled to unlimited rights for using
the technical data. However, if the
data are developed by a contractor or
subcontractor exclusively at private
expense, the government is entitled
to limited rights. Such data must be
unpublished and identified as limited
rights data.

*DSMC*

See also "Government Purpose
License Rights (GPLR)," "Limited
Rights," "Restricted Rights," and
"Unlimited Rights."

## RISK

(1) The probability of not attaining the
goals for which the party entered into
a contract. For the government, the
principal risks are the following:

- The total cost of the acquisition will
  be higher than expected or unreasonable in relation to the actual
  costs of performance.
- The contractor will fail to deliver or
  will not deliver on time.
- The final deliverable will not satisfy
  the government's actual need,

whether or not "acceptable" under the terms and conditions of the
contract.

- The government's need will change
  before receipt of the deliverable.

*FAI*

(2) A measure of the inability to
achieve program objectives within
defined cost and schedule constraints.
Risk is associated with all aspects of
the program (e.g., threat, technology,
design processes, or work breakdown
structure (WBS) elements). Risk has
two components: (a) the probability of
failing to achieve a particular outcome,
and (b) the consequences of failing to
achieve that outcome.

*DAAT*

## RISK ANALYSIS

A detailed examination of each identified
program risk, which refines the
description of the risk, isolates the
cause, and determines the effect
of the program risk in terms of its
probability of occurrence, its consequences, and its relationship to other
risk areas or processes.

*DAAT*

## RISK ASSESSMENT

The process of subjectively determining
the probability that a specific interplay
of performance, schedule, and cost as
an objective will or will not be attained
along the planned course of action.

*P&L*

## RISK MANAGEMENT

(1) The process for identification, analysis, and treatment of loss exposure, as well as the administration of techniques to accomplish the goals of a company in minimizing potential financial loss from such exposure.

*F&F*

(2) Risk management is the process of planning, analyzing, tracking, and controlling events that could put a project or contract in danger of not being completed on time, within schedule, or within budget. Risk management is a key component in reducing acquisition cycle time and in cutting costs.

*NES-00*

## ROBINSON-PATMAN ACT

Section 2(a) of the Clayton Act, as amended in 1936 by the Robinson-Patman Act (15 U.S.C.A. 13), makes it unlawful for any seller engaged in commerce to directly or indirectly discriminate in the price charged purchasers on the sale of commodities of like grade and quality where the effect may be to injure, destroy, or prevent competition with (a) any person who grants or knowingly receives discrimination, or (b) the customer of either.

*BLD*

See also "Clayton Act" and "Sherman Antitrust Act."

## RULE 4 FILE

A file containing the contracting officer's (CO's) final decision; the contract; and any pertinent correspondence, affidavits, or related information that is prepared pursuant to Rule 4 of the Rules of the Armed Services Board of Contract Appeals (ASBCA).

*GUIDE*

# S

## SAFETY STOCK
A minimum or buffer inventory as a cushion against reasonable expected maximum usage. The appropriate level of safety stock depends on the cost of running out of inventory versus the carrying cost of the safety stock.

*MGMT*

## SALVAGE
Surplus material or equipment that has a market value and can be sold.

*Commercial Practices*

## SAMPLE SIZE
Number of units to be selected for the random samples.

*DGCQI*

## SAMPLING
Method of obtaining statistics from a large body of data without resorting to a complete census of the data. Two broad methods of selecting samples are (a) probability sampling (in which sample units are selected according to the law of chance) and (b) nonprobability sampling (in which personal choice, expert judgment, or some other nonprobabilistic rationale is used to select sample units).

*Cohen*

## SCHEDULE CONTRACT
See "Federal Supply Schedule (FSS) Program."

## SCHEDULE VARIANCE (SV)
(1) Comparing the earned budget (the value of work accomplished) during a given period of time to the value of work scheduled (planned budget) during the same period of time provides a valuable indication of schedule status in terms of dollars worth of work accomplished. It represents the quantity (i.e., the value) of the work that is ahead of or behind schedule. In essence, it is an "accomplishment" variance.

(2) The difference between the Budgeted Cost of Work Performed (BCWP) and the Budgeted Cost of Work Scheduled (BCWS) (Schedule Variance (SV) = BCWP − BCWS).

*DAAT*

## SCRAP
(1) The loss of labor and material resulting from defects that cannot be economically repaired or used.

*DGCQI*

(2) Residual material resulting from machine or assembly processes, such as machine shavings, unusable lengths of wire, faulty parts.

*DOD-MMH*

## SEALED-BID PROCEDURE

A method of procurement involving the unrestricted solicitation of bids, a public opening, and award of a contract to the lowest responsible bidder.

*NCMA-SB*

See also "Invitation for Bids (IFB)."

## SECOND SOURCE

An acquisition strategy that establishes two or more producers for the same part, system, or service for the purpose of increasing competition or broadening the industrial base.

*P&L*

## SECONDARY COMPARISON

A means of accomplishing price analysis. Secondary comparisons are used to support primary comparisons. When no primary data are available, a combination of secondary comparisons may result in a determination that a price is fair and reasonable. Types of secondary comparisons are comparative analysis, historical prices, market data, index numbers, cost estimating relationships, government catalogs, and government estimates.

*W-ICPA*

Compare "Auxiliary Techniques" and

"Primary Comparison."
See also "Comparative Analysis," "Cost Estimating Relationships (CER)," "Historical Prices," and "Market Data."

## SECTION 8(a) SUBCONTRACT

(1) A subcontract between the Small Business Administration (SBA) and a socially and economically disadvantaged business concern.

*NES-89*

(2) Named after the section of the Small Business Act (SBA) that authorized it.

*TIPS(2-9)*

(3) Firms approved for the 8(a) Program cannot exceed nine years in the program.

*W-CC*

## SECTION 800 PANEL

A panel tasked with streamlining defense acquisition laws by Section 800 of the fiscal year (FY) 1991 National Defense Authorization Act. The panel's official name is the Advisory Panel on Streamlining and Codifying Acquisition Laws. The panel presented to Congress an 1,800-page study in January 1993 titled Streamlining Defense Acquisition Laws.

*TIPS(4-7)*

See also "National Performance Review (NPR)."

## SECTION 1207 PROGRAM
Named after the section of the Department of Defense (DOD) Appropriations Act of 1987 (P.L. 99-661) that authorized it, this program allows DOD to "set aside" contracts for socially and economically disadvantaged firms. The program also allows DOD to apply a 10 percent evaluation preference when awarding a contract to a socially and economically disadvantaged business that competes in unrestricted procurements.

*TIPS(2-9)*

## SECTOR
Certain commercial activities are common to more than one agency. Many of these commercial activities can be aggregated. For example, an agency may inventory transportation acquisition, operations, maintenance, and disposal as independent commercial activities.

*OMB A-76*

## SEPARABLE COST
A cost directly identifiable with a particular segment.

*NCMA-CA*

## SERVICE CONTRACT
(1) A contract for the time and services of individuals or organizations in support of a government objective.

*OPM*

(2) A contract that directly engages the time and effort of a contractor whose primary purpose is to perform an identifiable task rather than furnish an end item of supply.

*W-CCC*

See also "Contracting Out."

## SERVICE CONTRACT ACT
Federal law establishing labor standards for such matters as wages and working conditions, which applies to every government contract over $2,500 when its principal purpose is to furnish services to the government.

*GUIDE*

See also "Professional Services."

## SERVICE RECIPIENT
An agency organizational unit, programmatic entity, or chargeable account that receives information processing services from an information processing service organization (IPSO). A service recipient may be either internal or external to the organization responsible for providing information resources services, but normally does not report either to the manager or director of the IPSO or to the same immediate supervisor.

*OMB A-130*

## SET-ASIDE
(1) A kind or class of procurement reserved for contenders that fit a certain category (e.g., business size, region, minority status).

*OPM*

(2) A set-aside can be total or partial, or a class set-aside (whereby a class of acquisitions of selected products or services may be set aside for exclusive participation by small business concerns).

*FAR*

Compare "Unrestricted Procurement." See also "Partial Set-Aside" and "Total Set-Aside."

## SETTLEMENT PROPOSAL
A proposal for effecting settlement of a contract terminated in whole or in part.

*FAR*

## SEVERABLE CONTRACT
A contract divisible into separate parts; a default of one section does not invalidate the whole contract.

*FBL*

## SEVERABLE EXPANSION
A severable expansion is an expansion of currently contracted, in-house, or interservice support agreement (ISSA) provided work that could be provided using the current approach or could be provided, without severe additional administrative burden, by another competitive offeror. Economies of scale are not justification for dismissing new or expanded work as severable; these economies will be tested through competitive offer.

*OMB A-76*

## SHARP PRACTICE
Indirect misrepresentation, unscrupulous shrewdness, deceit, or trickery, practices that are just short of actual fraud. Such actions are usually designed for short-term gain, but typically act to the detriment of good long-term supplier relations on the basis of honesty, truth, and respect.

*Commercial Practices*

## SHERMAN ANTITRUST ACT
The Sherman Antitrust Act (15 U.S.C.A. 1–7) prohibits any unreasonable interference by contract, combination, or conspiracy with the ordinary, usual, and freely competitive pricing or distribution system of the open market in interstate trade.

*BLD*

See also "Clayton Act" and "Robinson-Patman Act."

## SHIFT PREMIUM
The difference between the contractor's regular rate of pay to an employee and the higher rate paid for extra-pay-shift work.

*FAR*

## SHOULD COST
(1) An estimate of what an item or system should cost according to evaluation by independent reviewers of all applicable contractor business methods (contrasting more efficient methods with present contractor

methods). This evaluation should include subcontractor procedures when subcontracting is part of the proposal. The result is used to develop realistic price objectives for contract negotiation purposes.

*L&P*

(2) An estimate of contract price that reflects reasonably achievable contractor economy and efficiency. It is accomplished by a government team of procurement, contract administration, audit, and engineering representatives performing an in-depth cost analysis at the contractor's and subcontractor's plants. Its purpose is to develop a realistic price objective for negotiation purposes.

*DAAT*

## SHOW CAUSE LETTER
A written delinquency notice informing a contractor of failure to perform within the specified terms of the contract, and advising that the government is considering termination for default. Affords the contractor the opportunity to show cause why it should not be terminated.

*OPM*
See also "Default Termination."

## SHRINKAGE
An additional quantity of material added to the quantity listed on the bill of materials (BOM) to provide for spoilage, scrap, waste, and natural attrition.

*DOD-MMH*
See also "Attrition."

## SIMPLIFIED ACQUISITION THRESHOLD
The threshold means $100,000, except for acquisitions of supplies or services that, as determined by the head of the agency, are to be used to support a contingency operation or to facilitate defense against or recovery from nuclear, biological, chemical, or radiological attack. The term means (a) $250,000 for any contract to be awarded and performed, or purchase to be made, inside the United States, and (b) $1 million for any contract to be awarded and performed, or purchase to be made, outside the United States. Definition and threshold revised in sixth edition.

*FAR*

## SIMPLIFIED PROCEDURES
(1) Methods for entering into contracts without using elaborate and formal solicitation techniques (i.e., invitation for bids (IFB) and request for proposal (RFP). Procedures are restricted to purchases under the simplified acquisition threshold (anticipated dollar value exceeding $2,500 and not exceeding $100,000). Threshold revised in sixth edition.

*McVay*

(2) Means the methods prescribed in Federal Acquisition Regulation (FAR), Part 13, for making purchases of supplies or services.

*FAR*

## SINGLE AWARD SCHEDULE (SAS)

Contracts made with one supplier, pursuant to the Federal Supply Schedule (FSS) Program, to cover delivery to one geographic area.

*W-PSP*

See also "Federal Supply Schedule (FSS) Program."

## SINGLE PROCESS INITIATIVE (SPI)

The process for making block changes to existing contracts to replace multiple government-unique manufacturing and management systems with common facility-wide systems, so as to unify the manufacturing and management requirements of these contracts on a facility-wide basis.

*DAAT*

## SINGLE SOURCE

One source among others in a competitive marketplace which, for justifiable reason, is found to be most advantageous for the purpose of contract award.

*OPM*

## SIZE STANDARDS

Measures established by the Small Business Administration (SBA) to determine whether a business qualifies as a small business for purposes of implementing the socioeconomic programs enumerated in Part 19 of the Federal Acquisition Regulation (FAR). SBA size standards establish ceilings on either the number of employees or the amount of annual revenue for each standard industrial classification (SIC) code.

*F&F*

See also "Standard Industrial Classification (SIC) Code."

## SMALL AND DISADVANTAGED BUSINESS (SDB) CONCERNS

A business whose size meets government size requirements for its particular industry type, or a business owned (at least 51 percent) by members of socially and economically disadvantaged groups (i.e., groups that have been subjected to racial or ethnic prejudice or cultural bias).

*OPM*

## SMALL AND DISADVANTAGED BUSINESS UTILIZATION SPECIALIST (SADBUS)

An advocate for small, minority, and women-owned businesses who is located at each military and civilian activity that has a procurement office.

*McVay*

## SMALL BUSINESS ACT (SBA)

The Small Business Act (15 U.S.C. 631 et seq.) is a federal law providing preferences for small and small disadvantaged businesses in government contracting.

*GUIDE*

## SMALL BUSINESS ADMINISTRATION (SBA)

The government agency whose function is to aid, counsel, provide financial assistance to, as well as protect the interests of, the small business community.

*McVay*

## SMALL BUSINESS COMPETITIVE-NESS DEMONSTRATION PROGRAM (SBCDP)

A test program established by the Business Opportunity Development Reform Act (P.L. 100-656) whereby 8(a) small business set-asides in four designated industry groups (DIGs) were eliminated for a test period initially set for January 1989 through December 1992, but later extended through September 1996 by the Small Business Credit and Business Opportunity Enhancement Act (P.L. 102-366). The four DIGs are (a) construction, (b) refuse, (c) nonnuclear ship repair, and (d) architect and engineering services including surveying and mapping.

*TIPS(5-1)*

## SMALL BUSINESS CONCERN

A business that is independently owned and operated and that is not dominant in its field; a business concern meeting government size standards for its particular industry type.

*OPM*

## SMALL BUSINESS CREDIT AND BUSINESS OPPORTUNITY ENHANCEMENT ACT

See "Small Business Competitiveness Demonstration Program (SBCDP)."

## SMALL BUSINESS INNOVATION RESEARCH (SBIR) PROGRAM

A program that requires federal agencies with research and development (R&D) budgets in excess of $100 million to set aside a fixed percentage of their budgets exclusively for small business participation.

*McVay*

## SMALL PURCHASE PROCEDURES

Actions involved in the purchasing, rental, or lease of supplies or services as an exception to the statutory requirement to procure by means of formal advertising in order to ensure rapid delivery of a large volume of purchases, to reduce administrative costs and paperwork, and to improve opportunities for small and disadvantaged business concerns. The procedures include imprest fund (cash) actions, purchase orders, orders under blanket purchase agreements (BPAs), or orders issued under federal supply schedules (FSSs).

*OPM*

See also "Simplified Acquisition Threshold."

## SMART CARDS

Purchase cards defined as "plastic cards the size of standard credit cards containing a microchip that can store user data, provide security features, and provide computational capability." The government uses purchase cards such as these as part of its simplified acquisition process.

*NES-98*

## SOCIOECONOMIC PROGRAMS

Programs designed to benefit particular groups. They represent a multitude of program interests and objectives unrelated to procurement objectives. Some examples are preferences for small businesses and American products, required sources for speci-fied items, and minimum labor pay levels mandated for contractors.

*Sherman2*

## SOLE SOURCE ACQUISITION

A contract for the purchase of supplies or services that is entered into or that is proposed to be entered into after soliciting and negotiating with only one source.

*FAR*

## SOLICITATION

A document requesting or inviting offerors to submit offers. Solicitations basically consist of (a) a draft con-tract, and (b) provisions on preparing and submitting offers.

*FAI*

## SOURCE DATA

Data generated in the course of research, development, design engineering, and production of systems, material, and services.

*AFIT*

## SOURCE SELECTION

The process wherein the requirements, facts, recommendations, and policies relevant to an award decision in a competitive procurement of a system or project are examined and the decision made.

*DSMC*

See also "Rating System."

## SOURCE SELECTION ADVISORY COUNCIL

A group of people who are appointed by the Source Selection Authority (SSA). The Council is responsible for reviewing and approving the source selection plan (SSP) and the solicita-tion of competitive awards for major and certain less-than-major procure-ments. The Council also determines what proposals are in the competitive range, and it provides recommenda-tions to the SSA for final selection.

*Navy*

## SOURCE SELECTION AUTHORITY (SSA)

The person who makes the final source selection in a competition. The

SSA is responsible for ensuring that the entire source selection process is properly and efficiently conducted.

*Navy*

## SOURCE SELECTION EVALUATION BOARD (SSEB)

A group of personnel representing the various functional and technical disciplines relevant to the acquisition whose function is to evaluate proposals and report its findings.

*NCMA-SS*

## SOURCE SELECTION INFORMATION

Information that is prepared or developed for use by the government to conduct a particular procurement. The procurement is determined by the head of the agency or the contracting officer (CO) to be information that, if disclosed to a competing contractor, would jeopardize the integrity or successful completion of the procurement involved. Source selection information is required by law, regulation, or order to be secured in a source selection file or other facility to prevent such disclosure.

*GSA*

## SOURCE SELECTION PLAN (SSP)

(1) The document that describes the selection criteria, the process, and the organization to be used in evaluating proposals for competitively awarded contracts.

*Navy*

(2) The SSP is written by the Program Office and approved by the Source Selection Authority (SSA). Typically, the SSP consists of two parts. The first part describes the organization and responsibilities of the source selection team. The second part identifies the evaluation criteria and detailed procedures for proposal evaluation.

*DAAT*

## SPEARIN DOCTRINE

A rule that takes its name from a 1918 Supreme Court case. The case stated that by providing the contractor with specifications to be followed in carrying out the contract work, the government implied warrants that, if the contractor complies with those specifications, an adequate result will follow.

*BP(91-8)*

Also known as "Implied Warranty of Specifications."

## SPECIAL TEST EQUIPMENT

Either single- or multi-purpose integrated test units that are engineered, designed, fabricated, or modified to accomplish special-purpose testing in performing a contract. The equipment consists of items or assemblies of equipment that are interconnected and interdependent so as to become a new functional entity for special testing purposes.

*FAR*

## SPECIAL TOOLING

Jigs, dies, fixtures, molds, patterns, taps, gauges, other equipment and manufacturing aids, all components of these items, and replacement of these items are termed special tooling. The items are of such a specialized nature that without substantial modification or alteration their use is limited to the development or production of particular supplies or parts thereof to the performance of particular services.

*FAR*

## SPECIFICATION

(1) A description of the technical requirements for a material, product, or service that includes the criteria for determining that the requirements have been met.

*NCMA-SP*

(2) There are generally three types of specifications used in government contracting: performance, functional, and design.

*FAR*

(3) Performance-based specifications define an item's functional requirements or capabilities, the environment in which the item must operate, the item's interface and interchangeability characteristics, and the criteria for verifying the item's compliance. These specs do not describe how a requirement is to be achieved, nor do they require the use of specific materials or parts or give any detailed design or construction requirements beyond those that are needed to ensure interchangeability with existing items. Detailed specifications prescribe the design requirements, such as how the item is to be fabricated or what materials must be used. A spec that contains both performance and prescriptive requirements is still considered a detailed spec.

*NES-97*
See also "Spearin Doctrine."

## SPECULATIVE BUYING

Purchasing material in excess of current and future known requirements, with the intention of profiting on price movement.

*Commercial Practices*

## SPIRAL DEVELOPMENT

See "Evolutionary Acquisition (EA)."

## SPLIT-OFF POINT

See "Joint Products Costs."

## SPOILAGE

A form of waste material resulting from misuse of material or errors in workmanship.

*DOD-MMH*

## STANDARD

A document that establishes engineering and technical limitations and applications of items, materials, processes, methods, designs, and engineering practices. It includes any related criteria deemed essential to achieve the highest practical degree of uniformity in materials or products, or interchangeability of parts used in those products.

*FAR*

## STANDARD ABSORPTION COSTING

The type of product costing in which the cost of the finished unit is calculated as the sum of the standard allowances for the factors of production, without reference to the costs actually incurred.

*NCMA-CA*

## STANDARD COST

A cost determined to represent an expected value; a goal or baseline that is used to expedite the costing of transactions, and that is determined from historical experience or contrived from the best information available. Excepting costs attributable to precise and highly predictable operations, actual costs will almost always vary from standard costs due to factors (usually called variances) that affect performance, such as employee fatigue, unforeseen interruptions, and other delays.

*Cohen*

## STANDARD DIRECT COSTING

That type of product costing in which the cost of the finished unit is calculated as the sum of the costs of the standard allowance for the factors of production, excluding fixed factory overhead, which is treated as a period cost, and without reference to the costs actually incurred.

*NCMA-CA*

## STANDARD FORM (SF)

A set of standard provisions or terms issued for use by all government agencies in regard to procurement matters.

*GUIDE*

## STANDARD HOURS ALLOWED (EARNED OR WORKED)

The number of standard hours that are chargeable to production for the actual goods produced.

*NCMA-CA*

## STANDARD INDUSTRIAL CLASSIFICATION (SIC) CODE

A code representing a category that is within the SIC system and is administered by the Statistical Policy Division of the U.S. Office of Management and Budget (OMB). The system was established to classify all industries in the U.S. economy. A two-digit code designates each major industry group, which is coupled with a second two-digit code representing subcategories. SIC codes are published in the Standard Industrial Classification Manual.

*F&F*

See also "Size Standards."

## STANDARDIZATION, INDUSTRIAL

The process of establishing agreement on uniform identifications for definite characteristics of quality, design, performance, quantity, service, etc. A uniform identification is called a "standard."

*DBL*

## STANDARDS

- Private-sector or nongovernment standards are documents that are developed by companies, consortia, industry and trade associations, and technical societies. The groups are collectively referred to as standards-developing organizations

- Voluntary or consensus standards are standards established by a private sector body and available for public use. The term does not include private standards of individual firms.

- De facto standards are widely recognized by the companies in an industry but are not formally docu-mented by an accepted standards-developing organization. Because they are usually not documented, de facto standards should not generally be used for government procurement.

- Company or consortium standards are developed by a company or group of companies and are maintained for internal use. These standards are usually developed without outside comment. They are usually applied across products and may be licensed to outside parties.

- Association standards result from agreements that have been reached between the key economic players in a sector: suppliers, users, and often governments. The players agree on specifications and standards that are to be applied consistently in their sector's (a) classification of materials, (b) manufacture of products, and (c) provision of services.

- American National Standards are those standards that have been approved by the American National Standards Institute (ANSI), which is a private, not-for-profit membership organization that coordinates the U.S. voluntary, consensus-based standards system and that represents the United States in the International Standards Organization for Standardization (ISO).

- The ISO is a worldwide federation of national standards bodies from approximately 100 countries. The ISO develops, coordinates, and promotes international standards. ISO standards cover all fields except electrical and electronic engineer-ing, which is the responsibility of the International Electrotechnical Com-mission. Work in the field of informa-tion technology (IT) is carried out by a joint ISO/IEC technical committee.

- The IEC develops and promotes standards in electrical and electronic engineering. It is composed of national committees, of which 49 exist at the present. These committees represent the major industrial countries.

- MILSPECS was born from the lessons learned during the period of World War II. MILSPECS is a broad term referring to a variety of technical military documents, to include military standards, military handbooks, military bulletins, and other documents listed in the Department of Defense (DOD) Index of Specifications and Standards (DODISS).

- GSA specs and standards are defined as either of the following:

    - FEDSPECs—nonmilitary federal documents that are issued or controlled by the General Services Administration (GSA) and that are listed in the GSA Index; or
    - CIDS (commercial item descriptions)—a standard product specification that is written by the government and that describes a commercial item's essential functional, performance, or physical requirements. The government uses CIDs to buy items that are sold in commercial markets and that have established prices.

*NES-97*

## STANDARDS OF CONDUCT

The ethical conduct of personnel involved in the acquisition of goods and services. Within the federal government, business shall be conducted in a manner above reproach and, except as authorized by law or regulation, with complete impartiality and without preferential treatment.

*Garrett*

## START DATE

This term is used in two ways. First, it is the date when a cost comparison begins, generally defined as the date that a local study team is formed and actual work on the performance work statement (PWS), management plan, and in-house cost estimate begins. Second, it may refer to the actual date work is scheduled to begin under a contract, as provided in the solicitation.

*OMB A-76*

## STATEMENT OF OBJECTIVES (SOO)

The portion of a contract that establishes a broad description of the government's required performance objectives.

*DAAT*

## STATEMENT OF WORK (SOW)

(1) The portion of a contract describing the actual work to be done by means of specifications or other minimum

requirements, quantities, performance date, and a statement of the requisite quality.

*DSMC*

(2) The SOW for the project should reflect all work to be performed. The SOW communicates the work scope requirements for a program and should define the requirements to the fullest extent practicable. It is a basic element of control used in the processes of work assignment and establishment of program schedules and budgets.

*EVMIG*

## STATIC BUDGET
A budget prepared for only one level of activity and, consequently, one that does not adjust automatically to changes in the level of volume.

*NCMA-CA*

## STATISTICAL PROCESS CONTROL (SPC)
The application of statistical methods to monitor variation in a process over time. SPC displays variation in a process to identify special or assignable causes of variation versus common or chance causes of variation.

*DGCQI*

## STATUTE
A law enacted by the legislative branch of government and signed by the president. It is identifiable by a

Public Law (P.L.) number.

*FAI*

## STATUTE OF LIMITATIONS
A statute that sets limits to the time in which a lawsuit may be filed in certain causes of action.

*FBL*

## STEVENSON-WYDLER TECHNOLOGY INNOVATION ACT
This Act (P.L. 96-480) emphasized a national policy of transferring technology from federal laboratories to industry by setting aside 0.5 percent of each agency's research budget to fund technology transfer.

*IIPS(1-14)*

## STOCKLESS PURCHASING
See "Systems Contract."

## STOCKOUT
Occurs when items normally carried in stock are exhausted.

*Commercial Practices*

## STOP WORK ORDER
A request for interim stoppage of work as a result of nonconformance, funding, or technical considerations.

*Garrett*

## STREAMLINING
(1) Allows flexibility for application of contractor's expertise, judgment, and creativity in meeting requirements. It

insures only cost-effective requirements are included in solicitation and
contracts.

*DAAT*

(2) It is broadly used to denote efforts
to shorten the acquisition process.

*DAAT*

Also See "Acquisition Streamlining."

## SUBCONTRACT
A contract between a buyer and a
seller in which a significant part of the
supplies or services being obtained
is for eventual use in a government
[prime] contract.

*DSMC*

## SUBCONTRACT DATA REQUIRE-
## MENTS LIST (SCDRL)
See "Contract Data Requirements List
(CDRL)."

## SUBCONTRACTING
## MANAGEMENT
A concept that addresses subcontracting issues and the government's
(buyer's) role in ensuring successful
prime contractor interaction with
subcontractors in order to satisfy
prime contract requirements.

*DSMC*

## SUBCONTRACTING PLAN
A subcontracting plan is required
for an acquisition that is expected to
exceed $500,000 and that has subcon-

tracting possibilities. It must contain
goals for both small businesses and
small disadvantaged businesses.
The goals are stated in terms of
percentages of dollars awarded and
are negotiated with the contracting
officer (CO) or the agency's small and
disadvantaged business utilization
specialist (SADBUS) before the contract is awarded. The negotiated plan
is subsequently incorporated into the
contract by reference. Small businesses
themselves are exempt from the
requirement to submit a subcontracting
plan (FAR 19.702).

*TIPS(2-9)*

See also "Subcontracting
Preference."

## SUBCONTRACTING PREFERENCE
A government policy that encourages
prime contractors to assist minority
companies by requiring that prime
contractors develop subcontracting
plans. On all contracts over the
simplified acquisition threshold,
contractors must agree to allow small
and small disadvantaged businesses
(SDBs) opportunities to participate in
contract performance (FAR 19.702).
In acquisitions that are expected
to exceed $500,000 and that have
subcontracting possibilities, the bidder
selected for award must formalize its
intent to allow small businesses and
SDBs opportunities by submitting a
subcontracting plan. Threshold
revised in sixth edition.

*TIPS(2-9)*
See also "Subcontracting Plan."

## SUBCONTRACTOR
A contractor that enters into a contract with a prime contractor or a subcontractor of the prime contractor.

*DSMC*

## SUBJECT MATTER EXPERTS
Term used to describe those people who have a good understanding of particular user requirements and of the technology and tools available to meet those requirements.

*NES-96*

## SUBSTANTIAL PERFORMANCE
Doctrine that prohibits termination of a contract for default if a contractor's performance deviates only in minor respects from the contract's requirements.

*GUIDE*

## SUNK COST
A cost that has already been incurred and that, therefore, is irrelevant to the decision-making process.

*NCMA-CA*
See also "Historical Costs."

## SUPERIOR KNOWLEDGE
Government liability for nondisclosure of information is based on an implied duty to disclose information that is vital for the preparation of estimates or for contract performance. This implied duty is consistent with the general contract law concepts of good faith and fair dealing. The contractor must show that the government possessed the undisclosed information.Knowledge of one government agency will not be attributed to another government agency without some meaningful connection between the agencies.

*NC-A*

## SUPPLEMENTAL AGREEMENT
(1) Any contract modification that is accomplished by the mutual action of the parties.

*OPM*

(2) Bilateral written modification to a contract by which the government and the contractor settle any price or performance adjustments to the basic contract.

*DAAT*

## SUPPLEMENTAL APPROPRIATION
An appropriation enacted as an addition to a regular annual appropriation act. Supplemental appropriations provide additional budget authority (BA) beyond original estimates for programs or activities that are too urgent to be postponed until the next regular appropriation.

*DAAT*

## SUPPLIER
The individual or concern that is actually performing services, or that

is manufacturing, producing, and shipping any supplies required by the contract or subcontract.

*AFIT*

## SUPPLIER RATING SYSTEM

A system used to evaluate and rate suppliers' performance, which generally involves quality, service, delivery, and price. Rating formulas vary depending on the nature of the item being purchased, the quality required, and the competition within the supplying industry.

*Commercial Practices*

See also "Performance Risk Assessment Group."

## SUPPLY MANAGEMENT

(1) A systems management concept that is used by some organizations and that is designed to optimize the factors of material costs, quality, and service. This optimization is accomplished by consolidating the following operating activities: purchasing, transportation, warehousing, quality assurance for incoming materials, inventory management, and internal distribution of materials. These activities normally are combined in a single department, similar to the arrangement under a materials management form of organization.

*Commercial Practices*

(2) A continuing evolving management philosophy that seeks to unify the collective productive competencies and resources of the business functions found both within an enterprise and outside a firm's allied business partners along intersecting supply channels into a highly competitive, customer-enriching supply system that is focused on developing innovative solutions and on synchronizing the flow of marketplace products, services, and information to create unique, individualized sources of customer value.

*NES-00*

## SURETY

An individual or corporation legally liable to the debt, default, or failure of a principal to satisfy a contractual obligation.

*FAR*

## SURPLUS

The materials that are in excess of a firm's operational requirements. Surpluses typically originate from three primary sources: (a) scrap and waste; (b) surplus, obsolete, or damaged stocks; and (c) surplus, obsolete, or damaged equipment.

*DBL*

## SURPLUS, DISPOSAL OF

When material is declared surplus, the materials management, purchasing, or other such department, as appropriate, is informed. Following this action, disposal is made by one of seven methods: (a) use within the firm,

(b) return to the supplier, (3c) direct sale to another firm, (d) sale to a dealer or broker, (e) sale to employees, (f) donations to educational institutions, or (g) some combination of the preceding.

*DBL*

## SUSPENSION

Action taken by a suspending official to disqualify a contractor temporarily from government contracting and subcontracting.

*FAR*

Compare "Debarment."
See also "Consolidated List of Debarred, Suspended, and Ineligible Contractors."

## SUSPENSION OF WORK CLAUSE

Allows the buyer the right to temporarily halt the work. It may provide a maximum time period for such suspension.

*Cohen*

## SWITCH TRADING

This term refers to the use of a third-party trading house in a countertrade arrangement in which switch traders frequently trade countertrade credits for cash, and the trading house then sells the credits to another country that needs the goods in that particular country.

*Commercial Practices*

## SYNOPSIS

An abbreviated description of a procurement that is published in the Commerce Business Daily (CBD) in advance of the procurement, along with the contracting officer's (CO's) name, for the purpose of informing the commercial world of the opportunity to bid or submit an offer.

*OPM*

## SYSTEM

The organization of hardware, software, material, facilities, personnel, data, and services needed to perform a designated function with specified results, such as the gathering of specified data, its processing, and delivery to users. It can be a combination of two or more interrelated equipments (sets) arranged in a functional package to perform an operational function or to satisfy a requirement.

*DSMC*

## SYSTEM ACQUISITION PROCESS

The sequence of acquisition activities that start from an organization's delineation of its requirement needs, with its capabilities, priorities, and resources, and that extend through the introduction of a system into operational use.

*DSMC*

## SYSTEM ENGINEERING

The application of scientific and engineering efforts to transform an operational need into a description of a system configuration that (a) best satisfies the operational need according to the measures of effectiveness; (b) integrates related technical parameters; (c) ensures compatibility of all physical, functional, and technical program interfaces in a manner optimizing the total system definition and design; and (d) integrates the efforts of all engineering disciplines and specialties into the total engineering effort.

*DSMC*

## SYSTEMS CONTRACT

A contract that authorizes designated employees of the buying firm, using a predetermined release system, to place orders directly with the supplier for specified materials during a given contract period. One principal objective of systems contracting is to reduce the buyer's inventories to a level as low as is consistent with assured continuity of supply; thus, systems contracting is sometimes referred to as "Stockless Purchasing." Order releases under systems contracts should usually be made by personnel from the using department.

*DBL*

## TAILORING

The process by which individual sections, paragraphs, or sentences of a specification or solicitation are modified to meet the minimum requirements and the specific needs of the requestor.

*NCMA-SP*

## TARGET FISCAL YEAR

The fiscal year (FY) that is two FYs into the future from the current FY; the year for detailed consideration in programming.

*AFIT*

## TARIFF

A schedule or rate of duties imposed on imports includes the following:

- General Category
- Special Group A Category
- Special Group E Category
- Other Category

*NES-94*

## TAX ACCOUNTING

Involves the measuring, recording, and reporting of relevant financial information in accordance with tax rules and regulations to interested users

(primarily, government authorities).

*NCMA-CA*

## TEAM ARRANGEMENT

An arrangement in which either (a) two or more companies form a partnorchip or joint venture to act as a potential prime contractor, or (b) a potential prime contractor agrees with one or more other companies to have them act as its subcontractor(s) under a specified government contract or acquisition program.

*FAR*

See also "Joint Venture."

## TEAMING

An agreement of two or more firms to form a partnership or joint venture to act as a potential prime contractor; an agreement by a potential prime contractor to act as a subcontractor under a specified acquisition program; or an agreement for a joint proposal resulting from a normal prime contractor–subcontractor, licensee–licenser, or leader company relationship.

*DAAT*

## TECHNICAL ANALYSIS

Evaluation, ordinarily conducted by engineering, technical, or specialized personnel, of the (a) technical and managerial qualifications of a contractor to perform a particular contract requirement, and (b) applicability or sufficiency of the technical solution proposed to fulfill contemplated contract requirements.

*P&L*

## TECHNICAL DATA (TD)

(1) Recorded information, regardless of the form or method of the recording, of a scientific or technical nature (including computer software documentation).

*DSMC*

(2) Scientific or technical information recorded in any form or medium (such as manuals and drawings) necessary to operate and maintain a defense system. Documentation of computer programs and related software are TD. Computer programs and related software are not TD. Also excluded are financial data or other information related to contract administration. One of the traditional elements of logistics support (LS).

*DAAT*

## TECHNICAL DATA PACKAGE

The documents, drawings, reports, manuals, revisions, technical orders, or other submissions as set forth as a Contract Data Requirements List (CDRL) line item to be delivered as required by contract.

*DOD-MMH*

See also "Contract Data Requirements List (CDRL)."

## TECHNICAL FACTORS

Factors other than price-related that are used in evaluating offers for award. Examples include technical excellence, management capability, personnel qualifications, prior experience, past performance, and schedule compliance.

*FAI*

## TECHNICAL LEVELING

Helping an offeror to bring its proposal up to the level of other proposals through successive rounds of discussion, such as by pointing out weaknesses resulting from the offeror's lack of diligence, competence, or inventiveness in preparing the proposal. This practice is not allowed in federal government contracting.

*FAR*

## TECHNICAL TRANSFUSION

Disclosure of technical information pertaining to a proposal, which results in improvement of a competing proposal. This practice is not allowed in federal government contracting.

*FAR*

## TECHNOLOGY INVESTMENT AGREEMENTS (TIAs)

Initially, TIAs were mainly used to fund development projects that had both military and civilian applications. These dual-use projects were primarily with consortia of interested organizations, which generally were composed of co-business partners who bonded together under articles of collaboration for the project. However, in 1994 the authority for other transactions (OTs) was expanded by the Department of Defense (DOD) National Authorization Act, Section 845, to acquire prototypes exclusively for military purposes. Prototypes have not been defined in detail in the law, so broad application is possible. TIAs are especially useful in the area of intellectual property rights.

*NES-99*

## TECHNOLOGY TRANSFER

The process by which federal scientific research and development (R&D) is transformed into commercially viable products and services.

*TIPS(1-14)*

## TERMINATION

An action taken pursuant to a contract clause in which the contracting officer (CO) unilaterally ends all or part of the work; it can be "Termination for Convenience," in which the ending of work is in the best interest of the government, or "Termination for Default," in which the contractor has not performed according to the terms of the contract.

*OPM*

See also "Convenience Termination" and "Default Termination."

## TERMINATION CLAIM

Any claim or demand by a prime contractor for compensation because of the termination before completion of any contract or subcontract for the convenience of the government.

*AFIT*

See also "Claim."

## TERMINATION CONTRACTING OFFICER (TCO)

The contracting officer (CO) assigned responsibility for settling terminations for default or convenience and for, in some cases, settling claims and actions involving extraordinary relief.

*OPM*

## TERMINATION INVENTORY

Any property purchased, supplied, manufactured, furnished, or otherwise acquired for the performance of a contract that was subsequently terminated and properly allocable to the terminated portion of the contract. It includes government-furnished property (GFP). It does not include facilities, material, special test equipment, or special tooling that is subject to a separate contract or to a special contract requirement governing its use or disposition.

*FAR*

## TERMS AND CONDITIONS
All language in a contract, including time of delivery, packing and shipping, applicable standard classes, and special provisions.

*OPM*

## TESTING
(1) The determination by technical means of the physical and chemical properties or elements of materials, supplies, or components, involving not so much the element of personal judgment as the application of established scientific principles and procedures.

*AFIT*

(2) An element of inspection.

*DOD-MMH*

## THEN-YEAR DOLLARS
See "Current Year Dollars."

## THIRD-PARTY NETWORK
In Electronic Data Interchange (EDI) operations, a third-party network firm functions as a central communications clearinghouse. It accepts the buyer's purchase orders (POs), separates them by supplier, and, at appropriate times, transmits them to the computer in each supplier's organization. In addition, the firm can provide format

translation and other value-added functions.

*Commercial Practices*

## THIRD-PARTY SERVICES
Services performed by any person or firm other than the buyer and supplier.

## TIERING
The incorporation of standards and specifications resulting from cross-referencing of successively lower levels. Automatic tiering occurs when documents are invoked implicitly by reference in the primary document.

*W-GSD*

## TIME AND MATERIALS (T&M) CONTRACTS
A type of contract providing for a fixed hourly rate, including overhead plus profit and material at cost plus handling charges. T&M is used when it is impossible to estimate the schedule and costs at the time of contract award.

*OPM*

## TIME VALUE OF FUTURE CASH FLOWS
See "Present Value of Future Cash Flows."

## TORNCELLO RULE
In Torncello v. United States (1982), the Court ruled that the Termination for Convenience clause could not

be used to avoid anticipated profits, unless there had been some change in circumstances between the time of award of the contract and the time of termination.

*NC-A*

## TOTAL COST

Sometimes called all-in costs. In purchasing, total cost generally includes the price of the purchase and transportation cost, plus indirect handling, inspection, quality, rework, maintenance, incremental operations, and all other follow-on costs associated with the purchase.

*Commercial Practices*

## TOTAL COST BASIS

(1) A means of pricing equitable adjustments when the costs associated with a claim are not clearly identifiable. When one uses the total cost approach, an equitable adjustment is calculated as the difference between the contractor's proposed price on the original contract and the actual total cost of performing the contract as changed.

*TIPS(2-12)*

(2) This method assumes that (a) all costs expended by the contractor were caused by the change, and (b) the contractor's original estimate was correct and reasonable.

*W-ATCC*

See also "Actual Cost Basis," "Jury Verdict Basis," and "Modified Total Cost Basis."

## TOTAL PRODUCTION CYCLE TIME

Total activity time required to produce one unit of the product.

*Commercial Practices*

## TOTAL QUALITY MANAGEMENT (TQM)

The government term for the philosophy and principles that guide a continuously improving organization. TQM is the application of quantitative methods and human resources to improve the material and services supplied to an organization, the processes within an organization, and the degree to which the needs of the customer are met.

*DGCQI*

## TOTAL SET-ASIDE

Most small business set-asides reserve the entire amount of an acquisition for small businesses. This reserve is known as a "total set-aside."

*W-SBC*

See also "Set-Aside."

## TOXIC SUBSTANCES CONTROL ACT (TSCA) (1976)

The Act controls the entry of toxic chemicals into the environment through a system of testing, inspections, and regulation. The purpose of the Act is to prevent or limit the use of chemicals in the first instance before conditions become hazardous.

*NES-94*

## TRADE ACCEPTANCE

A time draft or bill of exchange for the amount of purchase, which was drawn by the seller on the buyer and which bears the buyer's acceptance and the place of payment.

*Commercial Practices*

## TRADE AGREEMENTS ACT

The Trade Agreements Act of 1979 (19 U.S.C. 2501–2582) specifically prohibits the purchase of end product items from nondesignated countries, as determined by the U.S. Trade Representative. In particular, federal agencies are currently prohibited from procurements with certain Communist areas and with certain sanctioned persons.

*TIPS(1-15)*

## TRADE BALANCE

The shift between trade surplus (when a country is exporting more than it is importing) and a trade deficit (when the value of the goods being imported and that is greater than those being exported).

*NES-94*

## TRADE DISCOUNT

A discount from list price offered to all customers of a given type (e.g., discount offered by lumber dealer to building contractor). Contrast with a discount offered for prompt payment or a quantity discount.

*BLD*

## TRADE-OFF

Selection among alternatives with the intent of obtaining the optimal, achievable system configuration. Often, a decision is made to opt for less of one parameter in order to achieve a more favorable overall system result.

*DAAT*

## TRADE SECRET

A form of legal protection for any information used in a commercial trade or business that (a) is not generally known in the trade, (b) is used in secrecy, and (c) affords a competitive advantage. The Trade Secrets Act (18 U.S.C. 1905) restricts disclosure of trade secrets and provides for civil and criminal penalties for violations. A company does not need to request "trade secret" status from anyone. Rather, it can declare such a status by adhering to certain practices.

*TIPS(2-5)*

## TRADE TERMS

Conditions offered, or offered and accepted, as terms for a sale or payment for goods or services.

*Commercial Practices*

## TRANSPORTATION, MODES OF

Transportation is a means of moving freight traffic. A surprisingly large number of transportation methods are available: parcel post; private parcel delivery service; bus service; air cargo; rail freight, car load (CL), and less-than-car load (LCL); motor freight, truck load (TL), and less-than-truck load (LTL); freight forwarder; coastal, intercoastal, and inland water freight; piggyback and fishyback; and pipeline.

*DBL*

## TRAVELING (PURCHASE) REQUISITION

A purchase requisition designed for repetitive use (e.g., inventory items). It contains stock level data, potential suppliers, lead times, and, frequently, prices and predetermined order quantities, as well as other data needed for ordering. The requisition is sent to the purchasing department where a purchase order (PO) is prepared directly from it.

*Commercial Practices*

## TREASURY MEMORANDUM ACCOUNT

See "M" Account.

## TRUTH IN NEGOTIATIONS ACT (TINA)

Federal law enacted as P.L. 87-653 to provide the government with sufficient information before the contract award to ensure that it does not pay excessive prices for its procurements. TINA requires contractors to submit cost or pricing data and to certify that, to the contractor's best knowledge and belief, the data submitted are accurate, complete, and current.

*GUIDE*

## TUCKER ACT

The Act, 28 U.S.C. 1346(a) and 1491, waives sovereign immunity from suit for all claims founded upon any contract, express or implied, with the U.S. government.

*NS*

## THE 1207 PROGRAM

See "Section 1207 Program."

## TWO-STEP SEALED BIDDING

A combination of competitive procedures designed to obtain the benefits of sealed bidding when adequate specifications are not available. An objective is to permit the development of a sufficiently descriptive and not an unduly restrictive statement of the government's requirements, including an adequate technical data package, so that subsequent acquisitions may be made by conventional sealed bidding. This method is especially useful in acquisitions requiring technical proposals, particularly those for complex items. Step one consists of the request for submission of technical proposals, evaluation, and discussions without pricing. Step two involves the submission of sealed-priced bids by those who submitted acceptable technical proposals in step one.

*FAR*

## TYING AGREEMENTS

An agreement or understanding to sell a desired product on the condition that the customer must buy another of the supplier's products.

*BCG*

## UNALLOWABLE COST

Any cost that, under the provisions of any pertinent law, regulation, or contract, cannot be included in prices, cost-reimbursements, or settlements under a government contract to which it is allocable.

*FAR*

## UNCOMPENSATED OVERTIME

Work that exempt employees perform above and beyond 40 hours per week.

*OPM*

Also known as "Competitive Time," "Deflated Hourly Rates," "Direct Allocation of Salary Costs," "Discounted Hourly Rates," "Extended Work Week," "Full-time Accounting," and "Green Time."

*TIPS(2-11)*

See also "Exempt Employee" and "Professional Services."

## UNCONSCIONABILITY

The basic test of "unconscionability" of a contract is whether, under circumstances existing at the time of making the contract and in light of general commercial background and the commercial needs of a particular trade or case, clauses involved are so one-sided as to oppress or unfairly surprise the party. Unconscionability is generally recognized to include an absence of meaningful choice on the part of one of the parties to a contract, together with contract terms that are unreasonably favorable to the other party. Typically, the cases in which unconscionability is found involve gross overall one-sidedness or gross one-sidedness of a term disclaiming a warranty, limiting damages, or granting procedural advantages.

*BLD*

## UNDEFINITIZED CONTRACT ACTION

(1) Any contract action for which the contract terms, specifications, or price are not agreed upon before performance is begun under the action.

*Navy*

(2) Any contract action for which the terms, specifications, or price are not agreed upon before performance is begun under the action. Examples are letter contracts, orders under basic ordering agreements, and provisioned item orders for which the price has not been agreed upon before performance has begun. Letter contracts await

negotiation to definitize prices.

*DAAT*

## UNEXPENDED BALANCE
The amount of budget authority (BA) previously granted to an agency but still unspent and available for future payments.

*DAAT*

## UNEXPIRED COST
A cost that may be properly carried forward to future periods as an asset to measure.

*NCMA-CA*

## UNICOR
See "Federal Prison Industries (FPI)."

## UNIFORM COMMERCIAL CODE (UCC)
Uniform law governing commercial transactions, developed by the National Conference of Commissioners on Uniform State Laws and the American Law Institute, which has been adopted by all states in the United States except Louisiana, and which is sometimes used to aid in the interpretation and enforcement of government subcontracts.

*GUIDE*

## UNIFORM CONTRACT FORMAT
The format (Section A through Section M) that must be used in most invitations for bids (IFBs) and requests for proposals (RFPs).

*McVay*

The uniform contract format is as follows:

Part I—*The Schedule*:
- Section A—Solicitation/contract form
- Section B—Supplies or services and prices
- Section C—Description/specifications
- Section D—Packaging and marking
- Section E—Inspection and acceptance
- Section F—Deliveries or performance
- Section G—Contract administration data
- Section H—Special contract requirements

Part II—*Contract Clauses*:
- Section I—Contract clauses

Part III—*List of Documents, Exhibits, and Other Attachments*:
- Section J—List of documents, exhibits, and other attachments

Part IV—*Representations, Certifications, and Other Statements of Bidders*:
- Section K—Representations, certifications, and other statements of bidders
- Section L—Instructions, conditions, and notices to bidders
- Section M—Evaluation factors for award

*FAR*

## UNIFORM PROCUREMENT SYSTEM (UPS)

An interagency group of senior procurement officials, known as the Council on the Uniform Procurement System (CUPS), chaired by the Administrator, Office of Federal Procurement Policy (OFPP).

*DAAT*

## UNILATERAL

Means that the contracting officer (CO) (buyer) does something without the concurrence of the contractor. For example, a unilateral modification would be a change to a contract where the procuring contracting officer (PCO) signs but the contractor does not. Unilateral modifications are used for the following:

- making administrative changes
- issuing change orders
- making changes authorized by clauses other than the Changes clause (e.g., Options clause, Property clause, etc.)
- issuing termination notices

*Navy*

## UNILATERAL CONTRACT

See "Bilateral Contract."

## UNIT COST

A total cost divided by some related base, such as labor hours, machine-hours, or units of product.

*NCMA-CA*

## UNITED STATES CLAIMS COURT

(1) Federal court that, upon dissolution of the United States Court of Claims in 1982, assumed the role of the Court of Claims' trial division.

*GUIDE*

(2) Renamed the United States Court of Federal Claims in 1992 by the Federal Courts Administration Act (P.L. 102-572).

Compare "United States Court of Appeals for the Federal Circuit." See also "Federal Courts Improvement Act."

## UNITED STATES COURT OF APPEALS FOR THE FEDERAL CIRCUIT

Federal court that, upon dissolution of the U.S. Court of Claims in 1982, assumed the role of the Court of Claims' appellate division.

*GUIDE*

Compare "United States Claims Court." See also "Federal Courts Improvement Act."

## UNITED STATES COURT OF CLAIMS

Until its dissolution in 1982, the federal court that resolved most government contract disputes brought in federal court.

*GUIDE*

See also "Federal Courts Improvement Act."

## UNITED STATES COURT OF FEDERAL CLAIMS

See "United States Claims Court."

## UNITED STATES FOREIGN CORRUPT PRACTICES ACT (1977) (Amended 1988)

This Act prohibits payments intended to influence foreign officials' behavior.

*NES-94*

## UNITED STATES SUPREME COURT

Highest of all federal courts that can review a government contracts case, but that does so very infrequently, reserving review primarily for cases involving important questions with far-ranging implications.

*GUIDE*

## UNJUST ENRICHMENT

Where one of the parties to the contract receives benefits far in excess of the amount of money involved.

*Cohen*

## UNLIMITED RIGHTS

Rights (a) to use, duplicate, release, or disclose technical data or computer software in whole or in part in any manner and for any purpose, and (b) to have or permit others to do so.

*DSMC*

See also "Rights in Technical Data."

## UNLIQUIDATED PROGRESS PAYMENTS

See "Liquidation."

## UNOBLIGATED BALANCE

The amount of budget authority (BA), previously granted to an agency but not yet committed, that continues to be available for commitment in the future.

*DAAT*

## UNRESTRICTED PROCUREMENT

The acquisitions available to all contractors, and not reserved to satisfy social or economic programs of the federal government.

*TIPS(2-9)*

Compare "Set-Aside."

## UNSOLICITED PROPOSAL

(1) A research or developmental proposal that is made by a prospective contractor without prior formal or informal solicitation from a purchasing activity.

*AFIT*

(2) A written proposal that is submitted to an agency on the submitter's initiative for the purpose of obtaining a contract with the government, and that is not in response to a formal or informal request.

*DAAT*

See also "Proposal."

## VALIDATION

Acceptance by auditors of reported cost reduction savings and cost
reduction reports, which are based on
a selective review of cost reduction
reports and supporting documentation.

*AFIT*

## VALUE ADDED

The value added to a product or
service at each stage of its production
and distribution on the basis of its
increased value at that stage.

*Commercial Practices*

## VALUE ANALYSIS

(1) A systematic and objective evaluation
of the function of a product and its
related cost; a pricing tool that
provides insight into the inherent
worth of a product.

*OPM*

(2) Value analysis assumes that value
is a function of three variables:
demand, use, and aesthetics.

*W-CC*

See also "Auxiliary Techniques."

## VALUE ENGINEERING (VE)

An organized effort directed at
analyzing the function of systems,
subsystems, equipment, facilities, procedures, and supplies for the purpose
of achieving the required function
at the lowest total cost consistent
with performance, reliability, quality,
maintainability, and producibility.

*AFIT*

## VALUE ENGINEERING CHANGE PROPOSAL (VECP)

A proposal that requires a change
to the contract to implement and
that results in reducing the overall
projected cost to the agency without
impairing essential functions or
characteristics, provided that it does
not involve a change in deliverable
end-item quantities, research and
development (R&D) quantities, or the
contract type.

*FAR*

## VALUE ENGINEERING (VE) PROPOSAL

An in-house, agency-developed
proposal, or a proposal developed by a

contractor under contract (a) to provide VE services and (b) to provide VE studies for a government project or program.

*OMB A-131*

## VARIABLE BUDGET
See "Flexible Budget."

## VARIABLE COST
(1) A cost that changes with the rate of production of goods or performance of services.

*OPM*

(2) Costs associated with production that change directly with the amount of production (e.g., the direct material or labor required to complete the build or manufacturing of a product).

*Garrett*

## VARIABLE COSTING
See "Direct Costing."

## VARIANCE
The difference between projected and actual performance, especially relating to costs.

*AFIT*

See also "Standard Cost."

## VARIANCE ANALYSIS
(1) Comparing the total budget with the estimate at completion (EAC) at the control account (CA) level provides a variance expected at the completion of the CA.

*EVMIG*

(2) The process of examining differences between actual costs and budgeted costs. In management control system terms, a variance can be positive or negative (parallel to the accounting terms of favorable or unfavorable). A positive variance indicates the program is under budget or ahead of schedule; a negative variance indicates that the program is over budget or behind schedule.

*W-ATCC*

## VENDOR
An individual, partnership, corporation, or other entity from whom items are acquired in the performance of a contract.

*AFIT*

## VISUAL ANALYSIS
The visual inspection of an item or its drawings, from which a general estimate of probable value may be made.

*AFIT*

See also "Auxiliary Techniques."

## VOLUNTARY DISCLOSURE PROGRAM

Created in April 1990 for the Department of Defense (DOD), this program offers a means by which defense contractors can identify their own potential civil or criminal fraud violations. In return for this disclosure, DOD generally grants the contractor the opportunity to conduct an internal investigation, which the government later verifies. DOD agrees not to pursue administrative actions until its verification process is completed.

*TIPS(3-2)*

## VOUCHER

See "Invoice."

## WAGE AND CLASSIFICATION
Guidelines to be used by the contracting office in determining applicable wages for specific classes of employees expected to be employed by the contractor to perform the required services under a proposed service contract. Determinations are made by the Department of Labor in accordance with the Service Contract Act.

*OPM*

## WAGE DETERMINATION
A determination of the Department of Labor that a certain scale of wages is the prevailing wage in a locality. Wage determinations are issued under the Davis-Bacon Act and the Service Contract Act, and they establish the minimum wages that government contractors may pay their employees.

*NS*

## WAIVER
(1) The voluntary relinquishment by a person of a right that he or she has.

*FBL*

(2) Acceptance by the government (buyer) of a minor nonconformity that does not degrade the function of the item.

*McVay*

(3) Specifications. A written authorization to accept a configuration item (CI) or other designated item, which, during production or after having been submitted for inspection, is found to depart from specified requirements, but that, nevertheless, is considered suitable "as is" or after rework by an approved method.

*DAAT*

(4) Decision to not require certain criteria to be met for certain reasons, such as national security.

*DAAT*

## WALSH-HEALEY PUBLIC CONTRACTS ACT
A law (41 U.S.C. 35–45) that requires a contractor that furnishes supplies to the government to be either a manufacturer or regular dealer of the supplies. The Act includes stipula-

tions on minimum wages, maximum hours, labor practices, and working conditions.

*FAR*

## WARRANT

(1) A contracting officer's (CO's) certificate of appointment.

*McVay*

(2) An official document (Standard Form 1402) designating an individual as a contracting officer (CO). The warrant will state as reference the limits of the CO's authority.

*DAAT*

(3) An official document issued by the Secretary of the Treasury (SOT) and countersigned by the Comptroller General of the United States by which monies are authorized to be withdrawn from the Treasury. Warrants are issued after appropriations and similar congressional authority has been enacted.

*DAAT*

## WARRANTY

A promise or affirmation given by a seller to a buyer regarding the nature, usefulness, or condition of the supplies or performance of services furnished under the contract. Generally, a warranty's purpose is to delineate the rights and obligations for defective items and services, and to foster quality performance.

*NES-92*

## WARRANTY, EXPRESS

A written statement arising out of a sale to the consumer of a consumer good pursuant to which the manufacturer, distributor, or retailer undertakes to preserve or maintain the utility or performance of the consumer good or to provide compensation if there is a failure in utility or performance. It is not necessary to the creation of an express warranty that formal words, such as "warrant" or "guarantee," be used, or that a specific intention to make a warranty be present.

*BLD*

## WARRANTY, IMPLIED

A promise arising by operation of law that something that is sold shall be merchantable and fit for the purpose for which the seller has reason to know that it is required. Some types of implied warranties are as follows: implied warranty of fitness for a particular purpose, implied warranty of merchantability, implied warranty of title, and implied warranty of wholesomeness.

*BLD*

See also "Spearin Doctrine."

## WEIGHTED AVERAGE COST METHOD

A method of determining the average unit cost of inventory and, by implication, an aid in determining the cost of goods made, sold, or held for future sale or incorporation into higher level end items. Under this technique, costs are periodically computed by adding the sum of the costs of beginning inventory with the sum of the costs of subsequent purchases and dividing by the total number of units.

*P&L*

## WEIGHTED GUIDELINES METHOD (WGM)

A cost analysis technique used to ensure consideration of the relative value of appropriate profit factors in establishing profit objectives and conducting negotiations. WGM is used as a basis for documentation and explaining final pricing factors, including contractor's input to total contract performance, contractor's assumption of contract risk, record of contractor's performance, and other selected factors.

*UPM*

## WHISTLEBLOWER

See "Qui Tam Action."

## WHOLESALE SUPPLY SOURCES

Certain government agencies have been tasked to maintain a stock of common-use items for all government agencies to use. The Defense Logistic Agency (DLA) and Veterans Affairs (VA) both have stock programs. However, by far the largest program is under the General Services Administration (GSA). GSA offers two methods of accessing its wholesale supplies: (a) distribution centers and (b) customer supply centers. Wholesale supply sources are a required source of supply.

*W-PSP*

See also "Required Sources of Supplies and Services."

## WILL COST

(1) A concept of contract pricing that requires an evaluation of what an offeror estimates it will cost to do the job in a specified future period.

*OPM*

(2) A projection by an offeror as to what a contract will cost, which is based on the offeror's best estimate using current methods, historical costs, and forecasts.

*L&P*

## WIN–WIN

A philosophy whereby all parties in a defense acquisition scenario come away gaining some or most of what they wanted (i.e., everyone "wins" something, even though it may not be 100 percent of the goal); the ideal outcome.

*DAAT*

## WORK BREAKDOWN STRUCTURE (WBS)

(1) A product-oriented family tree division of hardware, software, services, and other work tasks. WBS organizes, defines, and graphically displays the product to be produced, as well as the work to be accomplished to achieve the specified product.

*DSMC*

(2) The WBS is a direct representation of the work scope defined in the program statement of work (SOW) and breaks down that work scope into appropriate elements for cost accounting and work authorization. It is a multi-level hierarchical breakdown that shows how program costs are summarized from the lower elements to the total program level.

*EVMIG*

## WORK-IN-PROCESS INVENTORY

The cost of uncompleted goods still on the production line.

*NCMA-CA*

## WORK PACKAGES (WP)

(1) Work packages are natural subdivisions of control accounts (CAs) and constitute the basic building blocks used in planning, controlling, and measuring project performance. A WP is simply a low-level task, a grouping of similar tasks, or a job assignment.

*EVMIG*

(2) "Work package" is a generic term that translates into different terms in different companies and functions. It can be a design job, a tool design package, a build-to package, a shop order, a fabricated part, a purchase order (PO), or any other definable task at whatever level of control (LOC) is normal for program management within the company. It describes the work managed by a specific performing organization and serves as a vehicle for monitoring and reporting work progress.

*EVMIG*

(3) Work packages represent detailed jobs, except for those that are for material items. They are units of work at levels where work is performed and are clearly distinguishable from all other work packages. They are assigned to a single organizational element; have scheduled start and completion dates and, as applicable, interim milestones; have a budget or assigned value expressed in terms of dollars, labor hours, or other measurable units; have a duration limited to a relatively short span of time, or are subdivided by discrete value milestones to facilitate the objective measurement techniques of work performed, or they might be level of effort (LOE) work packages integrated with detailed engineering, manufacturing, or other schedules.

*NDIA*

## ZERO-BASED BUDGETING (ZBB)

An elaborate, time-consuming practice of having managers justify all their activities and costs as if they were being undertaken for the first time. ZBB is successfully used in many nonprofit organizations because most costs in many nonprofit organizations are discretionary. ZBB forces managers to define the output of various programs of expenditures and to relate inputs to the output.

*MGMT*

## ZERO-BASED PRICING

A form of cost analysis based on reviewing all cost elements and working with internal customers and suppliers to reduce the total combined cost of purchased materials, equipment, labor, and services.

*Commercial Practices*